Off the Leash
in Australia

The best of dog-friendly travel

SHANDOS CLEAVER

Hardie Grant
EXPLORE

Contents

Introduction iv
Travelling around Australia with your dog vi
Pet-friendly accommodation in Australia x
Dog-friendly sightseeing in Australia xiv
Preparing to travel with your dog xviii

New South Wales & Australian Capital Territory 1

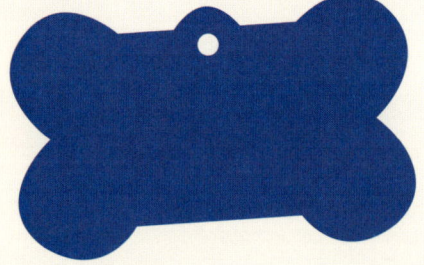

Victoria 69

South Australia **129**

Western Australia **163**

Northern Territory **206**

Queensland **223**

Tasmania/ Lutruwita **289**

Index **304**
About the author **313**

Introduction

Right: **Onboard Pacific Nature Cruises in Monkey Mia** Opposite: **Melbourne laneways**

When I travelled around Australia in a campervan, there was no question about leaving behind my miniature dachshund, Schnitzel. After all, he's part of my family and where we go, he goes too.

This is increasingly the case with many Australian families, whether you also have human children or are empty nesters with only a pampered fur-baby. And luckily it's become easier in recent years to holiday with pets in Australia, thanks to an increasing range of pet-friendly accommodation, from boutique motels and holiday rentals to caravan parks and farmstays.

But once your accommodation is sorted, what do you do during the day? When researching what to do with my dog on our trips, often the only options were lists of dog parks and off-leash dog beaches. Definitely handy, but not the only thing we wanted to do day in and day out!

So instead, I approached our holiday planning from a different angle. What are the popular attractions in different destinations around Australia that we would be visiting? And out of those, which places are dog-friendly?

While some places make it clear whether or not dogs are allowed, for other places it's a bit harder to find out. Even when it comes to national parks, there's not quite a blanket ban in Australia. For example, a handful of national parks in South Australia and elsewhere, plus many regional parks in New South Wales and Victoria, allow pets.

Along the way I ended up unearthing some surprising gems – attractions that I never would have expected to be dog-friendly, but which welcome dogs to join you. And overall, I uncovered more dog-friendly things to do in Australia than I expected!

So that you don't need to do the same difficult research, I've put together guides to many popular destinations in Australia, in every state and territory, full of fun sightseeing ideas for you to do together with your pup, plus tips on where to eat out and where to stay with your pet, and some great dog parks.

Have a fabulous time travelling together with your four-legged family members!

Shandos & Schnitzel

Travelling around Australia with your dog

Happy pups and happy snaps on the road

Whether you're travelling all the way around Australia on a Big Lap, just heading away for the weekend or out on a daytrip, the first thing to work out is how you'll be travelling with your dog: in your own car, a campervan or a hire vehicle.

⤵ YOUR OWN CAR

The easiest way to travel in Australia with your dog is in your own car. As well as your dog being allowed in your car (of course!), your dog will already be familiar with the vehicle.

Before taking your first long trip with your dog in your car, first make sure they're comfortable in your car on shorter trips. Puppies in particular often get car sick, but usually grow out of it; ginger chews can help, or a car seat for smaller dogs so they can see out of the window.

Always make sure your dog is securely fastened in your car, both for their own safety and the safety of other occupants. A seatbelt attachment is a common option, or consider a secured crate in the rear of your vehicle.

⤵ YOUR CAMPERVAN OR CARAVAN

On longer trips, an even better option is driving your own campervan or towing your own caravan. There are some parts of Australia where there are virtually no pet-friendly hotels or cabins, so with a caravan or campervan you'll always have your own comfortable accommodation (a big upgrade from a tent), and you only need to look for pet-friendly caravan parks or campsites. Plus, while advance bookings for pet-friendly accommodation are essential, it's not usually necessary for campsites – great for if you want to be flexible.

Your own campervan or caravan is the best option when completing a Big Lap (driving all the way around Australia). While some travellers are concerned before departing that their dog will limit what they can do, once you hit the road you won't regret it! Completing a Big Lap with your dog just requires some flexibility and the occasional kennel or pet- sitter (*see* p. xvii).

⤵ HIRING A CAMPERVAN

If you don't have your own campervan, it's possible to hire a pet-friendly campervan or motorhome. Both Apollo and Britz allow pets in selected campervans, and have locations throughout Australia. An additional cleaning fee applies for pets, so it's more cost effective if you hire the van for a longer trip, not just a weekend.

You can also use the Camplify website to rent private vehicles directly from their owners – make sure you apply the pet-friendly filter. As well as campervans and motorhomes, caravans and camper trailers are also available.

While some campervans are set-up for off-grid camping, other vans will require you to plug into a powered site at a caravan park at least every second night, or every night if you want to use certain features such as the air conditioning.

If your campervan doesn't have extra seats, consider ahead of time where your dog can travel comfortably within the van, as well as how best to keep them secured.

⬇ HIRING A CAR

If you don't have your own car, it's possible to hire a car for a trip away with your dog. I've done this when going away on short trips, when a campervan hasn't been necessary.

Finding a pet-friendly hire car in Australia can be tricky. Some of the large hire car companies in Australia ban pets from all of their vehicles, while other companies leave it up to the manager at the depot. It is best to call up a location directly and make inquiries.

If hiring a car, always return the car free of dog hair. Consider using a dog bed or blanket on the back seat of the vehicle, or wherever your dog is secured in the vehicle, to minimise the amount of hair left behind. Always dry and clean your dog before allowing them in the vehicle – extra dog towels are always handy! Plus consider vacuuming the car before you return it, particularly if your dog tends to shed.

Another option, if you're just heading away for a couple of days and live in a major city, is a car-share network such as GoGet or Popcar. These schemes usually allow pets in some vehicles, although naturally it's requested that you return them free of pet hair.

Keep your dog secure in your vehicle

↲ FLYING WITH YOUR DOG

The quickest way to travel long distances around Australia is, of course, by flying. And soon, you may be able to fly with your pet in the cabin on domestic flights in Australia.

In March 2024, Virgin Australia announced that they planned to allow pets to fly in the cabin, on selected flights, subject to regulatory approval. Only small dogs and cats would be permitted, and they would need to remain in an approved carrier underneath the seat in front at all times.

On flights overseas, generally a weight limit of 8 to 10kg applies. Both small and large pets can also fly in the hold on flights operated by Qantas, Virgin Australia and Regional Express. Bookings can sometimes be made directly with the airline or through a pet transport company, who can also sell or hire you a crate suitable for a plane.

↲ PETS ON PUBLIC TRANSPORT

If you're just heading out for the day or going away for the weekend with your pup, you may wonder whether it's possible to use public transport. This depends on where you are located, because the rules for pets on public transport vary greatly throughout Australia.

The most pet-friendly state when it comes to public transport is Victoria. Dogs of all sizes are allowed on metropolitan trains in Melbourne, as long as they are wearing a leash and muzzle or are in a container. Small pets in suitable containers are also permitted on trams, buses and regional V/Line train services.

In New South Wales, while pets are prohibited from trains and the Metro, small pets in enclosed carriers are allowed on buses, the light rail and ferries, if you receive permission from the driver or crew. The same applies on the light rail and buses in Canberra.

The only other state that allows pets on some form of government-run public transport is Queensland, where dogs are allowed onboard the Brisbane River ferries and CityCats, outside peak hour. Pet dogs need to be either wearing a leash and muzzle, or be in an enclosed carrier, and travel on the outside deck.

In the other states and territories of Australia – South Australia, Western Australia, the Northern Territory and Tasmania – there is a blanket ban on pets by the state-run public transport authorities. Only service animals are permitted.

Some smaller private companies have their own policies – in particular, I've found privately run ferries around Australia often allow leashed dogs.

Pet-friendly accommodation in Australia

Tucked up at dog-friendly hotel Alure in Stanthorpe, Qld

The next big consideration when travelling with your pet in Australia is where you can spend the night. Don't start making plans until you check that there's suitable pet-friendly accommodation available at your destination, especially if you're relying on pet-friendly cabins or motels.

↴ HOTELS AND MOTELS

A growing number of hotels and motels around Australia have put out the welcome mat for pet dogs. There are a surprising number of small country motels that have one or two pet-friendly rooms, plus in recent years many luxury and boutique hotels in the cities and popular tourist spots have started to offer pet staycation packages, complete with luxury dog beds, in-room dog dining menus and plenty of treats.

The rates charged for pets vary widely, from some properties that only charge $20 per stay (or pets even stay for free), up to fees of $100+ per night at some luxury hotels. While sometimes pet-friendly rooms can be booked online, many properties require direct bookings by phone or email. I recommend contacting the property directly to find out their rules, including how many pets they allow and if there are weight limits.

Double-check in advance what is provided for pets. While some hotels provide pet beds and bowls, others may not include any extras for pets. In any case, I often like to bring along my dog's own bed for familiarity. Generally, pets cannot be left alone in rooms, so double-check with the hotel for recommendations on what to do for dinner and breakfast.

↴ HOLIDAY HOMES AND AIRBNBS

For a relaxing getaway with your pet in your own space, consider booking a pet-friendly holiday home. All the major holiday home booking sites, like Stayz and Airbnb, have pet-friendly filter options. There are also multiple booking sites that specialise in pet-friendly holiday homes around Australia, including Pupsy.

Before booking a pet-friendly holiday home, it's essential to double-check the rules for pets. While some homes allow pets inside (though generally it's requested pets stay off the furniture and beds), other homes are advertised as allowing pets but they have to stay outside. Obviously this would not be suitable for indoor pets!

Other things to check include whether the yard is securely fenced (check the photos or previous reviews if in doubt) and if anything is provided for pets, such as beds and bowls. It's usually best to bring along your own supplies, just in case.

↴ CARAVAN PARKS AND CABINS

The most prolific form of pet-friendly accommodation in Australia are caravan parks. These days the majority of caravan parks allow pets – I'd estimate around three-quarters. Note, however, that some caravan parks only allow pets on selected sites, and many caravan parks in popular coastal areas have blackout dates during peak periods, most commonly over Christmas and the Easter long weekend.

Most pet-friendly caravan parks only allow pets on sites where you are camping in your own caravan, campervan or tent, often with a limit of one or two pets. Not as many caravan parks allow pets in cabins, although there are an increasing number of pet-friendly cabins. Some parks allow pets in all or most of their cabins, but most commonly only one or two cabins are pet-friendly. Advance bookings are essential.

The facilities for humans at caravan parks can vary greatly, from only basic facilities through to resort-style swimming pools and playgrounds. Some caravan parks also provide facilities for dogs, ranging from fenced dog parks to dog washes and even dog-sitting services. Keep an eye out for caravan parks located next to dog-friendly beaches and off-leash parks.

⤵ FREE AND BUDGET CAMPSITES

If you're looking to camp with your dog, don't overlook the many free and budget campsites throughout Australia. While campsites in national parks are largely off limits to dogs, there are still plenty of cheap or free dog-friendly campsites run by local councils, in state forests and at other natural reserves.

Also consider showground campgrounds. While only offering basic facilities compared to most caravan parks, usually pets are welcome and the rates are quite cheap. Just note that tents are often not allowed.

In outback areas, it's often permitted to stay for a night or two at many roadside rest areas, to break up your drive. Double-check the signs for time limits and other rules, and be prepared to supply your own toilet paper.

To uncover all the campsites out there, I recommend purchasing a guidebook, such as the latest edition of Explore's *Camping around Australia*. Comprehensive information is provided on campsites throughout Australia, most importantly whether they are dog-friendly.

Alternatively, there are a number of apps listing campsites as well as caravan parks, including Wikicamps Australia. You can filter by whether pets are allowed year-round or seasonally. Just don't be caught out when you don't have mobile reception!

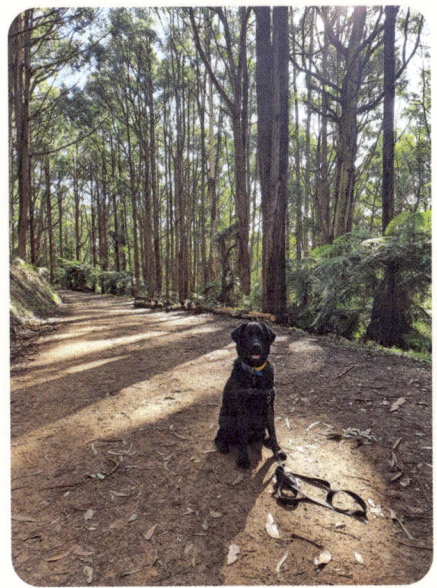

Whether it's local wineries and breweries, hikes or dog parks, there are plenty of dog-friendly experiences to discover

Dog-friendly sightseeing in Australia

Exploring silo art in Rochester, Vic.

One of the most common concerns dog owners have before travelling with their pet for the first time is whether they can do any sightseeing with their dog. It's common knowledge that many popular tourist attractions don't allow pets to join you. Luckily though, there are still plenty of interesting sights that you can enjoy together with your pup.

⬇ NATIONAL PARKS

It's often assumed that there's a blanket ban on pets visiting national parks in Australia. While this is generally the case (and fines apply for violating the laws), there are a few exceptions.

In South Australia and Victoria, there are a small number of national parks that allow pets in one or more areas. Some of the most popular pet-friendly parks are Belair National Park (*see* p. 133), just outside Adelaide, and sections of the Murray River National Park (*see* p. 145), around Renmark and Berri. In Great Otway National Park (*see* p. 124) in Victoria, leashed dogs are allowed at Johanna Beach.

There are also some types of natural reserves where dogs are generally allowed. In New South Wales and Victoria, dogs are allowed inside most regional parks, while in New South Wales pet dogs can join you in all state forests.

Carefully check the rules of the areas that you plan to visit and find out whether pets are permitted. If pets are not allowed, follow the rules and don't visit with your pet. The rules are in place both to protect the native wildlife found within national parks, and to protect your own dog from 1080 baits (*see* p. xx) used in most parks.

Note that it's generally permitted to drive through national parks on main roads with your pet in your vehicle, as long as you don't stop and use the facilities. But skip detouring down access roads.

⬇ DOG-FRIENDLY BEACHES

Australia is home to an astounding number of beautiful beaches. And while it's easy to think that dogs are prohibited from nearly all beaches if you live in the larger capital cities (particularly Sydney), there are plenty of dog-friendly beaches to visit, especially in regional areas.

The rules for dogs on beaches are determined by the local council and vary greatly. To find out which beaches are dog-friendly, check the council website or look out for signs at the beach.

Generally, dog-friendly beaches are divided into three main groups:

Off-leash beaches

These beaches allow dogs off-leash all day long, or at least from sunrise to sunset. Take note of the boundaries and if there are any exceptions: for example, if there are nesting seabirds during certain seasons.

Time-restricted beaches

In many popular tourist destinations, dogs are often only permitted off-leash on the beach during part of the day, such as before 9am and after 4pm. During the middle of the day, they may be prohibited or required to be kept on a leash. Often dogs are allowed off-leash all day long during the cooler months – so don't discount a beachside holiday during winter!

On-leash beaches

Dogs may be allowed on some other beaches, however, it may be a requirement that they are kept leashed while on the beach. Enjoy a leashed walk with your dog along the beach, but save off-leash fun for elsewhere.

⤵ OFF-LEASH PARKS

Nearly all towns in Australia provide off-leash exercise areas for dogs, but don't always count on something in the most remote regions.

The best source to find the local list of off-leash dog parks is the local council website. However, many dog parks can also be found if you search on Google Maps. Check the signage at the park, including whether there are any areas where dogs are not permitted off-leash, in addition to playgrounds and barbecue areas.

An increasing number of fenced dog parks are being built around Australia. While not everyone is a fan of fenced dog parks, they are a handy option when travelling, especially if you are concerned about your dog running off in an unfamiliar place. Plus, if you visit during the middle of the day, often you'll have the park to yourself.

Many fenced dog parks have a separate area for smaller dogs – something I usually mention in the listings of dog parks. There are also some excellent dog parks with agility equipment, swimming lagoons, picnic tables, barbecues and more!

⤵ DOG-FRIENDLY CAFES, RESTAURANTS AND PUBS

By default, dogs are permitted in the outdoor dining areas of cafes, restaurants and pubs throughout Australia, following a rule change by Food Safety Australia & New Zealand in 2012. However, the final decision still rests with the owner.

I always check in advance whether my dog is welcome in outdoor dining areas, before taking a seat, unless I can see other dogs at the venue or know in advance that it's dog-friendly. Some venues may also prefer that you sit in a certain area.

Some cafes provide water bowls for dogs, while others even have a menu for dogs, with options ranging from puppycinos to chews, and even doggy high teas!

⤵ WINERIES AND BREWERIES

Australia is home to a large number of wine-growing regions, plus a growing number of craft breweries. Luckily, both are great options for visiting with your dog, with most wineries and breweries welcoming pet dogs to join you.

The rules for visiting vary between venues. Some cellar doors and breweries even allow dogs inside – generally if they only offer tastings and don't have their own kitchen. However, always check in advance.

⤵ PET-SITTING AND KENNELS

Finally, of course there will be times when you want to do activities that can't accommodate your dog, whether you are visiting a national park or taking a boat trip to the Great Barrier Reef. On my trip around Australia, we used pet-sitting and kennels multiple times for Schnitzel, although we tried to minimise it.

Always research your options in advance – in some remote places there are only limited options available, or you may need to shuffle around the dates of your plans. If there is a vet, they may have kennels available during the day, although not usually overnight. Privately run kennels are better for overnight stays.

A popular website for finding pet-sitters is Madpaws, although this site works best in more populated areas. For remote areas, inquire with the local tourist information centre or caravan park whether they have a list of local pet-sitters. Contact details may also be provided on notice boards and shared in Facebook groups. As a final option, sometimes it's possible to swap pet-sitting duties with other campers travelling with their pets.

Preparing to travel with your dog

All packed up and ready for adventure

Before heading off travelling with your dog, make sure that you're fully prepared. Double-check that you've packed everything required for your dog on the road. Also find out more about some of the dangers for dogs (*see* pp. xx–xxi) throughout Australia that may not apply closer to home.

↓ TRAINING YOUR DOG

Before travelling with your dog, you may want to consider some dog training, whether informal or formal. While many puppies attend puppy preschool, there are some commands and situations that it would be helpful to focus on before travelling with your dog, including recall and dealing with strange environments.

If you don't trust your dog off-leash, visit fenced dog parks first and test different methods of calling your dog. Experiment with visiting different places close to home on daytrips before taking an extended trip with your dog.

Before travelling with my dog, Schnitzel, for the first time, we had some lessons with a dog trainer to help us calm him down when he joined us at cafes. It's often about training the owners, not the dogs!

↓ DOG PACKING LIST

The main things to pack when travelling with your dog are those things that you use every day at home with your dog, from their bed and bowls to their collar and leash. Make sure you pack the following items for your dog.

- Dog food and treats
- Food and water bowls (also consider a collapsible water bowl for outings during the day and a non-spill water bowl for inside your vehicle)
- Harness or collar and leash (and maybe a spare)
- Muzzle, for areas where 1080 baiting is used (*see* p. xx) and public transport
- Bed and blankets (even if provided by your accommodation, dogs often love the familiarity of their own bed)
- Dog seatbelt attachment (or another method for securing your dog in your vehicle)
- Plenty of towels
- Brush, shampoo and nail clippers
- Usual medication, including tick, flea and worming treatments
- Vaccination and registration papers (in case your accommodation or a kennel asks to see a copy; a digital copy is fine)
- Favourite toys
- Plenty of poo bags!

If camping with your dog, also consider packing extra things to make the campsite more comfortable for them, whether a long tether or fencing, or their own camp chair.

Depending on the length of your trip, you may need to stock up on supplies while on the road. Plan in advance where you can buy your dog's usual pet food. Click and Collect at larger pet stores is one of the easiest options.

⬊ CROSSING STATE BORDERS

Currently, Tasmania is the only state in Australia with biosecurity requirements for dogs crossing its border. Before entering Tasmania, your dog needs to be treated for the hydatid tapeworm, with a product containing praziquantel.

You will need to complete a declaration and provide proof of treatment. This can be an official statement from your vet, your own statutory declaration, or a pill packet and receipt. Additionally, since the outbreak of Ehrlichiosis in northern Australia, you need to also declare that you have inspected your dog for ticks and that they are free of ticks.

⬊ KEEPING YOUR PET SAFE IN AUSTRALIA

There are a number of dangers to pet dogs when travelling in Australia, particularly if you visit the more remote regions of the country. Before heading off on the road, be aware of these risks and make sure that you keep your pup safe.

1080 baits

One of the biggest concerns of dog owners travelling around Australia with their pets is 1080 baits. This is a type of bait that is used to control foxes and other pest species, but it is also deadly to dogs. These baits are used throughout Australia, including in many national parks and nature reserves, even in cities.

Keep an eye out for signs, and don't enter an area if there are signs warning of the current use of baits. Baits can also be transported by birds from their original location. It's best to keep your dog on a short leash and don't allow them to eat anything off the ground. In higher risk areas, consider training your dog to use a muzzle that prevents them from picking up anything off the ground.

Schnitzel prepares to cross the Nullabor Plain

Paralysis ticks

There are multiple types of ticks that are found throughout Australia, but the most problematic is the paralysis tick, which causes paralysis and can be fatal. It's found along the eastern seaboard of Australia, particularly from spring through to late autumn. Make sure you use a regular tick treatment for your dog and check them daily for ticks.

Ehrlichiosis

A relatively new danger for dogs in Australia is the tick-borne disease, Ehrlichiosis. Spread by the brown dog tick and potentially fatal, this disease is present mainly in northern Western Australia, the Northern Territory and northern South Australia. In addition to a tick treatment and daily checks, consider also using a tick collar.

Leptospirosis

This disease, spread through rat urine, is particularly concerning as it can be passed to humans. Most commonly found in rural areas of Queensland and the Northern Territory, there have also been recent outbreaks in Sydney and the Hunter region. Don't let your dog come in contact with stagnant water or rats or mice. Also consider a vaccine if visiting these areas during the wet season. Note there are two strains present in Australia, with separate vaccines.

Crocodiles

Crocodiles are a real danger to dogs in northern Australia, both around the coast and inland areas from Gladstone in Queensland to the Kimberley region in Western Australia. Always watch out for warning signs and don't let your dog swim in or even approach waterways where crocodiles are present.

Other dangers to be wary of include snakes, dingoes, cane toads and eagles. Keep your dog inside at night and on a leash most of the time in areas where these animals are present. It's also just as important to keep your dog up-to-date with regular vaccines and have your dog microchipped in case they get lost. Consider a pet first-aid kit and taking a first-aid course for pets.

01

New South Wales & Australian Capital Territory

Sydney/Warrang	2
Go hiking in the Blue Mountains	10
Wollongong & Kiama	12
Jervis Bay	18
South Coast	23
Central Coast & Newcastle	30
Taste wine in the Hunter Valley	36
Port Macquarie	38
Coffs Harbour	43
Byron Bay	50
Central West	56
Canberra/Ngambri/Ngunnawal	62

Sydney/ Warrang

Sydney is renowned for its natural beauty, from its sparkling harbour and iconic buildings to its world-famous beaches and national parks. While many of its most popular sights are off limits to dogs, there's a variety of dog-friendly beaches (mainly on the harbour), plus a wide range of walks where your pup can join you. There's even an increasing number of luxury hotels that roll out the red carpet to pet dogs!

Right: **On the Opera House steps** Opposite: **Walking across the Harbour Bridge**

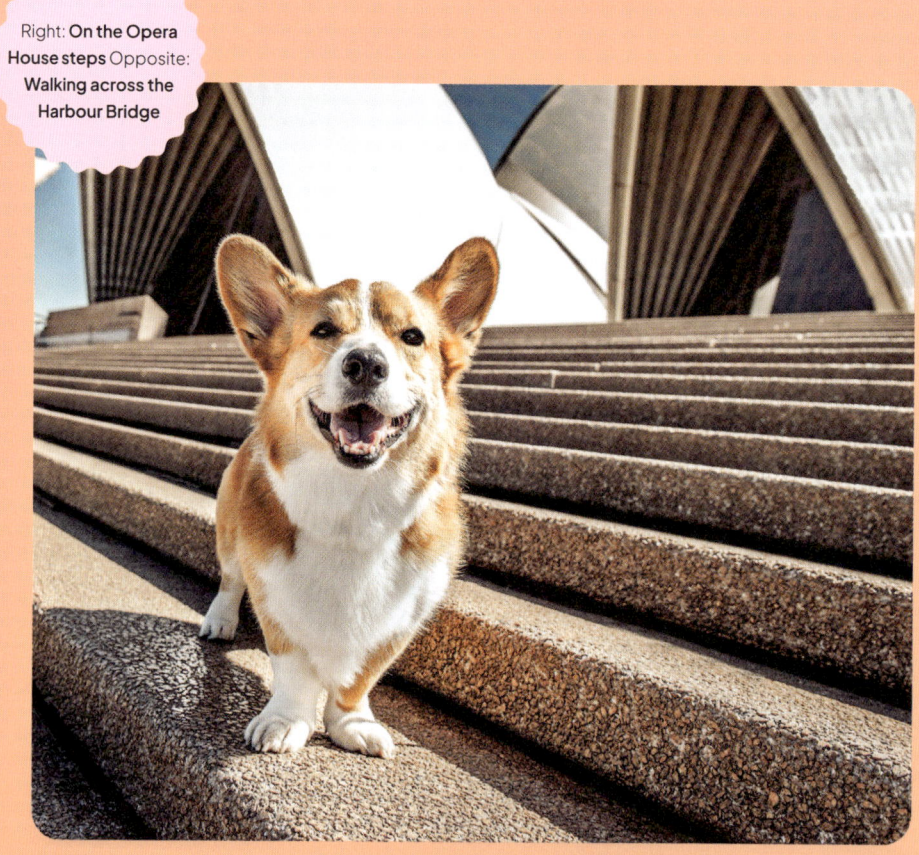

NEW SOUTH WALES & AUSTRALIAN CAPITAL TERRITORY

STROLL ALONG THE HARBOUR FORESHORE

While you won't spot many dogs in the Sydney CBD, they are welcome to join you on a stroll along its spectacular harbour foreshore, taking in views of the iconic Opera House and Sydney Harbour Bridge. Make sure you keep your dog on a leash, including in the wide expanses of Barangaroo Reserve, but avoid the Royal Botanic Garden Sydney, where dogs are not allowed.

Dogs are also permitted to join you in walking across the Harbour Bridge and enjoying the impressive views to the east along its length. At both ends there are steps up to the walkway, which stretches for nearly 1.5km north to Kirribilli, with secure fencing the whole way. (Consider skipping this walk if your dog is not happy walking close to noisy traffic.)

At the southern end of the bridge, don't miss stopping at Observatory Hill, where there's a handy off-leash dog exercise area and more fabulous views – just avoid the wedding parties and picnics on weekends! Or drop into the nearby Australia Heritage Hotel for a drink or a meal. This old-fashioned pub – best known for its Coat of Arms pizza – has plenty of relaxed outdoor seating, plus dogs are even allowed inside.

Another delightful section of the harbour foreshore to walk along with your dog is the Glebe Foreshore. Dogs are allowed off-leash on the Glebe Foreshore Walk, between Ferry Road and the tip of Glebe Point Road. There's even a small dog beach where dogs can enjoy a paddle in the harbour!

FOLLOW THE BONDI TO COOGEE COASTAL WALK

Another scenic walk in Sydney is the Bondi to Coogee Coastal Walk. Dogs are welcome to join you on the entire length of this popular walk, meandering along a 6km stretch of the coastline in the eastern suburbs, past some of the city's most famous beaches.

Sadly, none of the beaches along the way allow dogs on the sand, so I recommend skipping this walk during the heat of the day over summer; instead, head out with your dog either early in the morning or during the cooler months. Also skip sunny weekends during the annual Sculpture by the Sea festival (late October to early November), when the path becomes very crowded and puppy paws could be trodden on.

While the beaches are off limits, there are a number of off-leash parks along the way. Dogs are allowed off-leash at Marks Park, on the headland south of Bondi, before 8.30am and after 4.30pm, except during Sculpture by the Sea. Bronte Park, behind Bronte Beach, is off-leash before 10am and after 3pm. Best of all, detour through Burrows Park, just south of Waverley Cemetery, which allows off-leash dogs all day long.

There are multiple cafes with outdoor seating along the route, where you and your pooch can stop for a rest and grab brunch or just a coffee.

MAKE A SPLASH AT A HARBOUR BEACH

Sydney is home to only a small number of dog-friendly beaches, and most are on the harbour. Some allow dogs off-leash all day long.

One great off-leash dog beach, close to the centre of Sydney, is Rose Bay Dog Beach. Dogs are allowed off-leash on the sand in between Percival Park and Dumaresq Reserve, with the easiest entry at the end of Caledonian Road. There are no pesky time restrictions and the waters are fairly calm – great for dogs who aren't strong swimmers.

Another of my favourite off-leash dog beaches in Sydney is Sandy Bay at Clontarf. Located just north of The Spit Bridge, the off-leash dog beach is at the end of Sandy Bay Road. The beach is best visited at low tide, when the sand flats and shallow water extend a long way out – perfect for my short-legged Schnitzel.

Other off-leash dog beaches around Sydney Harbour include Sirius Cove in Mosman (only before 9am or after 4pm on weekends, but all day long on weekdays) and Callan Point Beach in Rozelle (no time

Schnitzel underneath the Sydney Harbour Bridge

restrictions). Alternatively, head south to Kyeemagh Dog Beach or Silver Beach on Botany Bay, or north to Pittwater.

A DAY OUT ON PITTWATER

Pittwater, among the Northern Beaches of Sydney, is home to another terrific dog beach. Bayview Dog Beach is part of the larger Rowland Reserve in Bayview, with a large grassy field and the adjacent beach allowing dogs off-leash all day long.

Being a harbour beach, it's relatively calm, with shallow waters close to shore and deeper waters further out for more confident doggy swimmers. Parking can be expensive, unless you grab one of the few free 1-hour spots next to the park.

Before or after a visit to the park, I recommend heading to The Newport, a fabulous waterfront pub that's visible just across the water. Dogs are welcome in most of their extensive outdoor areas. There's a wide variety of food options, from burgers to pizzas to seafood, and plenty of water bowls for pups.

WALK AROUND NARRABEEN LAGOON

One of the best longer dog-friendly walks on the Northern Beaches is the Narrabeen Lagoon Trail. This 8.4km easy loop around Narrabeen Lagoon is on a flat shared path passing through stretches of native bush and waterside parks.

My favourite part of the trail is on the northern side, where it passes through the bushland reserve of Bilarong Sanctuary and out above the lake. Although dogs need to be kept on a leash while on the walk, the nearby Deep Creek Reserve allows dogs to be off-leash and is also a handy free spot to park. There's a side path to the reserve from the northern part of the trail.

For more dog-friendly bushwalks around Sydney, head further south to Manly Dam, out to Lake Parramatta, or follow the track through Wolli Creek Regional Park near Earlwood.

GO BOATING ON THE HARBOUR

For a fun day out on Sydney Harbour with your dog, rent a boat and head out on the water. While many boats require a boat licence to operate, low-powered picnic boats are available that don't require a licence.

Multiple boat hire companies in Sydney allow dogs on their boats, including GoBoat at Cabarita Point. Their luxury electric picnic boats accommodate up to eight people (less if you're bringing a dog), with a picnic table, drink holders and shade onboard. Thanks to the electric motor, they're also whisper quiet.

Pack a picnic and head out onto the water for a couple of hours. I recommend finding a quiet bay to pull up in, then sit back and relax with your pup at your side, bobbing on the harbour. Schnitzel was fascinated by the salty smells on the water! Consider restraining your dog so there are no unexpected swims.

EXPLORE HISTORIC BERRIMA

One of the most gorgeous villages in New South Wales is a short 90 minute drive south of Sydney. The Southern Highlands town of Berrima is filled with well-preserved Georgian Colonial architecture, and is perfect for a daytrip.

I recommend exploring the town on foot (and four paws!). Follow the historic walk through the village, starting at the Berrima

Going for a paddle at Sirius Cove in Mosman

District Museum, where you can buy a map of the walk for a small fee. Highlights include the sandstone exteriors of the Berrima Court House and Old Berrima Gaol, both built in the 1830s. Naturally, dogs need to stay on a leash.

While spending the day in the Southern Highlands, consider visiting Bowral. It's home to the Bradman Oval and a statue of its namesake. Don't miss the Cherry Tree Walk, a colourful spot during spring and autumn. Or drop into Artemis Wines to enjoy a tasting of their wines and spirits, plus some pizza on the lawn at weekends.

SPLURGE ON A LUXURY HOTEL STAY

An increasing number of Sydney hotels are becoming pet-friendly, including many that offer luxury options. Whether you're visiting Sydney or are a Sydney local, consider treating yourself and your pup to a luxury hotel stay in Sydney.

Some options include the ultra luxurious Langham Sydney, the five-star Four Seasons Hotel Sydney, the W Sydney at Darling Harbour, the waterfront Ovolo Woolloomooloo and the hip QT Sydney.

Alternatively, head out of the city for a stay near the beach at the QT Bondi Beach or the Manly Pacific. Another option in the eastern suburbs is the InterContinental Double Bay, with its rooftop pool area where Schnitzel was permitted to sit with us.

If you are bringing along a pet, direct bookings with the hotel are often required. Note also that weight limits for dogs apply in some hotels. Many hotels offer luxury pet packages, featuring designer pet beds, dog minibars and special in-room dining menus for the ultimate pet-friendly splurge!

When to visit

Sydney is beautiful year-round, especially when the sun is shining. But while the beaches and water activities are best enjoyed between October and April, sunny days in winter are ideal for dog-friendly walks.

The boardwalk at Narrabeen Lagoon

 # Dog-friendly parks

 # Dog-friendly dining

Centennial Park,
Paddington

One of the largest off-leash dog areas in Sydney. Dogs are allowed off-leash in most areas around the edge of the park – outside the circle formed by the Grand Drive. Or enjoy a 3.6km on-leash walk along the Grand Drive walking path.

Sydney Park,
Alexandria

This large park, a few kilometres south of the city centre, allows off-leash dogs virtually everywhere, except in the wetland areas. Dogs even have their own pond.

Shale Hills Dog Park,
West Hoxton

I'm a big fan of this large dog park on the south-western fringe of Sydney. It's fully fenced, with a separate area for small dogs. There's also agility equipment and training stations, plus a scent garden – guaranteed to be a sniffing sensation!

The Grounds of Alexandria,
Alexandria

A Sydney institution with regular special installations in its laneways – perfect for Instagram pics. Dogs are welcome to dine with you on the terrace of the cafe, in the Potting Shed or you can grab something from the barbecue in the garden.

BrewDog,
Eveleigh

This massive brewpub near Redfern welcomes dogs in its large outdoor beer garden, plus in the bar section inside. As well as its extensive range of craft beers, expect to find burgers and tacos on the menu, plus kids' meals.

Carrington Hotel,
Surry Hills

One of the most dog-friendly pubs in Sydney, this pub has both indoor and outdoor dog-friendly areas. Dogs even have their own menu! Look out for the lunch and dinner specials on weekdays.

Dog-friendly accommodation

Pier One Sydney Harbour,
Dawes Point

One of my favourite dog-friendly hotels in Sydney. Stay right on the harbour, underneath the Harbour Bridge. Dogs are also welcome at outdoor tables at the on-site restaurant (perhaps order a Doggy Degustation?), plus they are supplied with their own minibar.

Kimpton Margot Sydney,
Sydney

This pet-friendly luxury boutique hotel has an 'if it fits in the lift' policy, with no other size or breed restrictions, as well as no pet fees. A pet nook will be set up in your room, including a luxurious pet bed and a special treat.

Hughenden Hotel,
Woollahra

Set in a historic mansion, this boutique hotel is just metres from the dog-friendly Centennial Park. Pets are welcome in selected Queen Courtyard rooms, with no restrictions on size, breed or number of dogs, although there is a pet fee.

Poplar Tourist Park,
Camden

Sydney doesn't have many caravan parks, and even fewer pet-friendly caravan parks, so this park on the south-western outskirts is a rarity. Up to two dogs are allowed on sites, plus in selected cabins.

The Grounds of Alexandria is dog-friendly

Go hiking in the Blue Mountains

Many people are surprised to learn that yes, you can visit the Blue Mountains with your dog. And you can even go hiking together! Much of this spectacular natural region on the doorstep of Sydney is within Blue Mountains National Park, but there are also plenty of reserves where leashed dogs are welcome. I'm constantly uncovering new gems every time I visit.

These are some of my favourite dog-friendly lookouts and hikes to enjoy in the Blue Mountains.

Echo Point Lookout

This lookout at Katoomba is deservedly the most popular in the Blue Mountains, since it's the closest viewpoint to the famous Three Sisters formation. Dogs on a leash are allowed at the lookout, although it's not possible to walk up to the Three Sisters with your pup, as the walking path crosses onto national park land. Note that parking on nearby streets is expensive.

Sublime Point

Jutting out into the Jamison Valley from the village of Leura, this is my pick of the next best dog-friendly lookout in the Blue Mountains. There are almost 360-degree views from the lookout at the end of the point. It's accessed by a short 175m walk, and there are even some picnic tables if you want to enjoy the views for longer.

South Lawson Waterfall Circuit

One of the most popular dog-friendly walks in the Blue Mountains is the South Lawson Waterfall Circuit. Despite being only a short 2.7km loop, this hike features not just one but four waterfalls. It's mainly an easy walk, but there are some tricky sections with steps, where I needed to carry my small dog. There's also certain to be some muddy stretches after rain! During summer, dogs will appreciate a dip in the many pools and streams.

Katoomba Falls Night-Lit Walk

For something completely different (and a mud-free walk!) head to the Katoomba Falls area at dusk to enjoy the surrounding walkways and cascades lit up by lights. I parked near the old Katoomba Falls Kiosk and completed a roughly 2km loop around the area, heading as far as the Cliff View Lookout. I had no idea dogs were even allowed in this area until this night-lit walk opened in 2021! You can also visit this area during the day with your dog.

Minnehaha Falls Track

This waterfall walk is located on the opposite side of Katoomba from Echo Point and Katoomba Falls. The 2.6km return hike starts off relatively easy on mainly flat ground, with some steps along the way. But the final descent to the base of the waterfall is quite tough for dogs, thanks to some steep metal stairs. Only complete this walk with agile dogs, or a dog that you're fine to carry on the steps (like I did with Schnitzel). However, the views of the waterfall, especially after recent rain, are spectacular!

Knapsack Viaduct via Lapstone Zig Zag Walk

You don't need to drive far from Sydney to access this dog-friendly hike at the base of the Blue Mountains. There are multiple walks that you can complete leading up to the imposing sandstone Knapsack Viaduct, a heritage-listed former railway bridge in the mountains. My pick is the Lapstone Zig Zag Walk that starts at the end of Knapsack Street in Glenbrook. It's about 2.6km return.

Hiking at Knapsack Viaduct

GO HIKING IN THE BLUE MOUNTAINS

Wollongong & Kiama

The city of Wollongong (immediately south of Sydney) combined with the tourist town of Kiama (a little further south) offers a wealth of beautiful natural, dog-friendly experiences. In particular, there are plenty of excellent surf beaches that allow dogs off-leash all day long.

While the region has limited pet-friendly accommodation, it's close enough to Sydney that you can easily visit on a daytrip with your dog.

The Sea Cliff Bridge near Wollongong

📍 TAKE IN THE VIEW FROM BALD HILL

One of the best ways to start a visit to the Wollongong region is by taking in the views from Bald Hill at Stanwell Tops, looking south along the rugged escarpment at the many headlands that jut out in between the region's golden beaches.

Turn off the motorway near Helensburgh and stop off at the lookout when you hit the coast. There's a kiosk at one end of the carpark, and an ice-cream van operating most days.

🐾 WALK ACROSS THE SEA CLIFF BRIDGE

From Bald Hill Lookout you'll glimpse the Sea Cliff Bridge a few kilometres south, one of the landmark attractions in the Wollongong region. Opened in 2005, the 665m long bridge soars out over the rock platforms and sea below, mimicking the curve in the cliffs.

Don't just drive across the bridge, but also stop and walk across it. The closest parking spots are located just south of the bridge, convenient if you're driving south. Alternatively, pull into the small carpark near the Clifton School of Arts, then walk down the hill.

Dogs are fine to join you in walking across the bridge; there's even a handy poo-bag dispenser at the southern end of the bridge. However, perhaps skip the walk if your dog is skittish around traffic noises.

At the northern end of the bridge, Schnitzel and I detoured down the gravel road leading underneath the bridge, to view it from a different perspective. Note though that dogs are not allowed on the adjacent rock platform.

📍 WATCH THE KIAMA BLOWHOLE

At the southern end of this stretch of coastline, the town of Kiama is synonymous with its blowhole. Situated on the point at the end of Kiama's main street, dogs on a leash are welcome in the Blowhole Point Reserve, including next to the blowhole.

The Kiama Blowhole is best visited when seas are a bit higher, with larger waves, to experience the boom and spray flying up high. While underwhelming on calm days, it's quite an experience when the conditions are right!

Just be warned that neither dogs nor humans should venture beyond the fences and signs, as the conditions on the surrounding rock platforms can be quite dangerous.

HIKE ALONG THE KIAMA COAST WALK

One of the best dog-friendly walks I've discovered in Australia is the Kiama Coast Walk. This 20km walk follows the beautiful coastline either side of the town of Kiama, extending from Minnamurra in the north to Gerringong in the south.

Dogs on a leash are allowed along the entire length of the walk. Just skip walking on the sand of some of the beaches along the route where dogs are prohibited. Instead, detour onto the streets behind the beaches. The walk also passes some of the area's dog beaches, where you can allow your dog off-leash.

Rather than attempting the entire walk, choose one short section to complete. There are plenty of access points along its length. A section of the walk passes the Kiama Blowhole, so you can start at the blowhole and go either north or south along the walk.

I loved the southernmost section of the walk, which starts at the northern end of

Werri Beach in Gerringong. This section follows the cliffs south of Kiama, with gorgeous views of the sea on one side, green paddocks on the other, a wide and grassy path in between. Just note that the Werri Lagoon can connect to the sea following heavy rain – so be prepared to remove your shoes and wade across to the starting point!

WANDER THROUGH PUCKEYS ESTATE

Another fun dog-friendly coastal walk is the track through Puckeys Estate Nature Reserve, just north of the centre of Wollongong. Even better, you can combine a walk through the reserve with a walk on the adjacent off-leash beach!

Puckeys Estate is an extension of the Wollongong Botanic Garden, and contains a rare remnant of littoral rainforest, along with coastal dunes and a lagoon. Dogs on a leash are allowed inside the bush reserve, with the flat and largely shady walk through the forest suitable for all but the hottest days of summer.

In my experience, it's easiest to park at Fairy Meadow Beach Reserve, at the northern edge of the reserve. Then follow the 1.5km walking track through the reserve, towards Squires Way. However, just before you cross the bridge over the lagoon, detour to the left towards the beach. The off-leash dog beach starts north of the lagoon. Then loop back to your starting point along the beach.

HIT THE BEACH

It wouldn't be a visit to the Wollongong and Kiama region without hitting one of the many dog-friendly beaches in the area.

Some of the dog-friendly beaches in the northern suburbs of Wollongong include Sharkey's Beach in Coledale, Little Austinmer Beach, McCauley's Beach in between Thirroul and Bulli, and East Corrimal Beach on the southern side of Bellambi Point. Further south, head to Coniston Beach in Wollongong, MM Beach in Port Kembla or the long Perkins Beach in between Port Kembla and Windang.

Kiama is home to three off-leash dog beaches, with the southern end of Jones Beach, the centre of Bombo Beach and the centre of Werri Beach allowing off-leash dogs all day long.

EXPLORE THE MAIN STREET OF BERRY

Just south of Kiama is the charming country town of Berry, with a range of shops and cafes lining its main street, Queen Street. It's always been a great spot for a stroll, but it's been greatly enhanced by the recent bypass, reducing traffic.

Vineyards of Mountain Ridge Wines

Many of the buildings in Berry date to the late 19th century, including the two-storey Wilson's General Store building and the ES & AC Bank building, now the Berry Museum. If you're interested in learning more, follow the heritage walk around the town. The shorter version along Queen Street takes only half an hour.

Try to time your visit for the first Sunday of the month (except in February), when the Berry Country Fair is held at the Berry Showground. Well-behaved dogs on a leash are welcome to join you browsing the stalls.

A visit to the Berry Donut Van is also a must. A fixture in Berry for over 50 years, order just one or half a dozen of the delicious steaming hot cinnamon donuts – but be prepared for a queue!

🍷 TASTE SOME SHOALHAVEN WINE

The area around Berry is dotted with multiple wineries, part of the Shoalhaven Wine Region. And many of them welcome well-behaved dogs to join you at their cellar doors, plus in their outdoor dining areas.

One of the most dog-friendly cellar doors in the region is Cambewarra Estate, just west of Bomaderry. The cellar door and restaurant are open Friday, Saturday and Sunday. I recommend making a booking for high tea, with pet dogs welcome at their outdoor tables for a relaxing hour or two overlooking their vineyard. Or splurge on the VIP high tea option for you and your pup, held in a gorgeous oversized pink teacup!

Other dog-friendly cellar doors in the region include Crooked River Wines, Silos Estate, Two Figs Winery, Coolangatta Estate and Mountain Ridge Wine. Double-check the opening hours and where dogs are permitted. Advance bookings are generally appreciated.

Walking through Puckeys Estate

How to get there

It's an 80km drive south from the centre of Sydney to Wollongong; generally a 90 minute drive. It's a further 35 minutes' drive south to Kiama.

When to visit

Wollongong and Kiama are great to visit on a sunny day any time of the year. Hit the beaches during the warmer months, or enjoy a walk along the coast and try to spot a whale in the wintertime.

Dog-friendly parks

Dog-friendly dining

Oak Flats Dog Park,
Oak Flats

Just off the motorway with plenty of parking, there are two fenced areas for large and small dogs, water fountains and shade.

Bombo Beach Headland,
Bombo

Practise with your dog on the agility equipment or explore the unusual basalt columns of the former quarry. While unfenced, it's an isolated headland surrounded by the sea on three sides and larger dogs will appreciate the wide open spaces.

Scarborough Hotel,
Scarborough

Dogs are welcome in the large beer garden of this pub perched on the cliff-tops, where you can enjoy lunch or just a drink. Arrive early to nab a table and be warned that you're paying for the views!

Headlands Hotel,
Austinmer

Headlands has plenty of outdoor tables for walk-in guests. It's open all day long. Also check out the Airstream serving up more casual options. The off-leash Little Austinmer Beach is just metres away.

Diggies Kiama,
Kiama

With a prime location next to the blowhole, make a booking for breakfast, lunch or sundowners. I recommend the generously portioned fish and chips, accompanied by a piquant tartare sauce.

Flagstaff Point Lighthouse in Wollongong

One of the many off-leash dog beaches

Dog-friendly accommodation

Mantra Wollongong,
Wollongong

This city-centre hotel has a number of pet-friendly rooms, with direct bookings essential and an additional fee applicable.

Werri Beach Holiday Park,
Gerringong

Pets are welcome on powered and unpowered sites, outside peak season. Plus there are three pet-friendly cabins. It's walking distance to off-leash Werri Beach (*see* p. 14) and the start of the Kiama Coast Walk (*see* p. 13).

Red Dog Retreat,
Beaumont

Located halfway between Berry and Kangaroo Valley, this rustic country retreat on 18 acres has a pair of two-bedroom cottages available to book. There's plenty of room for dogs to run and play.

Jervis Bay

Jervis Bay, renowned for its beautiful white beaches and calm waters, is a popular holiday destination. Many of its beaches are dog-friendly, with both off-leash and on-leash options abounding. There's also plenty of pet-friendly accommodation, places to dine out and fun walks to do with your dog. It all adds up to a great dog-friendly destination, especially for a beach weekend away with your pooch!

Sea cliffs at the mouth of Jervis Bay

🌊 STROLL ALONG A WHITE SANDY BEACH

By default, the beaches around Jervis Bay allow on-leash dogs. Only a few local beaches are off-limits to dogs (check the signs), as well as the beaches in nearby national parks, where dogs are strictly not allowed.

The most famous beach at Jervis Bay is Hyams Beach – the subject of endless discussions about whether it has the whitest sand in the world.

It's possible to visit Hyams Beach with your dog, as long as you keep them on a leash. Choose between a stroll along the squeaky white sand, lazing together on your beach towel or paddling with your pup in the crystal-clear waters, keeping an eye out for the local dolphins.

However, it may be better to head to one of the bay's off-leash beaches (and where parking is easier; the small carpark at Hyams Beach can fill up even on weekdays during winter, in my experience). Dogs are allowed off-leash during part of the day at a number of beaches around Jervis Bay – before 8am and after 4pm between October and April, extending to before 10am and after 3pm during the cooler months.

One of the best alternatives is Nelsons Beach in Vincentia, where the sand is nearly as white as Hyams Beach, and there's plenty of parking along the shore. Huskisson Beach, between Nowra Street and Tapalla Avenue, and most of Callala Beach also permit dogs off-leash during selected hours. Alternatively, head to the ocean-facing Currarong or Culburra beaches.

🌊 GO DOLPHIN- OR WHALE-WATCHING

The crystal blue waters of Jervis Bay are renowned for their local population of dolphins that resides year-round in the bay. Additionally, between the months of May and November, whales are often spotted, sheltering in the bay's calm waters.

While it's possible to glimpse dolphins and whales from the surrounding shores, the best way to spot them is by taking a dolphin- or whale-watching cruise. If you have a small dog, you're welcome to bring them along on the cruises run by Jervis Bay Wild.

Cruises operate daily, with departure times depending on whether the 90 minute dolphin-watching cruises or seasonal 2 hour whale-watching cruises are operating. The cruises depart from Huskisson, to the west of the public wharf.

🍺 SIP A LOCALLY BREWED BEER

The perfect way to cap a day at the beaches of Jervis Bay is by enjoying a locally brewed beer. In recent years, two breweries have opened just outside Huskisson.

Jervis Bay Brewing Co. has a great dog-friendly beer garden. It's generally open from Wednesday to Sunday, with a food truck on-site most days. Check in advance for the latest opening hours. I recommend starting with a tasting paddle, selecting from the core range of beers and seasonal specials.

Just a few streets away is Flamin Galah Brewing Co, with its distinctive pink designs. This brewery also has a dog-friendly beer garden and permanent food truck, open from Wednesday to Sunday. Dogs are allowed both inside and out until 8pm, when the family-friendly hours end.

The white sands of Hyams Beach

 HIKE AT ABRAHAMS BOSOM RESERVE

While many of the walking tracks around Jervis Bay don't allow dogs because they're located in national parks, for a great bushwalk where on-leash dogs are permitted, go hiking at Abrahams Bosom Reserve.

The walking track starts at the southern end of Currarong, where there's a handy carpark and a picnic area. After crossing a bridge, you have two options. The shorter Wreck Walk is an easy 1 hour long walk. Mainly flat, there are views of the *S.S. Merimbula* wreck along the way and the chance to spot whales during the winter and spring months.

Alternatively, for a longer hike follow the Coomies Walk. This 3 hour walk is graded as medium and is great for energetic pooches. The trail passes Lobster Bay, the Cliff Edge Lookout and a Dharawal rock shelter. Check whether you can also access Gossangs Tunnel and Mermaids Inlet. Hiking boots are recommended after rain!

 VENTURE OUT ON A MANGROVE BOARDWALK

For a shorter walk that keeps your feet dry, a fun walk with your dog is the Mangrove Boardwalk in Huskisson. The boardwalk starts at the rear of the Jervis Bay Maritime Museum, with the easiest parking on Dent Street.

The boardwalk passes through the wetlands of Currambene Creek. It's best explored at low tide, when you can spot the creatures in the mud and mangrove roots below. Schnitzel was tantalised by all the smells. At the end of the boardwalk is a peaceful spot to sit and take in the view. Allow about 30 minutes for the walk.

A tasting paddle at Jervis Bay Brewing Co.

🪑 SEE THE GARDENS AT MERIBEE

About a 30 minute drive north of Jervis Bay, east of the local hub of Nowra, lies Meribee. What was once dairy pasture land with a few dilapidated buildings has been turned into an ornate garden over the last 20 years.

Within the garden are a variety of 'botanical rooms', including the Parterre Garden, the Italian Garden, the Heritage Rose Garden and the Lavender Paddock where it's easy to imagine you've been transported to the fields of Provence during flowering season. New and existing gardens are being developed continuously.

The gardens hold regular open days, generally weekly on a Sunday during flowering season, with limited openings during the winter months. Dogs on a leash are warmly welcome, with a kiosk and nursery also in operation.

How to get there

Huskisson, the main town on Jervis Bay, is about 200km south of Sydney. Allow up to 3 hours if driving from Sydney, longer in holiday traffic.

When to visit

Jervis Bay is most popular during the warmer months from October through to April. Advance bookings are essential during busy holiday periods. However, it can still be delightful on sunny winter days, with off-leash hours for dogs on beaches extended.

 # Dog-friendly parks

Clifton Park,
Sanctuary Point

The only off-leash dog park close to Jervis Bay. There's a fenced dog exercise area at the rear of the park. Keep your dog leashed when walking over to it.

 # Dog-friendly dining

Albert N Miso,
Vincentia

Named after the owner's dogs, it's no surprise that dogs are welcome at this cafe, open daily for breakfast and lunch. There are multiple outdoor tables and a water bowl for dogs.

Huskisson Hotel,
Huskisson

Leashed dogs are welcome on the Pavilion Terrace, which can be accessed through the side gate at the bottom of the carpark on the right hand side of the hotel. Note that reservations are not possible.

Dog-friendly accommodation

Jervis Bay Holiday Park,
Woollamia

One of the only parks in the area that allows pets year-round. Pets are allowed both on powered and unpowered sites, and in pet-friendly villas. Schnitzel and I enjoyed relaxing on its jetty, plus it's within walking distance of both local breweries.

Life's a Beach,
Culburra

This colourful beach shack has three bedrooms, an outdoor shower and a fenced backyard, with dog beds and toys included. It's also only metres from the dog-friendly beach.

South Coast Retreat,
Greenwell Point

Just north of Jervis Bay, choose between the African-style glamping tents or the standard and deluxe cabins. Two dogs are permitted per tent or cabin.

The waterfront Jervis Bay Holiday Park

South Coast

The South Coast of New South Wales stretches for almost 250km, from Ulladulla and Mollymook, south to the Victorian border. It's home to an endless string of beautiful beaches, many of them dog-friendly, and plenty of other things to do with your pup, from coastal walks and whale-watching to enjoying local brews and oysters.

Sunrise at Mystery Bay near Narooma

HEAD TO THE BEACH FOR THE DAY

One of the top attractions of the South Coast is its many wonderful beaches, and the same applies if you're visiting with a dog. A huge number of South Coast beaches are dog-friendly. The 40km stretch of coastline around Batemans Bay alone is home to a dozen beaches that allow off-leash dogs all day long, year-round. Plus there are even more time-share beaches that allow dogs all day long during winter.

These are some of my favourite dog-friendly beaches on the South Coast.

Washerwomans Beach,
Bendalong

Bendalong is a small village on the northern side of Lake Conjola. Dogs are allowed off-leash all day long at the delightful Washerwomans Beach, a calm and sheltered beach where I've spotted kangaroo prints on the sand in the early morning.

Durras Main Beach,
Batemans Bay

Head 20 minutes north of Batemans Bay to Durras Main Beach, one of the best off-leash surf beaches in the area. Enjoy a long walk on the off-leash section of the beach, which extends from near the caravan park to the headland. Bigger dogs will enjoy a play in the waves.

Wimbie Beach,
Batemans Bay

While the surf at Durras Main Beach can be rough, I love Wimbie Beach, 9km south of Batemans Bay, for its calm waters. Perfect for even the smallest dogs to enjoy a paddle (Schnitzel was a fan!), the beach is well away from the road, with dogs also allowed off-leash in the adjacent reserve.

Lions Park Beach,
Pambula Beach

Pambula Beach is blessed with multiple delightful beaches, with the most dog-friendly option at Lions Park Beach. Dogs are allowed off-leash on the northern end of the beach, which is enclosed by cliffs. There's a handy carpark adjacent to the beach, along with a picnic area.

Aslings Beach,
Eden

While visiting Aslings Beach, keep an eye out for dolphins off-shore, like the ones I spotted when I last visited this beach. Dogs are allowed off-leash along a nearly 1km stretch of this beach, starting just north of the skate park, as well as along the adjacent footpath.

ENJOY A SOUTH COAST BEER

In recent years, a number of breweries have sprung up along the South Coast. Most of them welcome dogs, making them a great spot to visit with your pup.

One of my favourite breweries on the coast is Camel Rock Brewery, located at Wallaga Lake near the turn-off to the famous Camel Rock formation. The beers are best enjoyed at the on-site bar and restaurant, which has a huge dog-friendly outdoor area. Expect plenty of burgers and wings on the Americana-style menu.

Further south is the Oaklands complex on the southern side of Pambula, home to the Longstocking Brewery. Enjoy a small or large tasting paddle from their rotating selection of beers and ciders, all brewed on-site. There are

The vineyard at Cupitt's Estate

also wood-fired pizzas available and an oyster bar serving up the local delicacies. And yes, dogs are welcome to join you.

SPEND THE AFTERNOON AT CUPITT'S ESTATE

When visiting Ulladulla or Mollymook, a must-visit destination is Cupitt's Estate. Although most of the wine produced by this winery is grown elsewhere throughout the state, they have a farm-to-table restaurant and casual dining area overlooking their plantings of sauvignon blanc. There's also a brewery on-site.

If visiting with your dog, make a booking for the Garden section of Dusty's Garden Bar where you can order a wine or beer flight to sample their range, since dogs are not permitted inside the cellar door.

STROLL ON THE MERIMBULA BOARDWALK

One of my favourite boardwalks, and one of the best dog-friendly short walks on the coast, is the 2km long Merimbula Boardwalk. This popular walk is located on the northern edge of Merimbula Lake, just west of the bridge and not far from the centre of Merimbula.

Along the walk you'll pass some local oyster farms, plus signs about the local marine life and plants. Make sure you keep your dog leashed on the walk, plus make way for other people when walking along the narrower sections.

Allow 1 to 2 hours to complete the walk at a leisurely pace. You can park at either end of the boardwalk: immediately west of the bridge or in the carpark on Lakewood Drive.

Two other terrific dog-friendly boardwalks are at Narooma and Eden. In Narooma, walk

Schnitzel exploring the Narooma waterfront

along the 350m Mill Bay Boardwalk, keeping an eye out for local stingrays and seals. The Lake Curalo Boardwalk is 6km return and is located behind the off-leash Aslings Beach near Eden.

🍴 TASTE LOCAL OYSTERS

Oysters are grown in many of the lakes and estuaries along the South Coast, including Merimbula Lake. To sample some of its oysters, there are a number of spots around Merimbula you can visit with your dog.

Wheelers Seafood Restaurant is located just south of the airport. While dogs are not allowed inside the restaurant, leashed dogs are welcome in part of the alfresco Oyster Bar. Enjoy a plate of oysters or choose from the other snacks on the menu, accompanied by a glass of wine or a cocktail. Dogs can also join you in the Takeaway Shop area.

Another place to pick up some takeaway oysters at an affordable price is McKay's Oysters, a little further down the road. Don't expect any lemon at this no-fuss outlet – only cash was accepted when I visited. But their freshly shucked oysters were very tasty.

📍 VISIT THE CUTE VILLAGE OF CENTRAL TILBA

One of the cutest spots on the South Coast is the village of Central Tilba. Just south of Narooma, the district briefly boomed during the late 1800s and early 1900s due to the discovery of gold in the area. With many buildings from that era still standing, the district was classified by the National Trust in 1974.

Enjoy a stroll with your dog along the main street, lined with a variety of brightly painted shops and cafes. As well as the well-known ABC Cheese Factory (I can't resist their halloumi cheese), there are shops selling leathercrafts, woodturning products, gifts and local chocolates. Ask whether you can take your dog inside any of the shops.

📍 WATCH FOR WHALES FROM THE CLIFF-TOPS

Whales can be spotted from the cliffs along the South Coast twice a year: making their way north during winter and then returning home to the waters off Antarctica during spring. The best way to enjoy some whale-watching with your dog is by visiting one of the cliff-top lookouts in the region.

At Ulladulla, head to the Ulladulla Lighthouse, south of the harbour at Warden Head, where there's also a number of on-leash walking trails. Further south, some of the best dog-friendly lookouts for spotting whales are Tathra Headland, Short Point in Merimbula and Eden Lookout.

How to get there

It's about a 4 hour drive south of Sydney to Batemans Bay, or a shorter 2 hour drive from Canberra. From Batemans Bay, it's another 2.5 hour drive south to Eden.

When to visit

Peak period on the South Coast is from October to April, particularly during school holidays when towns become packed with visitors. However, pet-friendly accommodation can be limited, with many caravan parks not accepting dogs. The region can still be charming during winter, when many of the time-share beaches become off-leash for dogs all day long.

Colourful Central Tilba

 ## Dog-friendly parks

 ## Dog-friendly dining

Milton Showground,
Milton

The showground precinct is home to a 24-hour off-leash fenced agility area near the campground.

NATA Oval,
Narooma

This mostly enclosed oval is popular with local dog owners. Dogs are allowed off-leash all day long, except during events.

The Treehouse Cafe,
Ulladulla

Dogs are welcome on the large deck of this cafe. Open most days for breakfast and lunch, there are plenty of vegetarian options, plus a long list of cakes. I recommend their Mexican Naked Taco Bowl.

Grumpy & Sweethearts,
Mogo

This friendly cafe has a huge, partially covered outdoor area, with water bowls for pups and sometimes even treats. I enjoyed coffee and cake in the afternoon sun, but there's also a range of lunch options, including reasonably priced toasties and sandwiches.

Tuross Boatshed & Cafe,
Tuross Head

Relax with a waterfront beverage or simple meal on the wharf with your dog at your side – I even spotted the local dolphins! It's mainly open during the day, but the cafe stays open until 7pm on Friday and Saturday.

Bluewave Seafood,
Bermagui

I highly rate the fresh and tasty fish and chips and tender crumbed calamari from this takeaway outlet. Enjoy your meal on the benches along the adjacent wharf. Perhaps afterwards visit the nearby dog-friendly gelato shop.

Dog-friendly accommodation

Bannisters Pavilion,
Mollymook

For a luxury dog-friendly South Coast stay make a booking at Bannisters. Bannisters Pavilion has two pet-friendly classic rooms available, with pets up to 25kg allowed. They also have two pet-friendly tables at their on-site restaurant.

Abode Malua Bay,
Malua Bay

This chain of dog-friendly apartment-style hotels from Canberra has an outpost in Batemans Bay near the time-share off-leash Malua Bay Beach. Up to two pets are allowed per room for an additional fee per night.

NRMA Tathra Beachfront Holiday Park,
Tathra

This extra pet-friendly caravan park allows pets on sites nearly year-round, plus in their pet-friendly cottages and villas – each with either an enclosed verandah or a fenced yard. The local off-leash beach is next to the park.

Mystery Bay Campground,
Mystery Bay

A basic campground south of Narooma, Mystery Bay is popular for its affordable prices and location next to a time-share off-leash beach, where Schnitzel and I enjoyed a magical sunrise walk. Make sure you book online in advance for peak periods.

Heaven No. 1,
Pambula Beach

A short walk from the local off-leash beach, this truly pet-friendly two-bedroom cottage includes extras such as pet bowls and a dog-proof six-foot high fence.

Above: **Bannisters Pavilion in Mollymook**
Opposite: **Calm Wimbie Beach**

Central Coast & Newcastle

Immediately north of Sydney, the Central Coast and Newcastle region is a great natural playground. There's plenty of fun dog-friendly activities on offer, with a wide variety of beaches where dogs are allowed off-leash, plus some great dog-friendly hikes – both coastal and forest walks. Come the end of the day, snuggle up in your caravan at one of the dog-friendly holiday parks or splurge on a luxury pet-friendly stay.

Below: **Dog-friendly Nine Mile Beach**
Opposite: **Hiking at Strickland State Forest**

🌊 PADDLE AT THE BEACH

Whether you visit the Central Coast and Newcastle region for the day or longer, don't miss spending some time playing on the sand and paddling in the water with your pup by your side.

One of my favourite off-leash dog beaches on the Central Coast is Patonga Beach. Thanks to the calm waters of the lower reaches of the Hawkesbury River, this beach is perfect for small dogs who are nervous around waves. The off-leash beach is also just opposite The Boathouse Hotel (*see* p. 34), perfect for lunch before or after some fun on the sand.

There are also plenty of dog-friendly surf beaches (great for larger dogs) on the Central Coast. Popular options include North Shelly Beach at Toowoon Bay, North Avoca and Avoca beaches (next to the lagoon in between the two beaches), Copacabana Beach and the northern half of MacMasters Beach, and the southern end of Umina Beach.

One of the best off-leash beaches in Newcastle is Horseshoe Beach, just inside Nobbys Head. Due to its location on the harbour, hemmed in by dunes, it's a safe spot to let your dog run off-leash and enjoy a swim. It's a short walk from the city centre or there's a convenient carpark at the western end.

In the southern suburbs of Newcastle, dogs are allowed off-leash all day long on three beaches: a section of Nine Mile Beach in Redhead (between Second and Third creeks), at the northern end of Blacksmiths Beach and at Hams Beach in Caves Beach (adjacent to Mawson Close). Or head to Croudace Bay Dog Park on the shores of Lake Macquarie to let your dog paddle in the lake.

🔺 GO HIKING IN STRICKLAND STATE FOREST

Many popular hiking trails in the area are off limits to dogs because they're within national parks. However, dogs are allowed in all New South Wales state forests, and luckily Strickland State Forest near Gosford has some excellent walking tracks.

The most popular track is the Arboretum Track, a 2.3km hike through one of Australia's oldest arboretums. Schnitzel loved the chance to walk through the forest, stopping and sniffing constantly. There's also a fun swinging bridge at the start of the walk.

Other walking tracks in the state forest include the Bellbird Track, a 1.3km extension to the Arboretum Track; and the Strickland Falls Track, a 1.6km loop track to the falls.

North Shelly Beach at Toowoon Bay

Dogs are allowed off-leash, but must be kept under your control.

Note that the final road into the forest is unsealed. If you're driving a 2WD car shortly after heavy rain, it's probably best to only drive to the Banksia Picnic Area, not the lower carpark. The tracks will also be muddy underfoot after rain!

WALK TO NOBBYS LIGHTHOUSE

If you're after a drier, less muddy walk, an excellent dog-friendly walk around Newcastle is the walk out to Nobbys Lighthouse and the Newcastle breakwall. This fully paved walk is flat and easy, although there's no shade along it. Not surprisingly, during summer it's most popular at sunset, rather than the middle of the day.

The total length of the walk out to the breakwall and back is 3km. It starts and ends next to the excellent off-leash Horseshoe Beach. Just be warned there are no steps between the walkway and the beach, so a detour or a scramble is necessary.

If you'd like to extend your walk, continue along the Newcastle Harbour Foreshore. A flat concrete path leads past the city centre and Queens Wharf to the marina at Wickham. Or head 6km south along the Bathers Way to the Merewether Ocean Baths.

HEAD TO BLUE GUM HILLS

A popular dog-friendly bushwalking spot inland from Newcastle is Blue Gum Hills Regional Park near Minmi and the Pacific Motorway. Dogs on a leash are allowed throughout the park, except for in the picnic areas and playground.

A variety of walking tracks crisscrosses the park, like the 3km loop Heritage Walking Track. This track passes some interesting sites in the park, once a former mine site. I recommend using a map on your phone to navigate because signage is not the best.

VISIT STOCKTON

Stockton is just across the harbour from Newcastle. If you have a big dog, it's a 30 minute drive by road to reach the enclave, thanks to no direct bridge. If you have a small dog, it's just a 5 minute crossing on the ferry.

The rules for the Stockton ferry are the same as on Sydney ferries, with small dogs in a carrier bag allowed onboard, on the outside deck. Double-check with the ferry crew. The ferry between Queens Wharf and Stockton Wharf crosses roughly every half-hour.

From Stockton Wharf, it's a short walk to the two off-leash dog beaches. My pick of the two is Little Beach, part of the off-leash Pitt Street Reserve. This small calm beach looks across to Nobbys Lighthouse and is a great alternative to Horseshoe Beach for timid dogs (big and small), thanks to it being far quieter. Alternatively, there's a small stretch of beach at the off-leash Ballast Ground, next to the 16ft Sailing Skiff Club.

HEAD TO PORT STEPHENS

For a fun outing for dogs of all sizes, hop in your car and head to Port Stephens, under an hour's drive north of Newcastle. Largely situated along the southern shore of the natural harbour of the same name, it's a popular summer destination.

Top of the list of attractions in Port Stephens is getting out onto the water. If you don't have your own boat, inquire whether you can take your dog onboard if you hire a boat. Alternatively, take the ferry across to the town of Tea Gardens, on the northern shore of the harbour.

Both ferry companies that operate the route allow well-behaved leashed dogs with no size restrictions onboard at no extra charge. The picturesque crossing takes about an hour each way, with dolphins often spotted. Perhaps stop off and enjoy lunch in the dog-friendly beer garden of the Tea Gardens Hotel.

My favourite beach in the area is Bagnalls Beach, between Nelson Bay and Corlette. Dogs are allowed off-leash on the beach and adjacent reserve all day long, with the calm waters of Port Stephens ideal for dogs of all sizes. Dogs are also allowed off-leash at Birubi Beach, but not during the middle of the day during the warmer months.

How to get there

The Central Coast is immediately north of Sydney, with Newcastle just a little further north. Allow about 70 minutes to drive to Gosford on the Central Coast; Newcastle is at least a 2 hour drive from Sydney. Allow extra time for the return drive on Sunday afternoons.

When to visit

The Central Coast and Newcastle region is ideal to visit year-round, at least when the weather is sunny. While the beaches and holiday homes are most popular in summer, hit the walking trails on blue-sky days during the winter months.

Dog-friendly parks

Dog-friendly dining

Tuggerah Dog Park,
Tuggerah

This dog park has three large fenced areas, including one for small dogs, plus a fun obstacle course. There's plenty of easy parking and a small shelter with seats in each area.

Speers Point Dog Exercise Area,
Speers Point

Close to the shores of Lake Macquarie, this park is fenced, with plenty of shade, seating and agility equipment. Avoid the busy times of day if you have a timid dog.

Acacia Avenue Dog Park,
North Lambton

An excellent fenced dog park with high fences and separate areas for large or active, and small or quiet dogs, plus sheltered seating and water fountains.

Point Cafe,
Avoca Beach

Open daily for breakfast and lunch, this beachfront cafe welcomes dogs at the outdoor tables under the pine trees. Although a little pricey, my salad was delicious, and you can enjoy a beer or wine with your meal.

The Boathouse Hotel Patonga,
Patonga

Dogs are welcome at the large outdoor area of this trendy pub, opposite the local off-leash dog beach. There's also a takeaway outlet with decent prices, if you'd prefer a picnic.

Cafe Inu,
Carrington

Just west of the centre of Newcastle, this cafe serves brunch and lunch with a Japanese twist, plus a long list of drinks, including puppycinos. Dogs are welcome outside, plus at a few tables just inside the entry.

Cheeky Dog,
Soldiers Point

Not surprising given its name, this pub and bar near Bannisters (*see* p. 35) in Port Stephens welcomes dogs in the large beer garden outside.

Dog-friendly accommodation

QT Newcastle,
Newcastle

For a luxury stay in the heart of Newcastle, book a Pup Yeah! package at the QT, with a designer dog bed and dog minibar included. One dog up to 20kg is permitted per room, with an additional cleaning fee per stay.

Buccaneer Motel,
Long Jetty

Billing itself as a truly pet-friendly motel, dogs are allowed in any of the reasonably priced double, twin or family rooms at this basic motel. There is a small additional charge per night.

Blacksmiths Beachside Holiday Park,
Blacksmiths

Dogs are welcome year-round at this caravan park, both on powered and unpowered sites, plus in two dog-friendly cabins, each with its own doggy door and enclosed verandah.

Tantarra Bed & Breakfast,
Warners Bay

Pets are warmly welcome at this relaxing B&B. All three guest rooms are pet-friendly and set amongst Balinese-style gardens.

Bannisters Port Stephens,
Soldiers Point

Book a chic waterside stay at Bannisters. Choose between the pet-friendly ground-floor Ocean Deck and Luxury Suite rooms, both of which open directly to the resort's garden.

The walk to Nobbys Lighthouse

Taste wine in the Hunter Valley

The closest major wine-growing region to Sydney, the Hunter Valley is the perfect destination for a day of wine tasting or a luxury weekend away. And there's no need to leave your pup behind – there are plenty of dog-friendly options available in the Hunter Valley, including cellar doors that welcome your pup to join you.

During my most recent visit to the Hunter Valley, I visited the delightfully dog-friendly Briar Ridge Vineyard in Mount View. It's open daily, and you can enjoy a tasting either inside or outside on the deck with your pup, where there's also a handy pooch hydration station.

When making a booking, ideally add a dog treat platter (with enough treats for even a large dog) to your booking – your dog will be kept engrossed during your tasting, although maybe keep the platter up on the table so you can slowly distribute the treats, like I did.

I can also recommend the cheese platters for humans, with a charcuterie or mixed platter also available. With a wide variety of both red and white wines, you're sure to find some bottles to take home with you.

I've also previously had a delightful wine tasting experience with Schnitzel at Tintilla Estate – their cellar door was reminiscent of a Tuscan villa. Enjoy a tasting at the north-facing outdoor tables or inside their semi-enclosed space when the weather isn't so cooperative.

At Tintilla I recommend choosing a VIP wine tasting that includes a selection of their olive products and local cheeses – just the thing to go with wine! I particularly love their sangiovese wines.

More pet-friendly cellar door options include Pepper Tree, Hanging Tree Wines and Hungerford Hill. Alternatively, let someone else drive you and your pup around for the day. Grape to Glass welcomes dogs on Signature Tours, with everything from dog seatbelt restraints to handmade treats included. Or else contact Vino Paw Tours about their all-inclusive pet-friendly packages for the Hunter.

Take a break from wine tasting with a leisurely lunch in the Hunter. One of the most popular dog-friendly spots is The Deck Cafe Lovedale. Open daily for breakfast and lunch, enjoy a meal on their deck overlooking the dam, with heaters above keeping off the chill in winter months. The lunch menu is tapas-style and ideal for sharing, while my pick of the breakfast options is the delicious breakfast burgers.

Don't miss stopping in at the nearby Lovedale Smokehouse Cafe and Deli. As well as plenty of picnic supplies – from cheeses to smoked chicken – they stock a range of dog treats, with doggy donuts and pupcakes in the fridge. Water bowls are also provided if you dine at their cafe, plus there's a stick library!

If you're wanting to make a weekend of your trip to the Hunter (highly recommended after a tough day of wine tasting!) you can choose from a range of pet-friendly accommodation. One of the most popular pet-friendly hotels is Estate Tuscany, where four rooms have been designated as pet-friendly, and there's even a designated pet-friendly table outside their restaurant. Other pet-friendly options include Voco Kirkton Park Hunter Valley (for smaller dogs) and Misty Glen Cottage.

Wine tasting at Tintilla Estate

TASTE WINE IN THE HUNTER VALLEY

Port Macquarie

Just over a 4 hour drive north of Sydney, Port Macquarie is a beautiful coastal holiday town with lots to do. Top of the must-do list when visiting Port Macquarie with your dog is enjoying a stroll along its beautiful coastal walk, plus some off-leash time on its excellent dog beaches. Also consider heading inland for adventures in the local state forests.

The breakwall in Port Macquarie

NEW SOUTH WALES & AUSTRALIAN CAPITAL TERRITORY

FOLLOW THE PORT MACQUARIE COASTAL WALK

A number of walking paths have been combined to create the 9km long Port Macquarie Coastal Walk. Starting from Westport Park, on the western edge of the town centre, the walk follows the coastline south to Tacking Point Lighthouse.

While most of the southern half of the walk is not dog-friendly – including the section along Shelly Beach and through Sea Acres National Park – dogs are welcome to join you on the northern half of the walk. In particular, the two most popular dog-friendly stretches are along the Port Macquarie breakwall and near Nobbys Beach.

To walk along the breakwall with its colourful painted rocks, start from the town centre or the carpark behind Town Beach. There's also easy access from the adjacent NRMA Port Macquarie Breakwall Holiday Park (*see* p. 42), where Schnitzel and I stayed.

Note that dogs are prohibited from Town Beach, but you can walk your dog on the footpath behind the beach, continuing south to Flagstaff Lookout and the small Oxley Beach, where dogs on a leash are allowed on the sand.

Alternatively, head to the section of the Coastal Walk near Nobbys Beach, parking in the carpark at the southern end of the beach. Walk south along Kenny Walk in John Downes Park, as far as the start of Shelly Beach, before enjoying some off-leash fun on Nobbys Beach.

Make sure you keep your dog on a leash all along the walking path, especially in the evening when it can get busy around the breakwall.

ENJOY A DIP AT NOBBYS BEACH

The beaches in the Port Macquarie area alternate between prohibiting dogs, allowing dogs on-leash and allowing dogs off-leash. My pick of the off-leash beaches close to the town centre is Nobbys Beach. (While Rocky Beach is closer, access is difficult, with only a few rough tracks down onto it.)

There's a handy carpark at the southern end of Nobbys Beach, with a short staircase down onto the sand. Dogs are allowed off-leash along the whole length of the beach, with no time restrictions.

The beach is just long enough for a decent off-leash walk, with a handy stick and ball library set up by locals. The beach is partially sheltered, although the waters can still be rough depending on the wind, so keep a close eye on your dog when swimming.

HEAD TO LIGHTHOUSE BEACH

At the southern end of the Port Macquarie Coastal Walk is Lighthouse Beach and the Tacking Point Lighthouse. This unusual lighthouse is very short, a mere 8 metres tall. The rest of its height is provided by the headland on which it's perched. It's a popular spot for whale-watching during the whale migration season between May and November.

Down below, you can go 4WDing with your dog on Lighthouse Beach. There are two 4WD access points: at the southern end of Matthew Flinders Drive and 10km south at Lake Cathie, just north of Dirah Street.

Or just head to Lighthouse Beach for some off-leash time with your pup. While dogs are prohibited from the section of the beach immediately south of the lighthouse, they are allowed off-leash from the Watonga

Top: **Old Bottlebutt Tree** Bottom: **Nobbys Beach, Port Macquarie** Opposite: **Schnitzel found a koala sculpture**

Rocks (near Watonga Street) all the way south to Lake Cathie. It's a huge, wide expanse of sand, with plenty of room for off-leash fun for the most boisterous pups, although keep an eye out for 4WDs.

SEE THE OLD BOTTLEBUTT TREE

While dogs aren't allowed in many of the rainforest areas around Port Macquarie because they're located inside national parks, they are allowed at Burrawan State Forest, home to the impressive Old Bottlebutt Tree.

The Old Bottlebutt Tree is the largest red bloodwood tree in the Southern Hemisphere, estimated to be over 200 years old. A short 600m walking trail leads to the towering tree and passes through a delightful section of remnant rainforest.

It's about a 30 minute drive from Port Macquarie to the Old Bottlebutt Tree. Follow the signs from the southern end of Bago Road. The final stretch through the

state forest is along 3.5km of unsealed but well-maintained roads – I had no trouble in a 2WD campervan. Next to the small carpark, there's also a handy toilet and shelter.

🎨 SPOT A KOALA SCULPTURE

A popular sight around the Port Macquarie region are the many colourful koala sculptures, a tribute to the koalas that live in the area. While dogs are not allowed at the Koala Hospital (a popular local attraction), try to get a selfie with one of the sculptures and your pup.

There are over 70 koala sculptures in total; each is 1 metre high and painted in a unique design by Australian artists. I have spotted sculptures at Cassegrain Wines, outside McDonald's Port Macquarie and in Laurieton. Pick up a map with the latest locations from the Glasshouse visitor information centre, or download a map online.

📍 GO CAMPING AT DELICATE CAMPGROUND

One of the only dog-friendly beach camping grounds in New South Wales is located just north of Port Macquarie. Delicate Campground is in Goolawah Regional Park, just outside the national park of the same name.

The facilities are basic – there are no powered sites, only non-potable bore water, a mix of flushing and pit toilets, and only cold beach showers. However, it is beachfront, with dogs also allowed on the beach, and prices are far lower than for caravan parks in the region. You can also hire braziers from the campground manager on-site.

The campground is best accessed by taking the Crescent Head turn-off along the highway. The most direct route from Port Macquarie involves a ferry and 4WD-only track. Be sure to make an advance booking, with sites booking out quickly during peak periods.

How to get there

Port Macquarie is about a 400km drive north of Sydney. Allow at least 4 hours for the drive, longer during peak holiday periods.

When to visit

Port Macquarie is popular during the warmer months, particularly during the summer and Easter school holidays. If visiting with a dog, you'll have more accommodation options if you avoid these peak periods.

Dog-friendly parks

Dog-friendly accommodation

Stuart Park,
Port Macquarie

A fenced dog park is located in the centre of the park, adjacent to Woods Street. There's a separate section for small dogs, as well as agility equipment.

Dog-friendly dining

Sandbox Cafe,
Port Macquarie

Enjoy lunch with your pup at this cafe overlooking the beach, although dogs are not allowed on the sand below. I loved my warm chicken salad, and the side of chips was perfectly cooked. There's a dog water station for four-legged customers.

Abundance Cafe,
Sancrox

Located within a garden centre, this cafe has a large outdoor dining area next to a small lake. It's a tranquil spot to eat breakfast, lunch or just enjoy a Devonshire tea.

ibis Styles Port Macquarie,
Port Macquarie

This four-star hotel is located just behind Town Beach, close to the start of the Port Macquarie Coastal Walk (*see* p. 39), and has a handful of pet-friendly rooms. Call them directly to make a booking, with an additional fee applying per stay.

NRMA Port Macquarie Breakwall Holiday Park,
Port Macquarie

Centrally located next to the breakwall, pets are allowed on selected powered and unpowered sites, except during the peak Christmas and Easter holiday periods. Dogs often receive a welcome treat at check-in and there's also an on-site dog wash.

Nobbys Beach Cottage,
Port Macquarie

Located close to the off-leash Nobbys Beach, this cottage on Airbnb sleeps up to four, with a queen bed and sofa bed. Up to two small dogs or one large dog is allowed, including inside. Plus there's a fully enclosed yard.

Coffs Harbour

The coastal city of Coffs Harbour is located midway along the north coast of New South Wales, about halfway between Sydney and Brisbane. Stop at the Big Banana for an obligatory selfie with your pup, and then take some time to explore the natural wonders of Coffs, like strolling along the Urunga Boardwalk or heading up to the Forest Sky Pier.

Sunset at Coffs Harbour Jetty

The Urunga Boardwalk

GET A SELFIE AT THE BIG BANANA

Coffs Harbour is synonymous with the Big Banana. Built in 1964 on the grounds of a banana plantation right next to the highway, it was one of Australia's first Big Things and has been the site of countless family holiday snaps.

These days the Big Banana is surrounded by an amusement park. Dogs are allowed onto the grounds, although naturally they aren't allowed inside any of the attractions. Instead, I recommend simply taking a selfie with your dog at the Big Banana – I couldn't resist!

The adjacent cafe also has a convenient pet-friendly section of outdoor seating. Their chocolate-coated frozen bananas are a popular snack.

HEAD UP TO SEALY LOOKOUT

The area surrounding Coffs Harbour contains some beautiful rainforest, although most of it is off-limits to pets because it's within national parks. For a pet-friendly rainforest outing, head instead to the Orara East State Forest and Sealy Lookout.

Take the signposted turn-off not far north of the Big Banana and climb the hills through banana plantations. At the top you'll arrive at the Orara East State Forest, with Sealy Lookout located at the far end of the road. The highlight is the Forest Sky Pier, which extends out over the forest and provides beautiful views of the coast below.

There are also multiple walks close by, including the 650m Gumgali Track to Korora Lookout, starting just a short distance back down the road, and the longer Scenic Rim

Track. Make sure you keep your dog under your control on the walks.

During banana season, don't miss out on stopping at one of the many roadside stalls that line the road up to the lookout – there were plenty of cheap bananas available for sale when Schnitzel and I visited.

👣 VENTURE ALONG THE URUNGA BOARDWALK

About 25 minutes south of Coffs Harbour lies the sleepy coastal town of Urunga. Make sure you detour off the highway and venture out on the Urunga Boardwalk. This impressive 1.2km boardwalk starts just behind the caravan park and then follows the Bellinger River to the beach. A side branch of the boardwalk heads off into the mangroves, which is also worthwhile following.

Leashed dogs are permitted along the entire boardwalk. As a bonus, the beach at the far end permits dogs off-leash, if your dog still has the energy for a run. Make sure you take along poo bags, as there are limited bins and poo-bag dispensers along the walk.

🌊 ENJOY A PADDLE AT THE BEACH

You can't head to Coffs Harbour and not visit some of the beautiful beaches in the area. Even during the winter months, the water stays warm enough for swimming.

One of the most central off-leash beaches is North Wall Beach, just north of the marina in Coffs Harbour. There's plenty of parking, plus it's great to combine a paddle in the water with a visit to the nearby jetty, which permits on-leash dogs. Note that dogs are prohibited on the nearby Jetty Beach and Park Beach (to the north of Coffs Creek, including the reserve).

Schnitzel at the Big Banana

Alternatively, head further north to gorgeous Emerald Beach. Dogs are permitted off-leash at the northern end of the beach, north of Fiddamans Creek. This section of beach is most easily accessed from the adjacent pet-friendly caravan park in Emerald Beach (*see* p. 49), or walk through the reserve to the creek. Dogs are prohibited at the southern end of the beach and at the nearby Look at Me Headland which is popular for its many kangaroos.

Further north, dogs are permitted off-leash at Hearns Lake Beach, Woolgoolga Back and Darkum beaches (except during the little tern breeding season), and Corindi/Pipeclay Beach (south of Ocean Street). Dogs are also permitted off-leash on Boambee Beach, on the southern side of Coffs Harbour, plus at Urunga Beach, between the river mouth and the 4WD access point.

There's also a long list of beaches around Coffs Harbour where dogs are permitted on-leash, including Murray Beach at Sawtell, Korora Beach, Hills Beach, Campbells Beach, Sapphire Beach and the popular Moonee Beach.

Exploring Bellingen

📍 STOP OFF AT THE CLOG BARN

A Dutch-themed barn dedicated to clogs isn't something that I expected to find in Coffs Harbour. This attraction is located next to the pet-friendly caravan park of the same name. It features a beautiful miniature Dutch village, along with clog-making demonstrations and a coffee house.

There's free admission to the model Dutch village, accessible through the shop, and well-behaved dogs are welcome to join you on your visit. See what miniature buildings you can spot in the village!

SPEND A DAY IN BELLINGEN

One of the most charming spots near Coffs Harbour is the small town of Bellingen. Located in the hinterland, just over 30 minutes drive south-west of Coffs, this bohemian outpost on the Bellinger River is a delightful spot to visit with your pup, whether for the day or a longer stay.

Stroll along the main street, browsing cute boutiques (probably best to keep your pup outside) and stopping for coffee or chai at one of the many cafes. Don't miss visiting the Old Butter Factory Complex, just outside town. This sprawling complex is home to art and homeware shops, including The Woodcraft Gallery, as well as an excellent dog-friendly cafe (*see* p. 48).

Afterwards, head to Jarrett Park on the river. Dogs are allowed off-leash to the west of Lavenders Bridge, starting just behind the skate park. It's the perfect spot for doggy swims in the river during the hot summer months.

How to get there

Coffs Harbour is about a 5.5 hour drive north of Sydney, or just over 4 hours south of Brisbane.

When to visit

Coffs Harbour is ideal as a holiday destination year-round. The beaches are most popular during the summer months, but still warm enough during winter for a swim, at least if you're brave or have four legs.

The Forest Sky Pier at Sealy Lookout

 # Dog-friendly parks

 # Dog-friendly dining

West Coffs Reserve District Park, Coffs Harbour

This fairly new large park complex has two fully fenced off-leash areas, including one for small dogs under 10kg (but no puppies). There's also plenty to keep human kids entertained nearby.

Thompsons Road Reserve, Coffs Harbour

This fenced dog park is located on the southern side of Coffs Harbour. There's plenty of shade and benches, even a creek where your dog can have a freshwater swim.

King Tide Brewing, Coffs Harbour

Leashed dogs are welcome in the expansive beer garden, which includes undercover seating. Choose from their range of beers on tap. There are also some delicious share plates to order, as well as burgers on the menu.

Moonee Beach Hotel, Moonee Beach

A family favourite thanks to its minigolf, jumping castle and table tennis. Dogs are welcome in the outdoor dining area at this pub to the north of Coffs Harbour. There's even a dog wash next to the bottle shop!

Old Butter Factory Cafe, Bellingen

Located in the Old Butter Factory Complex just outside of Bellingen, this cafe is open daily for breakfast and lunch, with dogs welcome in the large sheltered outdoor area. The adjacent gelato shop is also dog-friendly.

Dog-friendly accommodation

Reflections Holiday Parks,
Moonee Beach

Regularly praised by pet owners, dogs are allowed year-round at this caravan park next to the on-leash Moonee Beach. Dogs are allowed both on sites and in selected cabins, with direct bookings required.

Discovery Parks,
Emerald Beach

I stayed at this park next to the off-leash section of Emerald Beach, about 20 minutes drive north of Coffs Harbour. Dogs are allowed on all types of sites outside the peak summer holidays and the Easter long weekend.

Friday Creek Retreat,
Upper Orara

A 20 minute drive inland from Coffs Harbour, the Friday Creek Retreat welcomes pets in all nine cottages, as long as you request pre-approval. With open fireplaces and beautiful views of the coastline, you can enjoy a toasty stay year-round.

Top: **The Silver Mill, Bellingen**
Bottom: **Old Butter Factory Cafe**

Byron Bay

Byron Bay in northern New South Wales is one of the most popular beach destinations on Australia's east coast. But what if you're visiting with a dog? Luckily, there's still plenty of fun things to do with your dog, including some excellent dog-friendly beaches and trendy cafes where your pup is welcome. Or head inland for a roadtrip through the Byron Bay Hinterland, stopping off at dog-friendly destinations like Newrybar and the hippie town of Nimbin.

Below: **Strolling around Byron Bay**
Opposite: **Beach time in Byron**

🌊 CHILL ON BELONGIL BEACH

One of the most popular things to do in Byron Bay is to head to its many beautiful beaches. While dogs are not allowed on some of the beaches – including Main Beach, Wategos Beach and Clarkes Beach – dogs are allowed off-leash on Belongil Beach. The off-leash section starts a little west of the Main Beach carpark and extends all the way west to Manfred Street.

Belongil Beach is the perfect spot to spend some time with your pup. Simply laze on beach towels on the sand, or go for a dip in the water – this beach is fairly sheltered, so it's ideal for dogs of all sizes. It's also the perfect spot to head late in the afternoon and enjoy the sunset. Just make sure your dog doesn't help themselves to a picnic like Schnitzel nearly managed!

Just near Belongil Beach is Treehouse Byron Bay (see p. 54), one of my favourite dog-friendly restaurants in Byron.

🌊 WALK ALONG TALLOW BEACH

The other off-leash dog beach close to the centre of Byron Bay is Tallow Beach. Located just south of Cape Byron, the off-leash section of the beach is a long 1.5km, stretching from just south of Arakwal National Park (where there's an access path to the beach) to Jarman Street in Suffolk Park.

This beach is much quieter than Belongil Beach, but with rougher waters. It's the ideal spot for a long off-leash walk with your pup, particularly for larger or more energetic dogs. Just take care in the water, especially if your dog is not used to waves.

Some other off-leash beaches in the region include the southern end of Brunswick Heads Beach, the northern end of Lennox

Head Beach, the Spit in Ballina, New Brighton Beach and South Golden Beach.

Note that dogs are not allowed inside the Cape Byron State Conservation Area, which includes Cape Byron and its lighthouse at the northern end of Tallow Beach.

📍 STOP OFF AT THE FARM AT EWINGSDALE

Next to the turn-off from the Pacific Motorway to Byron Bay is a must-visit stop, whether you're staying in Byron or just passing through. The Farm at Ewingsdale is more than just a farm; it's also home to the popular Three Blue Ducks restaurant, and a number of other foodie outlets.

Your dog will enjoy following a leashed 1km long tour around the property with you – a chance to view the animals and produce growing on the farm. Select between

Off-leash at Brunswick Heads Beach

a guided or self-guided tour. Perhaps also stop off at Baylato to buy a gelato for your walk, or the Bread Social Bakery for supplies for later.

📍 HEAD TO THE HINTERLAND

Head further inland to the Byron Bay Hinterland to explore plenty of cute dog-friendly towns and villages with your pup.

One of the most popular spots is Bangalow. Take a stroll along the main street of Bangalow, lined with many buildings over 100 years old. Keep an eye out for the Bangalow Heritage Walk signs on some of the buildings, for details about their history. It's also a great shopping destination, especially for homewares and clothing, even if you stick to window shopping like Schnitzel and I did.

Not far off the motorway is the delightful small village of Newrybar. Make a beeline for the Harvest deli and coffee stand. Don't miss buying one of their delicious sausage rolls and feasting on it out on the verandah, with your pup by your side. Afterwards, stroll past the gorgeous boutiques, including Harvest Marketplace and Luther & Co. The latter was named after the owner's old German shepherd, and you're likely to still encounter a dog or two out the front.

🔺 GO HIKING AT ROCKY CREEK DAM

Inland from Byron Bay are multiple national parks that are part of the Gondwana Rainforests World Heritage Site. While dogs are not allowed in any of these beautiful and precious national parks, you can instead head to Rocky Creek Dam, adjacent to Nightcap National Park.

A 55 minute drive inland from Byron Bay along some beautiful but rather bumpy roads, the dam is part of the Rous County Council Rainforest and Water Reserve. Dogs are permitted throughout the reserve, although owners are sternly reminded to keep them on a leash (so this privilege can remain).

There are multiple walks in the reserve, as well as a pretty picnic area. One of the longer dog-friendly walks is the Cedar Walk, which passes over the dam wall and spillway, before looping back along the edge of the reserve, through areas of regenerating rainforest. Allow about an hour to complete this 2.3km loop walk.

Note that dogs aren't allowed on the longer Scrub Turkey Walk, which enters the adjacent Nightcap National Park along part of its route.

EXPLORE THE HIPPIE TOWN OF NIMBIN

A little further inland from Byron Bay is the old hippie town of Nimbin. It's a 75 minute drive directly from Byron Bay, or 40 minutes past Rocky Creek Dam along a windy and bumpy road. If you're not visiting Rocky Creek Dam, I recommend following the slightly longer route through Lismore.

Originally just a small dairy farm, Nimbin became the hippie capital of Australia when it hosted the Aquarius Festival in 1973. The town is home to quirky boutiques and shopfronts, including the Nimbin Hemp Embassy, plus some New Age cafes and colourful murals – great for photo ops with your pup.

One of the best times to visit is on the weekend for the Nimbin Market, held on every fourth and fifth Sunday of the month.

How to get there

Byron Bay is over an 8 hour drive north of Sydney, not including any stops. Alternatively, it's just over 2 hours south of Brisbane, close enough for a weekend away.

When to visit

Head to Byron Bay any time of the year, with the milder winter weather a welcome break from the colder temperatures down south, although try to avoid the busy school holiday periods. The spring months tend to be the driest, with heavy rain most common in late summer.

The Nimbin Hemp Embassy

Dog-friendly parks

Lake Suffolk Park,
Suffolk Park

One of the few off-leash areas around Byron Bay that isn't a beach. Dogs are allowed off-leash at this reserve adjacent to Beech Drive, around the shores of the lake. There is a convenient walking path around the lake.

Weir Parklands,
Bangalow

Dogs are allowed off-leash in the Weir Parklands, adjacent to Deacon Street, except in the playgrounds.

Dog-friendly dining

Treehouse Byron Bay,
Byron Bay

Just metres from the off-leash Belongil Beach, this relaxed restaurant and bar under the palm trees welcomes dogs at its many outdoor tables. Open daily from early to late, for breakfast, lunch, dinner or just a drink.

Byron Bay General Store,
Byron Bay

This rustic chic cafe is a trendy spot serving up mainly vegan fare at breakfast and lunch. I highly recommend the smoothie bowls! There's plenty of dog-friendly outdoor seating.

Stone & Wood Brewery,
Byron Bay

Just west of town, this brewery welcomes dogs in its large outdoor space at this brewery. Tasting paddles are available to sample the large range of beer, plus there's a small food menu.

Left: **Stone & Wood Brewery**
Opposite: **Boutiques in Newrybar**

Dog-friendly accommodation

Byron Bay Hotel & Apartments,
Byron Bay

Just a few blocks back from the beach, selected rooms on the ground floor have been designated as pet-friendly, with a range of room sizes available. An additional charge applies per stay.

The Chalet Motel,
Brunswick Heads

A beautifully renovated classic 60s-style hotel. Pets are allowed with prior approval and an additional charge per stay. Brunswick Heads is a more relaxed alternative to Byron, with its own off-leash beach.

Ingenia Holidays Byron Bay,
Byron Bay

Pets are allowed on campsites and in selected studio cabins and standard villas, subject to blackout dates. The park has its own fenced off-leash dog exercise area, plus it's a short walk from the off-leash Tallow Beach, although the access path was flooded during my stay.

Central West

Located on the other side of the Blue Mountains from Sydney, the Central West region is close enough for a long weekend or ideal for a week-long roadtrip.

Base yourself in Mudgee, Orange or Dubbo, or stay in all three, and explore the region's wineries, rich history, good produce and more. There are also some surprising dog-friendly attractions that I've uncovered.

Right: **Bring your best fur-friend to a cellar door** Opposite: **Hanging out in Millthorpe**

🍷 VISIT A CELLAR DOOR OR TWO

The Central West region is home to not just one but multiple wine regions. My favourite wine region to visit is the Mudgee region, thanks to a wide variety of cellar doors, combined with the charms of an old-fashioned country town where the main street is still wide enough to turn around a horse and cart.

Many of the cellar doors around Mudgee allow dogs to join you, whether inside or outside. One of the top dog-friendly cellar doors, and definitely one to book in advance, is Lowe Wine. Best known for its organic wines, most of the tastings take place outdoors on the terrace, or inside the rustic barn. You'll likely spot the resident wine dog, and your own dog is welcome to visit, as long as they are friendly and kept leashed.

Other top dog-friendly cellar doors to visit around Mudgee include Robert Stein (choose between four different tastings and check out the collection of historic motorbikes), di Lusso Estate (match the Italian varietal wines with a wood-fired pizza) and Moothi Estate – where dogs are welcome both inside and outside at the heated seating area.

Another major wine region in the Central West is the Orange region, renowned for its cool-climate wines, grown on the slopes of Mt Canobolas. Make a booking in advance with Cargo Road Wines (also home to two resident kelpies; I enjoyed a tasting on the deck overlooking the vines with Schnitzel by my side) or Philip Shaw Wines (perhaps accompany your tasting with a plate of local cheese, lavosh and more).

If you'd prefer to go on a winery tour with someone else doing the driving, make an inquiry with Country Food Trails in Orange.

Their private wine tours can be tailored to include your dog. Alternatively, there are multiple tour operators in the Mudgee region that are pet-friendly – check the latest listings in the Mudgee region tourism brochure and then call for further details.

📍 STEP BACK IN TIME AT HILL END

Just over an hour west of Mudgee is the quaint town of Hill End. Once a thriving gold-mining town that was home to over 8000 residents, these days it's a picturesque ghost town looked after by the National Parks and Wildlife Service. While dogs are not allowed in national parks in New South Wales, they are allowed at Hill End, except for inside the Heritage Centre.

Only a fraction of the buildings that once lined the streets in Hill End remain. As you and your dog walk along the streets, historic photographs show what they once looked like. The atmospheric location has also been immortalised by many Australian artists, including Russell Drysdale and Margaret Olley.

Don't miss following the walking track to Bald Hill Mine. I also recommend stopping at Golden Gully to see the erosion resulting from the mining activities, although keep your dog on a short leash due to the unstable ground. You can also try fossicking for gold nearby at Tambaroora.

While in Hill End, drop by the Royal Hotel or the General Store, both still operating. At the General Store Cafe dogs are welcome in the outdoor seating area – Schnitzel was even offered a treat. It's an ideal destination to visit on a daytrip from Mudgee, or else stay overnight at either of the local campgrounds; both are pet-friendly.

A rustic cottage at Hill End

VISIT THE COWRA JAPANESE GARDEN

A surprising attraction in the Central West region is the largest Japanese garden in the Southern Hemisphere. Cowra was the site of a tragic escape of Japanese prisoners from the local prisoner-of-war camp during World War II, with the Cowra Japanese Garden later built as a gesture of friendship between Japan and the town.

These days the gardens are over 5 hectares in size, magnificently constructed with a lake, water cascade and tea-house pavilion. The gardens are at their most beautiful during the cherry blossom season (late September to early October) and when the many deciduous trees turn red, orange and yellow during autumn. But it was still beautiful on the sunny winter day when Schnitzel and I visited.

Leashed dogs are welcome to join you on a stroll around the garden, and also while you enjoy lunch or afternoon tea at the cafe overlooking the gardens. At the cafe, dogs are welcome in the outdoor area, with a gate providing direct access from the gardens. Cowra is about a 70 minute drive south of the city of Orange.

VENTURE INSIDE OLD DUBBO GAOL

One of the most surprising dog-friendly attractions in the Central West is Old Dubbo Gaol, in the city of Dubbo. While dogs are strictly prohibited from visiting the other major attraction in town – Taronga Western Plains Zoo – you're able to visit this historic 19th-century gaol with your pet, as long as they're friendly and leashed (or in a carrier).

Open daily, there's a mix of permanent displays and talks. Try to time your visit for one of the costumed talks on weekends and during school holidays. While it's been many years since I last visited this attraction as a kid and was left terrified, I'm relieved to know when I next return I can have my dog by my side to keep me safe!

 WANDER THROUGH MILLTHORPE

The Central West boasts a number of charming villages, but one of the cutest is Millthorpe. Just a 20 minute drive south-east of Orange, this village is a relatively undiscovered gem.

This National Trust heritage-listed village was home to a once-thriving flour mill, which has since closed, plus a railway station which still exists on the edge of town. These days its heritage buildings contain an enticing assortment of boutiques, cafes and cellar doors.

I recommend exploring the village on one of two self-guided walks. Maps and information are provided on the outside of the Millthorpe Corner Store, plus on the village website. Both walks are of course dog-friendly, as is much of the village.

TAKE A WALKING TOUR OF MUDGEE

Mudgee saw a boom during the late 1800s after gold was found in the surrounding region, and the town is home to many beautiful historic buildings from that era. The post office, police station, courthouse and Catholic church all date to around 1860 and have been heritage listed.

Every Saturday and Sunday morning a 1 hour Mudgee Heritage Walking Tour is held, highlighting the town's heritage buildings and sharing fascinating stories. The tours generally start outside the Clock Tower, on the corner of Market and Church streets, at 10am. Advance bookings are essential and can be made online. There is no charge for kids, and dogs on a leash are also welcome to join you for free.

 DRIVE AROUND MOUNT PANORAMA

Bathurst is also home to many fine buildings from the gold rush era. However, it's better known for the Mount Panorama Racing Circuit, home to the annual Bathurst 1000 car race.

For most of the year the racing circuit is a regular road. And yes, you can drive around it, with your dog in the car. Complete a lap around the track, stopping along the way at the Main Straight and the lookout at the top for some photos. Just keep to the signposted 60km/hr!

How to get there

Mudgee is about a 4 hour drive west of Sydney, with Orange also a similar distance. Allow over 5 hours for the drive from Sydney to Dubbo.

When to visit

The best time to explore the Central West is during spring or autumn, when the temperatures are mild and many of the region's food and wine festivals are held.

CENTRAL WEST 59

Dog-friendly parks

Jennie Blackman Dog Park, Putta Bucca

This excellent fully fenced dog park on the edge of Mudgee has double gates, seating and separate areas for small and large dogs. Drive to the park or walk there from town on the shared path.

Bloomfield Park, Orange

This park is my favourite off-leash dog park in Orange. Although unfenced, it's a huge area with plenty to explore, including multiple creeks – perfect for bigger dogs.

Dog-friendly dining

Mudgee Brewing Co, Mudgee

Dogs are welcome at the outdoor courtyard of this brewery in the centre of Mudgee. As well as tasting paddles and an extensive local wine list, there are pizzas, burgers and more substantial items on the menu.

Nile Street Cafe, Orange

Open for breakfast and lunch from Wednesday to Sunday, dogs are allowed in the lovely shaded courtyard.

Gracie's at 4 Pines, Orange

This craft beer and burger bar is open daily for both lunch and dinner. Dogs can relax at the tables in their beer garden, with photos of previous four-legged visitors decorating the wall.

Left: **Lowe Wine in Mudgee** Opposite top: **Lake Canabolas in Orange** Opposite bottom: **Driving around Mount Panorama**

Dog-friendly accommodation

Evanslea,
Mudgee

This five-star boutique guesthouse in Mudgee has four luxury cottages, as well as a house for larger groups, surrounded by beautiful grounds. Contact the property in advance for approval to bring along your pet.

Turon Gates,
Capertee

An authentic bush getaway between Lithgow and Mudgee, pets are welcome in the cottages and cabins, as well as when camping. Note that access is by a dirt road.

NRMA Dubbo Holiday Park,
Dubbo

This extra pet-friendly caravan park allows pets on sites and in their pet-friendly cabins – each cabin has its own fenced yard and kennel. There's also a fenced off-leash dog park on-site and pet-sitters can be recommended.

Millthorpe Motel,
Millthorpe

Centrally located in charming Millthorpe, selected rooms at this motel are pet-friendly for well-behaved dogs. Contact reception for full details.

CENTRAL WEST

Canberra/ Ngambri/ Ngunnawal

Many visitors with dogs are surprised by how dog-friendly Canberra is, myself included. While I wouldn't venture inside Parliament House with my dog, or visit the many excellent museums, there are still plenty of dog-friendly things to do in the nation's capital. Take in the views from Mt Ainslie, walk along the shores of Lake Burley Griffin, explore the National Arboretum and don't miss taking a selfie in front of Parliament House.

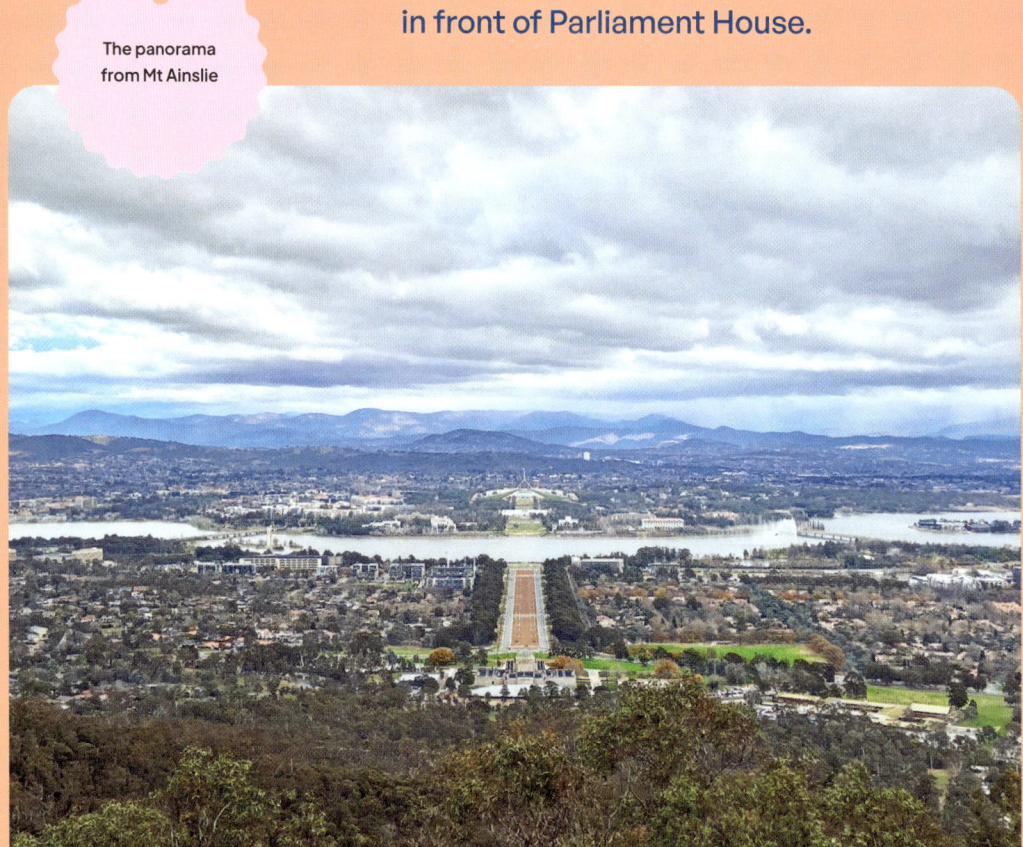

The panorama from Mt Ainslie

📍 VISIT PARLIAMENT HOUSE

Just as humans can walk on the lawns in front of Parliament House, dogs are also allowed access to this space, sometimes dubbed 'The Great Verandah of Australia'. For the ultimate Canberra dog-selfie, get a photo of your dog outside the iconic front of Parliament House.

While visiting Parliament House, also drive and explore on foot the rest of the Parliamentary Zone, which extends to the shores of Lake Burley Griffin. It's home to a number of important sites including Old Parliament House and the International Flag Display. It's fine for leashed dogs to walk around with you.

Across the lake, pet dogs are also allowed to visit the exterior of the imposing Australian War Memorial. Check out the sculptures and military vehicles on display, plus walk along Anzac Parade and view the many memorials.

📍 TAKE IN THE VIEW FROM MT AINSLIE

Canberra has a unique layout for an Australian city, thanks to the modern designs of Walter Burley Griffin. To best appreciate its layout, head to the summit of Mt Ainslie. One of the tallest peaks around Canberra, Mt Ainslie is deliberately situated at one end of the axis that extends through Parliament House to the Australian War Memorial.

The easiest way to reach the summit of Mt Ainslie is to drive up; there's a carpark at the top. However, it's also possible to walk up to the summit through the Mount Ainslie Nature Reserve, with dogs on a leash welcome in the reserve. A walking path starts behind the War Memorial.

A chilly day at the National Arboretum

🐾 STROLL THROUGH THE NGA SCULPTURE GARDEN

While dogs are naturally not allowed inside the National Gallery of Australia, the same restrictions don't apply to the Sculpture Garden outside. Just make sure you keep your dog on a leash and clean up after them!

The Sculpture Garden contains around 30 works by both Australian and international sculptors from the 19th, 20th and 21st centuries. One of the most famous works is a partial edition of Rodin's *The Burghers of Calais*, although my favourite work is Clement Meadmore's *Virginia*.

You can also enjoy a wander through the Sculpture Garden as part of a longer walk along the shores of Lake Burley Griffin, including the popular Bridge to Bridge Walk.

Dogs' Day Out at Floriade

👣 COMPLETE THE BRIDGE TO BRIDGE WALK

Multiple walking and cycling paths loop around Lake Burley Griffin. Around 30km of paths are divided into the Western, Central and Eastern loops, with dogs permitted on most of them; the main exception is the section of the Eastern Loop that passes through Jerrabomberra Wetlands Nature Reserve.

The most popular walk around the lake is the Central Loop, also known as the Bridge to Bridge Walk because it loops between the Commonwealth Avenue and Kings Avenue bridges. As well as passing the NGA Sculpture Garden, the 5km walk also passes the Captain James Cook Memorial water jet, Commonwealth Park and the International Flag Display.

📍 HEAD TO THE NATIONAL ARBORETUM

The National Arboretum on the western edge of Canberra was established in 2005 following the devastating bushfires of 2003 that swept through the area. It opened to the public in 2013 and still looks quite young, since many of its trees take years to mature.

My favourite section was the Himalayan cedars area. Predating the rest of the arboretum, the cedars were planted over 100 years ago. There are over 20km of walking trails throughout the arboretum. Schnitzel and I went for a walk through the cedar grove and up to the *Wide Brown Land* sculpture.

Dogs are welcome on all trails at the arboretum; just keep them on a leash and bring your own poo bags. Note they are not allowed inside the Village Centre, including the adjacent National Bonsai and Penjing Collection, plus the playground. The arboretum is particularly stunning to visit in autumn, thanks to its plantings of deciduous trees.

SNIFF THE FLOWERS IN SPRING

Every year between September and October, the month-long Floriade Festival is held in Canberra, with ornate flower displays in Commonwealth Park, between Lake Burley Griffin and the Canberra city centre.

Most days of the festival dogs are not allowed in Commonwealth Park, but the final day is usually designated as a Dogs' Day Out, with free entry to all pooches. Double-check the program to see if it's happening, and find out what other fun dog events are being held on the day.

Around the same time of year, Tulip Top Gardens in Sutton also opens to the public for about a month. These beautiful gardens are located just off the Federal Highway. Leashed dogs are welcome to join you any day the gardens are open.

GO FOR A DOGGY PADDLE

Just because Canberra is located a long way inland, doesn't mean there's nowhere for dogs to enjoy a swim during the hot days of summer, thanks to the many lakes dotted around the city.

While dogs are prohibited from the public swimming beaches, there are currently seven designated dog-swimming beaches. In Yarralumla, head to Orana Bay or Kurrajong Point Beach. At Belconnen, visit Lake Ginninderra or Diddams Close. Dogs are also allowed to swim at Point Hut Pond in Gordon, Lake Tuggeranong in Greenway and Yerrabi Pond in Gungahlin.

Further afield, head to the Murrumbidgee River outside the city. There are plenty of welcoming waterholes to cool down in at Uriarra Recreation Reserve Area, with dogs allowed off-leash at Uriarra East, Uriarra West and Swamp Creek picnic areas. Dogs are also allowed off-leash on the western riverbank of the Point Hut Crossing recreational area.

PLAY IN THE SNOW

If you're visiting Canberra during the depths of winter instead of summertime, you'll likely experience some bitterly cold weather. A few falls of snow are typical most winters in Canberra, but to be guaranteed enough snow to play in, head to the Corin Forest snow play area, 45 minutes south of Canberra.

While the picnic area is dog-friendly, generally the snow play area with paid entry is not open to dogs. However, they host a handful of designated Snow Dogs sessions each September, at the end of the season. Check their social media channels in August to find out the dates and make a booking.

How to get there

It's just over a 3 hour drive to Canberra from Sydney, along the Hume and Federal highways. From Melbourne it's at least a 7 hour drive.

When to visit

It's best to visit Canberra during spring or autumn, when many festivities ranging from Floriade to wine festivals are held. Summers can be uncomfortably hot, and overnight winter temperatures often fall below freezing.

Dog-friendly parks

Yarralumla Dog Park,
Yarralumla

This large fenced dog park has separate sections for small and large dogs, plus benches and water taps. Although when Schnitzel and I visited there wasn't much grass, mainly dirt under paw.

Barkley Dog Park,
Googong

Located just outside Canberra near Queanbeyan, this large and rather wild (but fenced) park is a great spot for adventurous dogs – it even has its own dam.

Dog-friendly dining

Local Press Cafe,
Kingston

Drop into this cafe while strolling around Lake Burley Griffin. It specialises in fresh and natural wholefoods, along with cold pressed juices. Dogs are welcome at the outdoor tables next to the water.

Snapper & Co,
Yarralumla

Enjoy a lakeside meal of fish and chips while lazing with your dog on the lawns at the Southern Cross Yacht Club. I loved the large, delectable chunks of fish on my burger.

Capital Brewing Co,
Fyshwick

Dogs are welcome both inside and outside at their Taproom. There's also a permanent food truck serving burgers and hot dogs.

Below: A stroll past the cherry blossoms at Lake Burley Griffin
Opposite: Schnitzel at Parliament House

Dog-friendly accommodation

Abode Hotels

Five of their seven locations around Canberra currently welcome dogs in selected rooms. All rooms are self-contained, with a small kitchenette. Pet-friendly rooms at the Narrabundah property have access to a dog run.

Mercure Canberra, Braddon

This heritage-listed hotel has dedicated pet-friendly rooms, each with its own courtyard. No size limits apply and pet-sitting can be arranged.

Capital Country Holiday Park, Sutton

Located just outside the Australian Capital Territory border, this pet-friendly caravan park has four fenced 'dog freedom sites', plus two dog-friendly bungalows. Dogs are also permitted on regular powered and unpowered sites.

02

Victoria

Melbourne/Naarm	70
Echuca	76
High Country	81
Play in snow at Dinner Plain	88
Gippsland	90
Step back in time at Walhalla	96
Mornington Peninsula	98
Yarra Valley & Dandenong Ranges	104
Daylesford & Macedon Ranges	110
Goldfields	116
Great Ocean Road	122

Melbourne/ Naarm

A discussion about which is the better city in Australia, Sydney or Melbourne, can elicit strong opinions on both sides. However, when it comes to which city in Australia is most dog-friendly, Melbourne wins hands down. Dogs are often allowed on public transport throughout the city (including larger dogs on trains), plus the city is home to plenty of dog-friendly attractions. From hiking and beaches to the city's street art and laneways, there's plenty of fun things to do with your dog.

Schnitzel explores Melbourne's laneways

CHECK OUT WORLD-CLASS STREET ART

Melbourne is deservedly world famous for its street art. And spending a few hours exploring it on foot is actually a fabulous activity to do in Melbourne's city centre with your pup. Unlike art galleries, there are no rules against pets walking down laneways! Although I think Schnitzel wasn't sure what all the fuss was about.

The best known destination for street art in Melbourne is Hosier Lane, not far from Federation Square. I also highly recommend visiting nearby AC/DC Lane and Duckboard Place, which are usually less crowded.

If you'd prefer not to head all the way into the city centre, there's lots more great street art in other inner-city suburbs of Melbourne, including Ftizroy, Brunswick and Prahran. It's an ideal activity to combine with brunch at a local cafe or a drink at a pet-friendly pub.

EXPLORE THE BOTANIC GARDENS

Unlike the Royal Botanic Garden in Sydney, dogs are welcome at the Royal Botanic Gardens Victoria in the centre of Melbourne. Leashed dogs are allowed to join you for a stroll around the gardens, whether around the ornamental lake, through the fern gully or past the 'volcano'.

Another highlight of a visit to the Botanic Gardens is going for a punt on the lake. Between September and May, private guided punt tours depart from the landing in front of the Terrace Cafe. Lasting 30 minutes, the punts can hold up to six passengers, with well-behaved dogs welcome to join you for free. It's best to book in advance, especially during busy holiday periods.

SPEND THE DAY AT ST KILDA

It's just a short drive or tram ride from the centre of Melbourne to the bayside suburb of St Kilda. A popular beach destination close to the city, it's also a terrific spot to visit with your pup.

While your dog won't be allowed inside the Luna Park amusement park (and they probably wouldn't appreciate the screams from ride-goers), you can take your leashed dog for a walk out on the long pier, or visit one of the surrounding beaches.

St Kilda Beach to the east of the pier only permits dogs on the sand during winter. Instead, head to the western side, near Pier Road, where dogs are allowed off-leash all day long, year-round. Dogs are also allowed year-round on the sand at St Kilda West, except for the sensitive dune area.

For a fun adventure with your pup, book one of the Paddle and Brunch events run by the local dog-friendly cafe, Chez Misty (*see* p. 74). Together with your dog you'll enjoy a 1 hour stand-up paddleboard session out on the bay, then breakfast together back at Chez Misty. The events run over summer, mainly on Saturdays, with group sizes kept small and life jackets included.

For a more sedate day out, check out the market along the Esplanade that is held every Sunday. And don't miss stopping at one of the old-school cafes along Acland Street for coffee and cake.

VISIT THE BRIGHTON BATHING BOXES

One of the most photogenic spots in Melbourne is Brighton Beach and its famous colourful bathing boxes. It's the perfect spot for photos with your pooch, as long as you get there early or late in the day if you visit during the busy summer months.

Along this stretch of Brighton Beach, dogs are allowed off-leash all day long between April and October. However, between November and March, dogs are forbidden from the sand during the middle of the day. They are only allowed off-leash before 10am or after 7.30pm. In any case, during summer it's best to head to Brighton Beach early to avoid the crowds.

For a terrific beach nearby where off-leash dogs are welcome all day long, head to Brighton Dog Beach at the end of Sandown Street. Thanks to its shallow water, it's a great spot for dogs of all sizes to enjoy a paddle. However, its most unique feature is that it's mainly fenced!

 FROLIC AT ALTONA DOG BEACH

For more beach fun with your dog in Melbourne, another popular dog-friendly beach is Altona Dog Beach. This beach is located west of the city and has plenty of easy, free parking.

Dogs are welcome off-leash at this beach all day long, year-round, both on the beach and in the adjacent fenced PA Burns Reserve off-leash park. It's best to visit at low tide, when it's possible to wade with your dog a long way off-shore.

Afterwards, make use of the dog wash-down area next to the carpark. I was impressed with the multiple spraying taps at different heights for dogs of all sizes.

HIKE IN THE YOU YANGS

For a fun day of dog-friendly hiking just outside Melbourne, head to the You Yangs Regional Park. Less than an hour south-west of Melbourne, not far from Geelong, this regional park welcomes dogs to join you, as long as they stay on a leash.

The You Yangs were named after the local Wathaurong phrase for 'big mountain in the middle of the plain', which is an apt description for Flinders Peak. The most popular walking track in the park leads to the summit of this granite outcrop, with superb views from the top back towards Melbourne and across the Bellarine Peninsula. The 3.5km return walk took Schnitzel and me about an hour to complete. Note that there are lots of steps along the way!

There's a variety of shorter and longer walks, including some flatter options. An easier walk is the 800m circuit around Big Rock. And don't miss the short walk to the top of Big Rock, just a 100m stroll from the carpark. There's also plenty of picnic areas throughout the park.

Below: **On top of Flinders Peak**
Opposite: **The St Kilda Foreshore**

GO BUSH AT YARRA BEND PARK

Yarra Bend Park is only 4km north-east of Melbourne's city centre, but it is home to the largest area of natural bushland left in the inner suburbs of Melbourne and is a tranquil respite from the city streets.

The park is situated on both banks of the Yarra River. There's a wide variety of walks on offer in the park, ranging from the rather short Bushland Circuit Trail to the 9.5km trail to the iconic Dights Falls, including the Westfield Extension.

Dogs are permitted in most areas of Yarra Bend Park, although there are a few areas where they are not allowed. The park also contains a number of off-leash areas – check the signage and make sure you always carry a leash. The best spot for a doggy swim in the river is just below Deep Rock.

If you're interested in taking your pup out on the river, head to Fairfield Park Boathouse. You can choose between renting a boat, a canoe or a kayak, with dogs welcome to join you. The outdoor tables at the adjacent restaurant are also dog-friendly.

 ## HIRE A BOAT ON THE YARRA

Hiring a boat at Yarra Bend Park isn't the only option for getting out on the Yarra with your pup. Another option is to hire one of the pet-friendly picnic boats available at GoBoat, located next to the city centre on the northern bank of the Yarra River near the Sandridge Bridge.

Accommodating up to eight people and not requiring a boat licence, these luxury electric picnic boats can be hired for between 1 and 3 hours, with optional extras including cheese boards and esky hires. BYO picnic and drinks!

The staff members will recommend a route for you based on the duration of your hire. Or you can just find a sheltered spot to park your boat and enjoy a leisurely time out on the river, with the city skyline as your backdrop.

When to visit

Melbourne is well-known for having four seasons in one day, and I can whole-heartedly agree, no matter what time of year I visit! Try to avoid summer when it can be oppressively hot, but winter has some bitterly cold mornings. Spring or autumn are the best options.

 # Dog-friendly parks

 # Dog-friendly dining

Kings Way Fenced Dog Park,
Southbank

One of the only fenced off-leash areas close to the centre of Melbourne, this park is ideal if you're staying nearby with your pup. This urban-style fenced park has gravel rather than grass. There are some interesting features for your dog to explore, from tunnels to logs, plus undercover seating.

Clayton Reserve Fenced Dog Park,
North Melbourne

On the western edge of North Melbourne, this spacious grassy park is a favourite amongst local dog owners. It's fully fenced with benches and lights, and it's even easy to park nearby.

Aranga Reserve Dog Park,
Donvale

This large and grassy fenced dog park, not far from the M3 motorway, stands out for its agility equipment. There are two obstacle courses for dogs to tackle, plus a smaller fenced area for more timid dogs.

The General Assembly,
South Wharf

Southbank is home to plenty of dog-friendly outdoor dining spaces, including The General Assembly. I loved that the outdoor area was mainly covered and fitted with outdoor heaters, plus they have weekday happy hour and meal specials.

The Commons Collective,
Melbourne

Often declared to be Melbourne's most beautiful garden cafe and wine bar, dogs are welcome in outdoor areas, including the beer garden. Treat your pup to a doggy daybed and a puppa-cino from their menu.

Chez Misty,
St Kilda

This French creperie has a whole menu of crepes and puppycinos just for dogs, as well as savoury galettes and sweet crepes for humans. Out the back are couches for canines, plus there's an indoor off-leash relaxing room.

Dog-friendly accommodation

The colourful bathing boxes at Brighton Beach

The Langham Melbourne, Southbank

For the ultimate dog-friendly luxury stay, make a booking for a Pampered Pets Staycation. One pet up to 20kg is permitted per room, with breakfast in bed included and a Private Dining Menu just for your pet.

Best Western Melbourne City, Melbourne

One of the first pet-friendly hotels in Melbourne's city centre, I've stayed in one of the pet-friendly courtyard rooms at this centrally located hotel. A small additional fee applies per night for pets.

Element Melbourne Richmond, Richmond

Stay 6km east of the city at this hotel focused on wellness, with eco-friendly features. Up to two dogs with a combined weight of 20kg are welcome in selected rooms, for an additional fee per night.

Crystal Brook Tourist Park, Doncaster East

One of the best pet-friendly caravan parks close to Melbourne, although a 30 minute drive from the city centre. Pets are allowed on sites plus in selected cabins. The park has its own off-leash dog exercise area with an agility course.

Echuca

Lying on the banks of the Murray River in northern Victoria, Echuca was home to the largest inland port in Australia during its heyday in the late 19th century. Today it is one of the most dog-friendly destinations in Victoria, with dogs welcome at a wide range of attractions. Take a paddlesteamer cruise on the Murray, enjoy lunch at a local winery, stroll through the largest cactus garden in Australia or explore a fine collection of historic Holdens, all with your dog by your side.

The Discovery Centre at the Historic Port of Echuca

📍 EXPLORE THE HISTORIC PORT OF ECHUCA

Echuca is known for its historic port and the role it played in the riverboat trade on the Murray River. Many of the old buildings and its wharf have been wonderfully preserved.

It's a must to wander through the Historic Port district, imagining what the town was like during its heyday. And, of course, your dog is welcome to join you, as long as they stay on a leash.

Dogs are even welcome to join you, both inside and outside, at the Discovery Centre. This free museum, situated at the old wharf, explores the history of the town and includes displays of steam engines and trains. Just make sure your dog is well behaved and stays on a leash, so this privilege remains.

You can also take a number of guided tours around the port that are dog-friendly, including the Port After Dark Lantern Tours, where hopefully your pup will keep you safe from any ghosts lurking around.

🐕 TAKE A PADDLESTEAMER CRUISE

One of the highlights of a visit to Echuca is heading out on the Murray River on a paddlesteamer cruise. The region is home to the world's largest operating paddlesteamer fleet, and you can experience a cruise on many of the original steamers, some built right on-site.

Luckily, your dog doesn't need to miss out, with many of the paddlesteamers welcoming dogs onboard for the trip. Generally only lunch and dinner cruises on the paddlesteamers don't allow dogs onboard, but double-check when booking.

Schnitzel and I took an hour-long cruise onboard the *PS Alexander Arbuthnot*, operated by Echuca Paddlesteamers. They operate multiple cruises daily. Dogs are welcome to join you for free, and even receive their own cute K9 Cargo Ticket.

Onboard the steamer there were no restrictions on where dogs could go, with a resident dog occupying the warm spot next to the engine during the chilly winter morning of our visit.

📍 VISIT THE HOLDEN MOTOR MUSEUM

For a different land-based Australian icon, walk around the corner from the Port of Echuca to the National Holden Motor Museum.

Over 50 Holdens are on display ranging from the earliest to the latest models, including a half-and-half car that compares the old models to the newest ones. It offers a fascinating insight into cars for everyone, not just Holden enthusiasts. There's also plenty of historical footage, memorabilia, prototypes and more.

Well-behaved on-leash dogs are allowed in the museum. Just like human visitors, they should also not touch any of the cars, so I kept Schnitzel on a very short leash.

🍷 ENJOY A CRUISE TO A WINERY

There are a number of wineries dotted around the countryside just outside Echuca, on both sides of the Victorian–New South Wales border. One of the best wineries to visit with your dog is Morrisons Winery in Moama. And instead of driving to the winery, thanks to its location near the banks of the Murray, you can visit it on a Wharf to Winery cruise.

Step onboard the *PS Canberra* paddlesteamer in the Port of Echuca for a 30 minute cruise upstream to the winery's wharf. After you disembark, enjoy a tasting of Morrison's fine wines, before sitting down for a two-course lunch with a complimentary glass of wine or beer.

The cruise generally operates from Thursday to Sunday each week – the days the winery and restaurant are open – with advance bookings essential on weekends. Dogs are welcome at the winery and on the cruise for no additional charge.

Other dog-friendly wineries in the region include Cape Horn Vineyard in Echuca, Old School Winery in Womboota and St Anne's Winery in Moama.

 MARVEL AT THE SILO ART

The countryside surrounding Echuca is home to some beautiful examples of silo art. For a great dog-friendly roadtrip, pick up the latest visitors guide for Echuca, where you'll find a listing of nearby silo art.

My favourite silo art near Echuca is in the town of Rochester, about a 20 minute drive south. As part of Rochester GrainCorp Silos, a pair of silos were painted with magnificent portraits of a squirrel glider and an azure kingfisher by Jimmy Dvate in 2018. The town is also home to a number of other murals – go for a wander and see what you find.

On your silo-art roadtrip, also drop into Colbinabbin and Kyabram. Most years at least one new silo is painted, so there's always something new to see.

Below: **Camping next to the Murray River**
Opposite: **Silo art in Rochester**

🪑 HEAD TO CACTUS COUNTRY

Something unexpected that you'll find in the Murray River Valley is Cactus Country. Located an hour east of Echuca, in Strathmerton, it's the largest cactus garden in Australia – a taste of Mexico in the Victorian countryside!

The picturesque farm has a number of walking trails, with dogs welcome to join you. Just make sure they stay on a leash close to your side – cacti spikes are very unforgiving! There are even multiple water bowls located throughout the garden.

Also on-site are a bar and restaurant, where you can enjoy freshly made margaritas or Mexican-style sodas, as well as sample some cactus ice-cream and cake. The farm is open from Wednesday to Sunday.

CAMP BY THE MIGHTY MURRAY

While Echuca is home to plenty of dog-friendly caravan parks and other accommodation options in town, a fun alternative is camping with your pup by the banks of the mighty Murray River. Three dog-friendly campsites close to town are Wills Bend, Betts Beach and Christies Beach.

Schnitzel and I spent the night at Wills Bend, located in the Murray River Reserve, about 17km west of Echuca. It was a wonderful peaceful spot with beautiful sunsets and sunrises, although the final 5km unsealed stretch of the access road (via O'Dwyer Road) was a bit rough.

Betts Beach and Christies Beach are located about 8km east of Echuca, both accessed by Simmie Road.

How to get there

Echuca lies along the Murray River, on the border between Victoria and New South Wales. It's under a 3 hour drive directly north of Melbourne.

When to visit

Echuca is a sunny destination, but experiences hot and sticky summers, and rather chilly winters. It's best to visit during spring or autumn, when it's not too cool in the morning, but the days are still warm and often sunny.

 # Dog-friendly parks

 # Dog-friendly accommodation

Moama Off Leash Dog Park,
Moama

This recently established off-leash dog park is just north of the river, on Perricoota Road in Moama. Fully fenced, it's a great naturally landscaped environment for dogs to play in, or just sniff and explore.

 # Dog-friendly dining

Henry's Bridge Hotel,
Echuca

Dogs are welcome in the large beer garden on the northern side of the pub, which has plenty of sunshine on wintery days (plus umbrellas for summer). I found the burgers well priced and tasty.

Johnny & Lyle's,
Echuca

This relaxed and friendly cafe is popular with both local and visiting pups. Open bright and early each morning for all-day breakfast plus lunch, portions are generous and it's fully licensed.

Rich River Caravan Park,
Echuca

Pets are welcome year-round, both on sites and in selected Standard and Deluxe cabins, for an additional fee. There's a dog wash on-site, plus an off-leash dog exercise area in one corner of the park.

Murray River Holiday Park,
Moama

We stayed in this park next to the Moama Recreation Reserve, perfect for dog walks. Pets are allowed on sites and in selected cabins. The park has a dog wash and an excellent camp kitchen.

River Country Inn,
Moama

The rooms at this country motel wrap around a garden with a pool and barbecue area. One of the rooms with both a queen and single bed is dog-friendly, with no size restrictions.

Henry's Bridge Hotel in Echuca

High Country

The High Country in north-east Victoria is home to snow-covered mountains, cascading rivers and a rich history. It's a charming region to visit and very welcoming to doggy visitors.

In the west is the town of Beechworth, full of fascinating old buildings to explore and interesting walks to follow. Or head east to Bright, the perfect base for outdoor activities, from hiking to cycling to swimming or doggy-paddling in the river.

Schnitzel on the Canyon Walk in Bright

The Historic and Cultural Precinct in Beechworth

EXPLORE HISTORIC BEECHWORTH

The High Country town of Beechworth boomed during the gold rush of the 1850s and is one of the best preserved towns in Victoria from that era. In particular, the row of honey-coloured granite buildings in its Historic and Cultural Precinct, opposite the Visitor Information Centre, is regarded as the finest group of provincial public buildings in Victoria.

Go for a walk with your dog through the centre of Beechworth to admire these and other grand buildings. I recommend picking up the self-guided walking tour brochure from the Visitor Information Centre for a small fee and using it to guide you and your pup.

Don't miss heading to the rear of the precinct to see the Stone Lock-Up, where Ned Kelly was once imprisoned. While dogs are not allowed in most buildings along the trail, you can step inside this small dark cell with your dog by your side.

FOLLOW THE GORGE SCENIC DRIVE

Adjacent to the town of Beechworth is Beechworth Historic Park. The bushland park encompasses many of the old mining sites around Beechworth, with dogs permitted on a leash within the park.

One of the easiest ways to see some of the highlights in the park is on the 5km Beechworth Gorge scenic drive, although you can also explore the park on foot. Head north along Wodonga Road for the start of the one-way road, which is mainly sealed.

Along the way, stop at the main sights, including the magnificent Powder Magazine building – used to hold gunpowder for mining operations during the gold rush and now listed by the National Trust, it's free to enter the grounds. There was no prohibition on dogs joining you at the time of my visit.

It's worthwhile stopping at Spring Creek Bridge, where you can follow a short trail to the Cascades. A brochure with a map is available at the Visitor Information Centre in town.

CYCLE ON A RAIL TRAIL

Cycling is one of the most popular activities in the High Country region, with the Murray to Mountains Rail Trail passing through. The town of Bright, near the start of the trail, is particularly popular with cyclists. The trail also passes through the towns of Myrtleford, Beechworth and Rutherglen.

If you don't have your own bike and you're travelling with a dog, you can still enjoy a ride. There are multiple bike-hire shops in Bright and at least one of the stores, Electric Bikes, has dog trailers for hire. Their trailers, which can only be fitted to their own bikes, are suitable for small to medium dogs up to 25kg.

One of the easiest introductory bike-riding routes around Bright is the cycle path to Wandiligong. It's only 5.5km from Bright, and relatively flat, making for a leisurely trip. Alternatively, it's 6km down the valley to Porepunkah.

WANDER ALONG THE OVENS RIVER

Bright is located on the banks of the Ovens River, the perfect spot for a delightful riverside walk with your dog. Head to Howitt Park next to the centre of town, where you can choose between two short walks heading in opposite directions: the Canyon Walk and the Cherry Walk.

Schnitzel and I followed the Canyon Walk. Head west along the concrete path to the walk's starting point on the far side of Star Road. The 3km walk loops through a section of the river known as the 'canyon', a historic gold-sluicing area. Note that the path is at times uneven, particularly on the northern bank of the river, and there are two swing bridges at the start and end of the canyon section.

In the opposite direction is the Cherry Walk. This 5km walk also follows the river and features swing bridges, with interpretive panels along the way. You can pick up a brochure detailing the local flora found along the walk at the Visitor Information Centre in Bright.

Even better, your dog can walk off-leash for parts of these walks. Dogs are allowed to walk off-leash in the Bright area outside the town centre, as long as they remain under effective control. On the Canyon Walk, dogs are allowed off-leash after the end of Riverside Avenue, while on the Cherry Walk, dogs are allowed off-leash after Centenary Park.

ENJOY A REFRESHING DIP

While Bright may certainly be a long way from the coast, there are still plenty of places where your dog can cool their paws and enjoy a swim on hot days, thanks to the Ovens River and other local creeks.

The most popular swimming spot in Bright is next to the Splash Park and River Pool. During the cooler months some dogs can be spotted having a swim here, but during summer find a quieter stretch of water a little further up river for your pup to enjoy a paddle.

Both the Canyon and Cherry walks (see previous entry) provide ample opportunities for paddling along quieter stretches of the river with easy access. Just be aware the water is quite cold, even during summer!

🍷 TASTE HIGH COUNTRY WINE

The High Country is home to multiple wine regions, from the Alpine Valleys wine region around Bright to the Rutherglen wine region, renowned for its fortified wines. Many cellar doors are happy for your dog to join you, at least in outdoor areas.

I visited Ringer Reef in Porepunkah, less than 10 minutes drive from Bright. Since dogs are not allowed inside the tasting area, I instead booked a dog-friendly table on the landing for lunch, where Schnitzel and I enjoyed wonderful views across to Mt Buffalo. I highly recommend ordering the grazing platter, full of local treats and perfect for a couple to share. Accompany it with their wines by the glass or bottle. Or order a set of tasting glasses, choosing from the wines that are currently available for tasting. The cellar door is open daily except on Wednesday, although double-check the hours during winter.

SIP A LOCAL BEER OR CIDER

The High Country region is one of the few places in Australia where hops are grown – they can be spotted on the drive up along the valley to Bright. It's no surprise then that there are plenty of local breweries.

One of the most popular breweries is Bright Brewery, in the centre of Bright. Open seven days a week, it was busy even

Exploring the streets of Bright

The dog-friendly Bright Brewery

on the Tuesday lunchtime that I visited. There's a large outdoor area, with a deck out the back, plus extra tables around the side, so there's plenty of room for your pooch to join you.

Choose between the 24 taps of beer on offer, or select one of the tasting trays of six beers. There's also an extensive menu with a focus on local produce, whether that's trout or mushrooms, spirits or wine. I really enjoyed the pizza, but the burgers and bowls also looked delicious.

If cider is more your thing, try some of the locally produced Nightingale Bros. Alpine Cider. Available from their Alpine Produce store in Wandiligong – plus on the menu at many local restaurants and bars – they produce both a sweet and dry cider, plus non-alcoholic sparkling apple juice. Dogs aren't allowed inside the store, but they're welcome at the tables outside.

How to get there

Beechworth is a little over 3 hours north-east of Melbourne, while Bright is a further 50 minutes' drive to the south-east.

When to visit

Unless you're visiting the area to experience the snow at nearby Dinner Plain (see pp. 88–9) with your pup, it's best to visit the High Country during the warmer months, from October to April.

 # Dog-friendly parks

 # Dog-friendly dining

Baarmutha Park Recreation Reserve, Beechworth

The only off-leash dog park in Beechworth. The unfenced area is shared with the local golf course.

Mitchell Avenue Reserve Dog Park, Wangaratta

This large dog park is located in the southern part of the reserve. Securely fenced with high fences, there's plenty of shade along one side, plus seats and bins.

Ginger Baker Cafe, Bright

A popular dog-friendly spot in Bright. It's open from Friday to Tuesday for breakfast, lunch or just a coffee.

Bridge Road Brewers, Beechworth

Located in an old coach-house in the centre of town, they have a huge pet-friendly courtyard. Open daily for lunch and dinner, there's a long list of pizzas to choose from, as well as local wines and 20 taps of beer.

Billson's Brewery, Beechworth

A different type of brewery; at Billson's, they brew a wide range of spirits and non-alcoholic traditional cordials on-site. Pet dogs will need to skip the tour, but can enjoy lunch in the dog-friendly beer garden. Open daily.

Dog-friendly accommodation

Must Love Dogs B&B,
Rutherglen

This luxury B&B is very welcoming to dogs! Dogs are permitted in both guest suites, plus the self-contained cottage on the 1849 property, which has a log fire inside and a fully-fenced garden. Pet-friendly wine tours, Devonshire teas by the fire and more can be organised.

Beechworth Holiday Park,
Beechworth

A peaceful spot just outside town. Dogs are allowed on sites (except over the Easter weekend), plus in the pet-friendly cabin. Located halfway along the often muddy dog-friendly walking track to Lake Kerferd, luckily there's a dog wash on-site.

Woolshed Cabins,
Beechworth

Dogs are welcome to stay for free in all but one of the two-bedroom cabins, including sleeping inside overnight. Dogs will love off-leash explorations of the surrounding 12 acres, including a seasonal dam.

BlueMill Bright,
Bright

Choose between the BlueMill Cottage, the BlueMill Lodge and the older but large Old Mill Park. Each holiday home is pet-friendly for a small fee, with generally two dogs permitted per house.

Left: Bridge Road Brewers in Beechworth
Opposite: Ovens River, flowing through Bright

HIGH COUNTRY

Play in the snow at Dinner Plain

With snow a far from common occurrence across much of Australia, most dogs never get to experience this cold white stuff. And if you're dreaming of a day in the snow together with your pup, it's trickier than expected to organise. Many ski resorts in Australia are situated in national parks, while most other resorts don't allow pets to enter without a permit, which is not granted for one-off visits. There is one exception.

Dinner Plain is the only alpine resort in Australia that is dog-friendly, with no permits required and even dog-friendly accommodation available. Located east of Mt Hotham, it's the perfect place to play in the snow with your dog during winter.

Make a booking well in advance for one of the pet-friendly houses, chalets or apartments at Dinner Plain during the winter months. The distinctively styled buildings of the resort are built using only timber, local stone and corrugated iron, inspired by the rustic style of old cattlemen's huts.

Alternatively, you can also stay in nearby Bright and drive to Dinner Plain for the day. Although you'll pass through Alpine National Park and the Mount Hotham resort area, your dog is fine as long as it stays in your car and you don't stop. Allow at least 90 minutes to complete the windy 65km drive (longer if conditions require), and make sure you hire snow chains for your car.

Dinner Plain features just one ski run with gentle slopes, ideal for beginners, plus a tobogganing area – although this area is off limits to dogs. Enjoy time with your pup by going for a walk through the snow and constructing a snowman together – with your dog on digging duties!

There are a number of trails suitable for walking with your dog, which don't enter the adjacent Alpine National Park. Fitzy's Cirque is a short and easy 1km loop on the northern side of the village. Or follow the 2km Collector's Cirque all the way around the village, staying just outside the national park. Snowshoes are available for hire (for humans).

Note that dogs should be kept on a leash throughout Dinner Plain, particularly as the village is partially surrounded by national park (mainly on the west) and there isn't a fence. If visiting during summer, there is an off-leash area near the treatment ponds at Appian Way, but this is not available in winter. Instead, the tennis courts are a defacto off-leash option when snow is on the ground.

If it's your dog's first experience of snow, keep a close eye on them and limit their time in the snow to only 20 or 30 minutes at a time. Rug them up with a jacket or sweater (short-haired and short of stature dogs in particular feel the cold), and consider buying them booties or using a paw balm to protect their paws from the cold.

While there aren't currently any indoor bars or cafes where dogs can join you at Dinner Plain, dogs are welcome to join you in most outdoor dining areas. Consider heading to the beer garden of Club Wyndham's Elements Bar & Dining or sit at the tables outside Hotel High Plain. Outdoor heaters are usually provided, but make sure you and your pup rug up!

The inviting snowy landscape at Dinner Plain

PLAY IN THE SNOW AT DINNER PLAIN

Gippsland

One of Victoria's largest regions, Gippsland extends across most of eastern Victoria, from Phillip Island in the west to Mallacoota in the east. Home to long windswept beaches, dense rainforest gullies and blink-or-you'll-miss-it towns, the region is deserving of a leisurely roadtrip with your dog.

The George Bass Coastal Walk

FOLLOW THE ENTRANCE WALK

One of the most popular destinations in Gippsland is the beach town of Lakes Entrance. There are plenty of footpaths around town and the local lakes for a stroll with your pup, but for a more varied walk, I recommend crossing over the Cunninghame Arm Footbridge to follow the Entrance Walk.

This on-leash walk starts on the beach side of the footbridge – veer to your right just before the surf club. The 2.4km walk meanders through coastal bush along the lake to its artificial entrance, after which the town is named. At the far end, you can explore the New Works Historic Precinct, home to old cottages, a lookout, boardwalk and amenities. Rather than returning by the same route, walk back along 90 Mile Beach.

Most of the beaches around Lakes Entrance don't allow dogs off-leash. And between November to April, dogs can't swim or stay on popular beaches, but can only pass through while leashed; this applies to the section of 90 Mile Beach near the surf club, plus the lagoon beach near the footbridge.

Allow about 2 hours to complete the entire walk, plus an additional hour to explore the Historic Precinct. Before or after the walk, I recommend stopping at the Riviera Ice-Cream Parlour, close to the footbridge, which has a huge selection of flavours to choose from.

STAY AT BEST FRIEND HOLIDAY RETREAT

One of the most dog-friendly holiday destinations in Victoria is the Best Friend Holiday Retreat. Nestled in the rainforested Tarra Valley in South Gippsland, this retreat has been specially designed for people travelling with their pet dogs, and is a wonderful place to enjoy a relaxing getaway.

As well as regular campsites, the retreat also features individually fenced caravan- and campsites (advance bookings essential), plus dog-friendly cabins with fenced yards. And yes, all dogs are expected to sleep inside at night.

Best of all, there are six securely fenced areas for dogs to enjoy some off-leash time, including one with agility equipment and a giant ball run. They even have luxury dog kennels and a hydro-bath hut, just the thing for the end of muddy days.

It was definitely muddy underfoot when Schnitzel and I stayed in late spring. But I treasure the moment I saw a mother koala passing through the park carrying a joey!

SPOT KOALAS AT RAYMOND ISLAND

The easiest dog-friendly place to spot koalas in Gippsland is Raymond Island. Drive to Paynesville, about 45 minutes from Lakes Entrance, then take the short ferry ride across to Raymond Island. The ferry departs every 20 minutes and is free for pedestrians and leashed dogs.

The Koala Trail starts just opposite the ferry terminal and is well signposted, or you can pick up a brochure at the start in return for a donation. The walk is about 1.2km long, although you can follow a longer version that continues until First Parade.

The sign states the walk can be done in 20 minutes, but I took far longer, continually peering up into the trees. I spotted about 20 koalas. The final stretch of the walk returns to the ferry terminal along a waterfront boardwalk.

Naturally dogs need to stay on a leash on the walk, although most of the time Schnitzel

was oblivious to the sleepy koalas in the trees above him. I rate this koala experience up there with any paid wildlife park, and it was delightful that my dog could join me.

🔶 HIKE THE GEORGE BASS COASTAL WALK

For another great dog-friendly walk in the Gippsland region, turn off before you cross the bridge to Phillip Island and head to the George Bass Coastal Walk.

The walk is most easily accessed from the Shelley Beach carpark in Kilcunda, just off the Bass Highway. Alternatively, drive to the end of the short but unsealed Punchbowl Road in San Remo, with the walk clearly signposted at the turn-off.

It's a 7km walk each way, a total distance of 14km – allow about 4 hours to complete the full walk or just do a section. The sections that I walked at either end were well-formed and fairly flat, although there are some stiles along the route.

The walk hugs the coast, mainly following the cliff-tops, with spectacular views along the way. At one point you can detour along a local beach at low tide. Just keep your dog leashed along the walk, and check for whether there are any signs about fox baiting, which occurs about once a year.

📍 STOP OFF AT AGNES FALLS

While some of the magnificent waterfalls of South Gippsland are within national parks and so off limits to dogs, Agnes Falls is an excellent dog-friendly waterfall, tucked away in a small reserve close to the town of Welshpool. The 59m high waterfall was thundering when I visited it after a few days of heavy rain, despite the weir on top of it.

Dogs are welcome on your visit to Agnes Falls Scenic Reserve, as long as they stay on a leash. It's a short 220m walk to the lookout, or take the longer 340m track along the bank of the river above the falls. It's an easy stroll, but there are some steps.

The reserve is also home to a picnic ground, including a picnic shelter with tables, plus toilets. Keep an eye out for wildlife while visiting, with echidnas and platypuses sometimes spotted.

🐾 CRUISE THE GIPPSLAND LAKES

The Gippsland Lakes are a network of lakes, marshes and lagoons throughout the region – Australia's largest inland waterway. If you don't have your own boat to get out on the lakes, hop onboard one of the many cruises that operate in the region.

To experience a cruise with your dog, make a booking with Lonsdale Eco Cruises. This 3 hour wildlife cruise that operates

Right: **Agnes Falls**
Opposite: **Koalas at Raymond Island**

out of Lakes Entrance permits one lucky dog onboard each cruise. Once onboard, pet dogs are allowed everywhere except the wheelhouse.

Cruises depart daily at 1pm (except on Wednesday), from the Cunningham Quay along the Esplanade. Previous passengers highly praise the scones served alongside afternoon tea and coffee.

VISIT THE MOUTH OF THE SNOWY RIVER

Heading into East Gippsland, an excellent dog-friendly coastal walking trail can be found near Marlo, an hour east of Lakes Entrance. On the eastern edge of town is the start of the 5.1km Snowy River Estuary Walk.

The walk runs alongside the estuary of this famous river, with many lookouts along the first half. It then descends next to the estuary after the Mots Beach carpark, continuing on to Frenchs Narrows, where it terminates at the wild ocean beach.

Allow about 1 hour and 40 minutes to walk the trail in each direction, or almost 3.5 hours in total. There are also multiple small carparks along the way, including at Frenchs Narrows, making it easy to just walk a shorter section. Dogs need to be kept on a leash.

How to get there

It's about a 4 hour drive east of Melbourne to the popular tourist town of Lakes Entrance, which is a great base to explore this vast region.

When to visit

It's best to head to the beaches and long coastlines of Gippsland with your dog during summer. Make sure you book your accommodation in advance if visiting during school holidays.

Dog-friendly parks

Dog-friendly dining

Brackenbush Unleashed Dog Park,
Lakes Entrance

Head 10 minutes outside town to this fenced dog park on private property, a 'Pick My Project' funded community facility. There are three gigantic off-leash areas, with one for timid dogs, as well as one for nature walks.

Palmers Road Fenced Dog Park,
Lakes Entrance

This smaller fenced dog park is closer to the centre of Lakes Entrance, next to the Aquadome. There's still plenty of room for dogs to have their own space, plus fun agility equipment and a water fountain.

Lakes Boatshed Cafe,
Lakes Entrance

Open daily for breakfast and lunch, or just a coffee or milkshake, this cafe is opposite the North Arm. The large outdoor deck area is dog-friendly.

Red Bluff Brewers,
Lake Bunga

Come Friday, Saturday or Sunday, head to this brewery just east of Lakes Entrance, where pets are welcome at their outdoor area. As well as a great range of beers, they have a resident food truck serving burgers and fish tacos.

San Remo Fisherman's Co-op,
San Remo

I thoroughly recommend the deliciously fried local gummy shark and chips at this highly rated shop. There are plenty of outdoor tables. Just be careful of the local pelicans who are fed metres away daily at midday!

Dog-friendly accommodation

Prime Pet-Friendly Tourist Park,
Lakes Entrance

The first child-free caravan park in Victoria, this park is designed for pet owners. Choose between the pet-friendly powered sites, cabins, cottages and vans. There's also a dog wash, an off-leash dog run, a washing machine for pet bedding and even dog daycare kennels.

NRMA Phillip Island Holiday Park,
Cowes

Located near the seasonal off-leash dog beach in Cowes, pets are welcome at this holiday park, except during the peak summer and Easter holiday periods. There are two pet-friendly cabins.

Eight Acres,
Lakes Entrance

Just outside Lakes Entrance in the countryside, dogs are allowed in the two-bedroom self-contained cottages. Up to two dogs are permitted per cottage, for an additional fee per stay.

Golden Beach Cabins,
Golden Beach

These cabins are located directly opposite 90 Mile Beach, close to two off-leash dog beaches. Both of the fully self-contained cabins sleep up to five guests, with well-behaved dogs allowed to join you.

San Remo Fisherman's Co-op

Step back in time at Walhalla

Top of the list for a visit to Walhalla is taking a ride on the Walhalla Goldfields Railway. The train line to Walhalla was only completed in 1910. Four years later the closure of its main mine made Walhalla a ghost town. However, heritage trains driven by diesel engines once again travel on the scenic 4km section of track between Walhalla and Thomson.

Winding through the narrow gorge beside Stringers Creek and crossing eight bridges along the way, it's a 20 minute journey in each direction. A return trip takes about an hour, including stopping time at Thomson. Train rides operate every Wednesday, Saturday, Sunday and public holidays, plus daily during school holidays, except the winter break.

Best of all, well-behaved dogs are welcome to hop aboard for free! When I arrived at Walhalla Station, a sign indicated dogs needed to ride in the guard carriage, but Schnitzel was allowed to ride on my lap. He was somewhat alarmed at first by the noisy old train, but settled down for the return trip.

The gold mining town of Walhalla is hidden in a deep mountain valley, about 2.5 hours east of Melbourne. A fascinating destination to visit, especially for lovers of history, it's also a surprisingly dog-friendly place.

Left: **Historic Walhalla** Opposite: **Onboard the Walhalla Goldfields Railway**

The railway isn't the only dog-friendly activity in Walhalla, with the underground tours of the Long Tunnel Extended Gold Mine also welcoming dogs. The tours take place in the original workings of the gold mine that closed in 1914. The guide shares fascinating stories about the heyday of the mine during the 50 minute tours.

Generally, one tour operates per day, with extra tours on days that the railway is operating. Since group sizes are limited, it's best to make a booking in advance. The mine tunnel is relatively flat, but dark and damp, so I carried my small dog for the tour.

While in Walhalla, don't miss walking through the village to discover more about its history. There are over 30 stops on the Walhalla Heritage Walk that meanders for 2.5km between Walhalla Station and the Chinese Gardens Camping Area. Signs explain individual buildings as well as the overall town's story, sharing interesting facts and fascinating old photos. Pick up a brochure with a map at the station.

It's also worthwhile walking along the Tramline Walkway. Climb the hill opposite the old post office, with the walk continuing for about 700m along the flat trail of the former tram route to the Long Tunnel Extended Gold Mine. Even if you don't complete the trail, the lookout at the top of the hill offers beautiful views of the village.

The valley of Walhalla is dotted with plenty of day-visitor facilities and barbecues, perfect if you bring your own picnic lunch. Alternatively, check if the Walhalla Lodge Hotel at the bottom end of the valley is open for a bite to eat, with friendly dogs welcome at its outdoor tables.

STEP BACK IN TIME AT WALHALLA

Mornington Peninsula

Located on the south-eastern side of Port Phillip, just past the edge of Melbourne's outer suburbs, the Mornington Peninsula is an ideal destination for a daytrip from Melbourne or a weekend away, thanks to its beaches, wineries and hot springs.

Aside from many of the beaches and the hot springs (which prohibit dogs), there's plenty to do with your dog in the region. You can enjoy a long off-leash walk through a local forest, taste some of the local pinot noir, or treat your dog at a delightful dog cafe and bakery.

Right: **Green Olive at Red Hill** Opposite: **Miss Drew's Bakery and Dog Cafe**

🍷 TASTE THE WINE AT RED HILL

The Mornington Peninsula is a premium cool-climate wine region, renowned for its pinot noirs and chardonnays. Luckily, some of the region's wineries welcome your pup to join you when visiting their cellar doors.

Many of the peninsula's wineries are dotted around Red Hill, including Green Olive at Red Hill. This farm, cellar door and restaurant are open Thursday to Monday and welcome leashed dogs on their deck. Make a booking for a tasting paddle, perhaps accompanied by a grazing platter, or a farm picnic including a bottle of wine. And keep an eye out for their resident kelpie.

Another dog-friendly winery to visit is the small family-run Paradigm Hill Winery. The cellar door is open Saturday and Sunday, except during winter, and leashed dogs are welcome on the timber deck, the perfect spot to enjoy the beautiful views. When booking, make sure you select the cellar door verandah option.

🍴 ENJOY A TREAT AT MISS DREW'S

For a different type of treat, head to Miss Drew's Bakery and Dog Cafe. While you won't find any human treats on the menu, your dog will drool over the menu of dog treats, including pugichinos, muffins and more. Schnitzel slurped up his pugichino and devoured his cookie in no time!

This dog cafe is located behind the Tyabb Packing House, surrounded by antique shops. It's generally only open on Saturday and Sunday – double-check the latest opening hours. As well as the dog cafe, with plenty of tables for pooches and their owners, there's also a shop selling treats and the option to order dog birthday cakes. Head to the cafe opposite for your own fix of coffee.

🎨 SEE MCCLELLAND SCULPTURE PARK

There are multiple sculpture parks at wineries on the Mornington Peninsula, but the best one to visit if you have a dog is McClelland Sculpture Park, located near Frankston, just off the Mornington Peninsula Freeway.

Situated on what was originally the site of local artist Harry McClelland's art studio, nearly 100 sculptures have been installed in the bushland park, including some impressive kinetic sculptures. It's a wonderful spot for an on-leash walk with your dog. While following the path with Schnitzel, I never knew what to expect around the next bend.

Naturally, dogs are not allowed inside the galleries, although they can join you at the outside tables at the cafe. The park is also the perfect spot for a picnic. The sculpture park is open from Wednesday to Sunday, with a small admission fee charged, except for locals.

Bayside views along the Millionaire's Walk

WALK IN THE BRIARS COMMUNITY FOREST

While I've visited plenty of excellent fenced dog parks with Schnitzel, the Briars Community Forest takes off-leash dog walking in a fenced area to the next level! It's a must-visit for adventurous dogs.

This huge tract of bushland on the edge of the coastal suburb of Mount Martha is entirely fenced and permits dogs off-leash throughout, with multiple walking tracks available and even a creek swimming spot. Just beware that it often gets muddy!

It's best to park along the Nepean Highway opposite Balcombe Grammar School. There's a rough carpark plus a bin outside the double-fenced entrance to the park.

HAVE A DIP AT TASSELLS COVE

While dogs are not permitted on many beaches on the Mornington Peninsula, particularly during the busy summer months, one of the most popular year-round off-leash dog beaches is Tassells Cove, in the suburb of Safety Beach.

This small sandy beach is located between Marine Cove and Bruce Road. A fairly sheltered beach, it's a great spot for dogs to enjoy a swim in the beautiful clean water or a play on the sand. It's also reasonably removed from the nearby road.

Be warned that there's only limited parking nearby. Since the beach is quite popular on warm sunny days, either get there early or park on the other side of the marina entrance and walk to the beach.

Other popular dog beaches that allow dogs off-leash year-round on the peninsula include Royal Beach and Hawker Beach. On other beaches, the standard rule is that dogs are allowed on-leash, except during daylight savings time (October to March) when they are prohibited from the sand between 9am and 7pm. Note though that dogs are always prohibited from the beaches in Mornington Peninsula National Park.

EXPLORE THE BALCOMBE ESTUARY BOARDWALK

On wet days, skip the sand and mud, and instead take a walk with your dog along the Balcombe Estuary Boardwalk. Starting close to the beach in Mount Martha, this raised boardwalk meandering through the saltmarsh is part of the Balcombe Estuary Nature Trail. Dogs are allowed on the trail, as long as they are kept on a leash.

The best spot to access the boardwalk is from Balcombe Estuary Reserve, a picnic area with a carpark at the end of Mirang Avenue. The walking track starts on the eastern side of the reserve, with the boardwalk starting after a few hundred metres.

The entire Balcombe Estuary Nature Trail is 2.5km, extending to the Nepean Highway and the Briars, and takes about an hour to walk one way.

STROLL ALONG MILLIONAIRE'S WALK

If you drive around the Mornington Peninsula, you will eventually reach the posh enclaves of Sorrento and Portsea, home to many expensive cliff-top properties. A popular walk in the area is the appropriately named Millionaire's Walk.

The walk, tucked in behind the mansions, runs for about 500m between Point King Road and Lentell Avenue. It feels like you're walking across private property, particularly as you pass through multiple gates, but there's a public right of way along the easement.

Parking can be tricky nearby. On quiet days you'll likely find a parking spot on Point King Road. Otherwise, park by the boat ramp in Sorrento and access the walk via Point Nepean Road. Dogs need to be kept on-leash along the walk.

Along the way you'll pass some stunning vantage points, the inspiration for some well-known Australian paintings, plus get a glimpse of the mansions.

How to get there

It's about an hour's drive to Mornington from Melbourne, while Sorrento is a further 45 minutes drive around the bay.

When to visit

The best time to visit the Mornington Peninsula with your dog is during the hot days of summer, or while the weather is still warm in the autumn months.

 ## Dog-friendly parks

 ## Dog-friendly dining

Murrowong Reserve Fenced Dog Park, Rosebud

A fully fenced dog park with multiple entrances. There are also benches to sit on and some shade, plus a water tap and bowl for dogs.

Grant Road Reserve Fenced Dog Park, Somerville

A fully fenced park with double gates, it's large enough for multiple groups of dogs to enjoy their own space. There's plenty of parking, plus a drinking fountain. Just beware of the mud at times.

Tar Barrel Brewery, Mornington

Dogs on a leash are welcome at the outdoor tables at this brewery and distillery, open from Wednesday to Sunday. Both beer and gin tasting paddles are available. I recommend the wood-fired pizzas, plus there are regular barbecue specials. Note that the tables are not sheltered from rain.

Morgan's Sorrento, Sorrento

Open from Wednesday to Sunday for lunch and dinner. Order from their coastal French menu while sitting in the alfresco area overlooking the beach.

Dog-friendly accommodation

Blue Moon Cottages, Rye

Located 250m from Rye Beach, pets are allowed inside both of these self-contained cottages, or you can ask for a kennel to be provided in the secure yard. Dog bowls and a towel for your pup are also included.

Merricks Cottage, Merricks

A gorgeous two-bedroom house nestled in a peaceful country lane on the eastern side of the peninsula. Pampered pooches are welcome, with all applications for pets considered. An additional pet fee is charged.

Portsea Hideaway, Portsea

Perfect for large groups, this four-bedroom luxury beach house can accommodate up to eight adults. Dogs are welcome to join you, including inside. There's also a seasonally heated swimming pool.

Stony Point Caravan Park, Crib Point

One of the only pet-friendly caravan parks on the Mornington Peninsula, with pets permitted at the discretion of the manager. Stay for the night in your caravan or campervan.

Right: **Vineyards at Red Hill** Opposite: **Off-leash in Briars Community Forest**

Yarra Valley & Dandenong Ranges

The Yarra Valley is one of the most popular wine-growing regions in Victoria. A long list of Yarra Valley cellar doors welcomes dogs and you can even enjoy a private winery tour with your dog. Then cap off your weekend in the Dandenong Ranges, with a dog-friendly train ride or a stroll in a beautiful garden.

Yering Farm Wines

VISIT DOG-FRIENDLY WINERIES

A must when visiting the Yarra Valley is tasting and buying some wines at a winery or two. Luckily many of the wineries welcome well-behaved dogs; sometimes they're even allowed inside the tasting room.

Rules can change, so it's always best to check in advance for the latest pet policies, ideally when making a booking. Since weekends in the Yarra Valley are quite busy, consider a relaxing midweek visit with your pup.

When planning a visit to the Yarra Valley with your pup, consider visiting some of my favourite dog-friendly wineries.

Helen's Hill Estate

This boutique family winery is home to both the Helen's Hill label and the more affordable Ingram Road range. The Breachley Block Chardonnay is one of my personal favourites. Schnitzel was warmly welcomed inside the cellar door – mention you have pets when you book a tasting.

Helen & Joey

Choose between a tasting inside or outside on their large deck where you and your pup can enjoy one of the most gorgeous vistas of the valley. Either way, don't miss out on saying hello to the resident unicorn!

Yering Farm Wines

Previously the site of a vineyard in the 19th century, Yering Farm Wines' cellar door is a resurrected hay shed full of rustic Australian charm. In addition to the wines, sample the Farmyard Apple Syder, made from the farm's own apples. I recommend enjoying a generous pruner's platter on their verandah, accompanied by a glass of wine.

Maddens Rise

At this winery the focus is on quality. The range of wines is smaller than elsewhere, but carefully curated. The Arcobaleno blend (Italian for rainbow) features many white varietals you won't find anywhere else in the valley.

 BE PAMPERED ON A WINERY TOUR

Rather than organise your own self-guided wine tour with your pup, take all the hassle out of wine tasting in the Yarra Valley by booking a private winery tour, where you're chauffeured around the valley. And luckily there's the perfect company for wine-loving dog owners: Pooches and Pinot.

On my most recent visit to the Yarra Valley, Schnitzel and I went on a winery tour with Pooches and Pinot. After asking about my tastes and requests, Jeff and Helen put together a dog-friendly itinerary for the day, driving us around the valley in style in one of their fabulous vans.

Up to two dogs can be accommodated on each tour (as long as they're already pals), either on beds in the back or in between the seats if there's room. Naturally Schnitzel insisted on sitting at my feet the whole time.

While I enjoyed the wine (and beer) tasting, along with a gourmet lunch, Jeff made sure Schnitzel was looked after, including the occasional walk and plenty of treats throughout the day. It's the VIP touches like these that make this a fabulous day out for both you and your pup.

🧭 HOP ONBOARD *PUFFING BILLY*

A famous attraction in the Dandenong Ranges is the *Puffing Billy* Railway, one of Australia's top historic steam railways. A ride on the steam train from either Belgrave or Emerald is a fun family outing, and there's now the option to bring along your four-legged family members.

Pet dogs are allowed on the *Puffing Billy Dog Express* that operates roughly two days per month. Advance bookings are essential, with tickets quickly snapped up. Up to two dogs are permitted per booking, with an additional charge for each dog ticket.

You'll be asked your dog's breed, so that you can be allocated to a suitable carriage. Note that all dogs riding on the train should be fine with being in close proximity to other humans and dogs.

It's a 40 minute journey onboard the train, departing from Emerald Lakeside Park and meandering through Wright State Forest, crossing over three old timber bridges. Then spend about 2 hours in Gembrook, plenty of time for a play in the adjacent dog-friendly J.A.C. Russell Park or to walk along a section of the Eastern Dandenong Ranges Trail, before returning to Emerald.

🍴 ENJOY HIGH TEA AT OLINDA TEA HOUSE

Topping my wish list for my next trip to the Dandenong Ranges is a visit to the Olinda Tea House. This gorgeous tea house, high in the ranges, is surrounded by historic flower gardens and forests, the perfect spot to enjoy a sumptuous high tea.

As well as offering high tea for humans – featuring a range of savoury and sweet options, including bottomless scones – there's also a special afternoon tea and range of

Alfred Nicholas Gardens

treats just for four-legged guests. Your pup will be treated to a peanut butter cookie, cranberry chews and a puppacino.

If visiting with a group during summer, consider upgrading to a picnic experience in the gardens. Either way, don't miss going for a stroll with your pup afterwards through the beautiful grounds.

🪑 STROLL THROUGH THE ALFRED NICHOLAS GARDENS

The original garden of the Burnham Beeches Estate, the Alfred Nicholas Gardens are renowned for their extensive water features. Open year-round with no entry fee, dogs on a leash are welcome to join you in exploring the gardens, with the highlights changing from season to season.

Follow the winding walking path down under the canopy of mountain ash trees to the ornamental lake with its quaint boathouse. During spring the many rhododendrons, azaleas, camellias and flowering cherries burst into bloom, while autumn is ablaze in colour from the foliage of maples, beeches and golden ginkgos.

HIKE TO LA LA FALLS

Heading further east to the Warburton Valley, La La Falls has been delighting visitors since the 1880s. Dogs are welcome to join you on the walking track up to the falls, south of the town of Warburton.

Park in the small carpark just off Old Warburton Road, then start the gently inclined walk up to the falls. About 1.6km in each direction, the track winds alongside Four Mile Creek, meandering through lush forest. Allow up to 90 minutes for the walk to the falls and back.

The falls are at their best during autumn and winter, after heavy rain. Although this is also when the track can become rather muddy – bring some old towels to clean your pup afterwards!

Top: **Onboard Puffing Billy** Bottom: **Pruner's platter at Yering Farm Wines**

How to get there

The Yarra Valley and Dandenong Ranges are immediately east of Melbourne. It's just over a 1 hour drive to Healesville in the Yarra Valley from Melbourne.

When to visit

The Yarra Valley and Dandenong Ranges are most vibrant during spring and autumn, although relaxing next to an open fire in winter also has its charm. Avoid the hottest days of summer when bushfires are a risk.

Dog-friendly parks

Dog-friendly dining

Coronation Park,
Healesville

Just a few blocks from the centre of town, this off-leash park has a short trail along the creek – ideal for dogs to cool off on warm days – plus plenty of large shady trees.

Maroondah Reservoir Park,
Healesville

Although dogs need to be kept on-leash, this beautiful park offers plenty of scenic walks. Skip the dam wall and the forest walking tracks to the north of the Watts River, as both are off-limits to dogs.

My Little Kitchen,
Healesville

Open daily for breakfast and lunch, this cafe offers a menu full of inventive takes on brunch favourites – I loved the house smoked salmon with poached eggs. The dog-friendly courtyard is covered, with heaters for chilly days.

The General Food Store,
Emerald

The menu at this highly rated cafe changes seasonally. Open daily for breakfast and lunch, take a seat at the dog-friendly tables out the front and add some Pawtastic dog treats to your order.

Coldstream Brewery,
Coldstream

Offering more than just beer, the brewery's kitchen is open for lunch and dinner from Wednesday to Sunday. There are eight parmigiana options on the menu, available in half and full sizes, plus multiple dog-friendly outdoor areas.

Dog-friendly accommodation

Leddicott Cottage,
Olinda

This luxury cottage for couples is surrounded by historic gardens, and has a wood-fired pot belly stove and clawfoot bath. Four-legged guests are warmly catered for, with their own blankets, towels and plenty of treats.

Wiggley Bottom Farm,
Badger Creek

The perfect luxe farmstay for dog owners. Choose between the Apartment, the Cottage with a fully-fenced outdoor kennel, or the new Tiny House. There are plenty of outdoor areas for your dog to explore and a doggy-care kit with bits you may have forgotten. Schnitzel loved the dog treat jar!

Enclave at Healesville Holiday Park,
Badger Creek

A friendly and quiet caravan park just a few kilometres outside Healesville. Pets are welcome to stay on powered sites, plus in selected pet-friendly two-bedroom cabins.

Below: **Wiggley Bottom Farm** Opposite: On a Pooches and Pinot wine tour

Daylesford & Macedon Ranges

Just a short drive north-west of Melbourne lie the cooler climes of Daylesford and the Macedon Ranges.

In Daylesford, skip a leisurely afternoon at the spa for some quality hiking with your dog. Enjoy a long lazy lunch at a local cafe or cidery, or buy food for a picnic at a farmers' market, with some great picnic grounds on offer. And don't miss the beautiful gardens in Mount Macedon.

Schnitzel at Forest Glade Gardens

STROLL AROUND LAKE DAYLESFORD

Lake Daylesford is a delightful spot, just a short distance from the centre of Daylesford. The picturesque lake is surrounded by an easy 2.8km walking path, perfect for a stroll with your dog on a leash.

Allow about an hour to complete the full lap. There are three carparks around the lake – at Foreshore, Fulcher Street and Wombat Flat – or you can walk from the town centre; just follow the signs.

SAMPLE THE LOCAL MINERAL SPRINGS

The Daylesford area is famous for its mineral springs, and while heading to a local spa for treatments is not a dog-friendly option, you can still sample the local springs.

On my walk with Schnitzel around Lake Daylesford, we made a short detour down to the Central Springs Reserve, where there's a historic pump for the mineral water. There are also mineral-water pumps at Wombat Flat Mineral Spring.

In Hepburn Springs, head to Hepburn Mineral Springs Reserve, which features a number of different tasting springs. Read the tasting notes and compare the taste of Locarno, Soda, Sulphur and Wyuna springs. On-leash dogs are allowed, including on the walking trails starting at the reserve that cross into the adjacent Hepburn Regional Park.

But can your dog drink the mineral water too? The general advice is that dogs shouldn't drink water high in minerals, especially if it's carbonated. However, a little taste should be fine – I let Schnitzel have a taste. Note that the water from these springs is untreated, although tested regularly, so there is a small risk for both humans and dogs.

ENJOY THE AUTUMN COLOURS

With a higher altitude and cool climate, the Macedon Ranges are home to many beautiful cool-climate gardens and plantings of deciduous trees. It's a popular destination to visit during autumn, with an Autumn Festival held in April each year.

One of the most popular spots to visit is Honour Avenue in Macedon, which is lined with an incredible 154 pin oaks. From late March to late April the oak leaves slowly turn red in a beautiful display. During the Autumn Festival, the road is closed on weekends and public holidays, with visitor parking available nearby. Dogs are welcome to visit Honour Avenue, plus many of the other events during the festival.

BE CHARMED BY THE GARDENS

No matter what time of year you visit the Macedon Ranges, there's a beautiful garden to enjoy with your dog.

Forest Glade Gardens, one of the private gardens that lines Mount Macedon Road, is dog-friendly and open daily. Schnitzel and I enjoyed a delightful visit on a quiet day in spring. The Japanese garden is a particular highlight, as well as the many fine sculptures situated throughout the gardens. Allow at least an hour for a stroll around the entire gardens. Just remember, it is a private garden, so follow the rules, including keeping your dog on a leash and cleaning up after them.

The region is also home to many beautiful botanic gardens, mainly established in the late 19th century. In Daylesford, head to Wombat Hill Botanic Gardens on the hill above town for a stroll or a picnic. Alternatively, head to the Kyneton Botanic Gardens on the banks of the Campaspe River or Malmsbury

Botanic Gardens with an ornamental lake and grand viaduct.

⚠ GO HIKING AT MOUNT MACEDON

If you keep going up Mount Macedon Road, you'll reach Macedon Regional Park and the forested heights of the Macedon Ranges. Since it's a regional park rather than a national park, your dog is allowed to join you on the walking tracks within the park, as long as they are kept on a leash.

There's a 30km loop track that links all the major sites in the park, along with Macedon Railway Station, but it's a gruelling full-day hike. Instead, walk a section of the loop, or the other short trails in the park.

A fun short walk Schnitzel and I enjoyed is the hike up to Camels Hump, the highest point in the Macedon Ranges. From the lookout there are wonderful views across to Hanging Rock and the surrounding countryside. It's a moderate 1km return hike, which took us less than 30 minutes, despite some stops to sniff along the way.

Another popular destination nearby is the 21m high Memorial Cross. It's close to the main picnic grounds and tea rooms, although trees now obscure much of the surrounding view. It's only a 200m gentle stroll each way, with a short side detour possible to Major Mitchell Lookout. For something more challenging, hike the 3.6km ascent up to the

Hanging Rock

Cross from the Old Scout Camp on Middle Gully Road – best for energetic dogs.

 HAVE A PICNIC AT HANGING ROCK

Another famous spot in the Macedon Ranges is Hanging Rock – the setting of the mysterious novel *Picnic at Hanging Rock* and the subsequent film. Situated just north of Mount Macedon, the reserve contains large picnic grounds and multiple walking tracks, including the popular walk to the summit of Hanging Rock.

Pet dogs on a leash are allowed in the reserve with you, except on major event days. While dogs are not allowed to ascend the summit of Hanging Rock to protect the local wildlife, they are allowed on the lower part of the Summit Walk, plus the other walks in the park. Note that an entry fee is charged, either per vehicle or per individual if you enter on foot.

 MARVEL AT TRENTHAM FALLS

Trentham Falls are located just outside the charming town of Trentham, about 20 minutes down the road from Daylesford. The falls are the longest single-drop waterfall in Victoria, cascading 32m over beautiful basalt columns, formed by a volcanic eruption five million years ago.

It's just a short stroll from the carpark to the lookout at the top of the falls, either down steps or a slope. Note that the older walking track to the bottom of the falls has been closed for a number of years, due to rockfalls and ongoing safety risks.

The falls are usually at their best in winter and spring, thanks to more abundant rainfall. Dogs need to be kept on a leash at the falls.

HEAD TO A FARMERS' MARKET

Each weekend one or two farmers' markets are held in the region, with many allowing leashed dogs to join you. It's the perfect spot to sample the local produce and pick up some picnic supplies.

The Daylesford Sunday Market is on every Sunday, from 8am to 3pm (closing earlier during bad weather), at Daylesford Railway Station on Raglan Street. Alternatively, check out the Trentham Farmers' Market on the 3rd Saturday of the month, or the Woodend Farmers' Market on the 1st Saturday of the month.

How to get there

Allow about 90 minutes to drive to Daylesford from Melbourne, while Mount Macedon is an hour's drive north of Melbourne.

When to visit

One of the best times of year to visit Daylesford and the Macedon Ranges is during autumn, particularly during April when the Autumn Festival is held in the Macedon Ranges.

Dog-friendly parks

Campaspe Park,
Woodend

Located alongside Five Mile Creek, the walking path that follows the banks of the creek in this off-leash park is a great spot for walking with dogs.

Centennial Park,
Macedon

Located adjacent to Honour Avenue and one of the most popular spots for viewing autumn leaves each April, this off-leash park is also home to mosaic statues that reflect the district's history, plus an Ash Wednesday Memorial.

Dog-friendly dining

Wombat Hill House,
Daylesford

Located in the grounds of Wombat Hill Botanic Gardens, this cafe is open during the day from Friday to Tuesday, with a seasonal menu focused on local produce. The semi-enclosed outdoor area is dog-friendly.

Daylesford Cider,
Musk

A few kilometres east of Daylesford, this restaurant welcomes dogs in its protected but unheated courtyard area. Open for lunch from Friday to Monday, with bookings recommended.

Mr Cafe Macedon,
Macedon

This highly rated cafe has a nice outdoor area that's dog-friendly. Open daily for breakfast and lunch, order off their seasonal menu or just grab a coffee.

Left: **Daylesford Cider** Opposite: **Kyneton Streamside Reserve**

114   VICTORIA

Dog-friendly accommodation

Hollow Log Estate,
Musk Vale

A delightfully dog-friendly estate just south of Daylesford. Choose between the Stoney Studio or the larger Cottage, both with indoor fireplaces. Dogs will love the on-site secure dog exercise area, plus walks in nearby Wombat State Forest.

Spring Creek Cottage,
Hepburn Springs

An extra pet-friendly cottage that sleeps up to four adults in Hepburn. Pets are allowed inside, even on beds if you pay for the 'furry friend linen' package. There's a secure yard, dog beds, blankets, treats and more.

Daylesford Holiday Park,
Daylesford

Pets are welcome year-round at this park near Lake Daylesford, plus in the new pet-friendly cabin. Up to two small dogs are allowed inside the Bark Royal studio cabin, with its own small enclosed yard.

Goldfields

The Goldfields region covers a vast swathe of inland Victoria. Many of the region's cities and towns, including Ballarat and Bendigo, formed during the heady gold-rush days of the 19th century. Explore this fascinating history with your dog by your side. Enjoy a ride on a vintage tram or steam train, stroll in historic botanic gardens or tour the grand buildings of Bendigo. The region is also home to some hidden surprises, including the largest stupa in the Southern Hemisphere.

The Vintage Talking Tram in Bendigo

HOP ON THE VINTAGE TALKING TRAM

One of the best ways to get around Bendigo's top sights, and learn plenty of history along the way, is to hop aboard its Vintage Talking Tram. And best of all, friendly leashed dogs are allowed to ride for free.

Choose between staying on for the whole trip, about 45 minutes, or hop-on and hop-off as many times as you'd like at the five stops, with tickets valid for the whole day. There's free all-day parking available at most stops, with the best parking for caravans and campervans at the Central Deborah Gold Mine stop.

VISIT THE CENTRAL DEBORAH GOLD MINE

The first stop on the Vintage Talking Tram route is the Central Deborah Gold Mine, just south of the Bendigo city centre, where almost a tonne of gold was extracted until its closure in 1954. While dogs aren't allowed on the underground mine tours, they are permitted to join you on the surface tours.

Surface tours are self-guided. At your leisure, explore the original change rooms, blacksmith's shop and engine room of the mine. I even carried Schnitzel up the stairs to the poppet head – the framework above the mine shaft.

Dogs are allowed in all areas on the surface, although the staff request that you minimise time in the reception area and museum. A small entry fee applies for adults on the surface tour, with tickets able to be pre-booked or purchased on the day. Allow about 30 to 45 minutes to explore, and keep your dog leashed.

MINE THROUGH HISTORY AT THE VICTORIAN HILL DIGGINGS

For another taste of the gold-mining heritage of Bendigo, head to the western side of town and the Victoria Hill Historic Mining Reserve. This reserve contains a number of old mining relics, including some open-cut mines.

There's a lot less to see here than at Central Deborah Gold Mine, with mining ceasing in 1913, although there's still a poppet head rising high. However, there are plenty of informative signs dotted around.

It's a popular spot for dog walking, with tracks crisscrossing the reserve. Just make sure you keep your dog on a leash and stay on the path, due to the presence of old mine shafts. There's an entrance and carpark just off the Calder Highway. Allow about an hour to walk around the entire reserve.

TAKE A TOUR OF GRAND BENDIGO

The city centre of Bendigo is still home to many grand old buildings. I recommend picking up a brochure from the Bendigo Visitor Centre (itself in an impressive old building) and spending an hour or two following a self-guided tour around the city's streets and impressive buildings.

Some of the city's highlights include the Law Courts, the Soldiers Memorial Hall with its rooftop band rotunda, and the opulent Hotel Shamrock. Dogs are welcome to join you, except inside most buildings.

Many of the buildings are built around the edge of Rosalind Park – the grand gardens located in the city's centre that are named after the heroine of Shakespeare's *As You Like It*. It's the perfect spot to enjoy an on-leash stroll with your pup, particularly during spring and autumn.

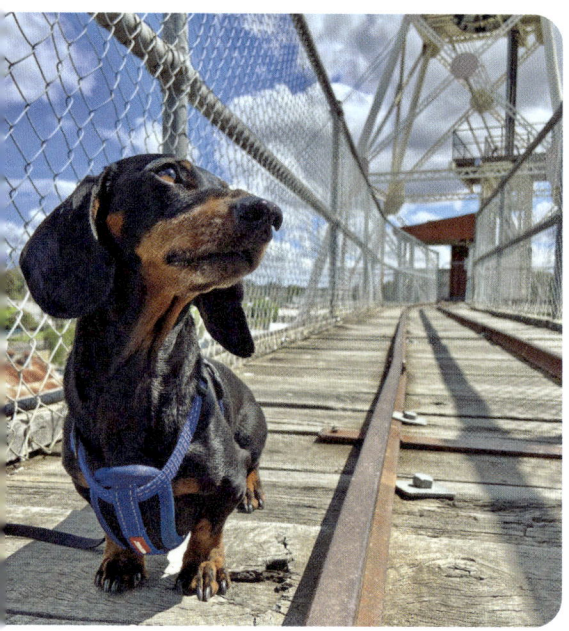

WANDER THROUGH HISTORIC MALDON

While some goldmining towns in the region grew into cities like Bendigo, others reverted to small villages. One of my favourite spots in the region is the small village of Maldon. The village was classified by the National Trust as Australia's First Notable Town, mostly thanks to its main street, which remains largely unchanged since its heyday in the late 19th century.

Wander along the main street, which is now dotted with boutiques and cafes. Perhaps stop off at one of the many cafes that have dog-friendly tables out the front. And don't miss heading to Maldon Historic Reserve, adjacent to the town, with its distinctive Beehive Mine Chimney. You can pick up a brochure with a map of the reserve in town.

RIDE ON THE VICTORIAN GOLDFIELDS RAILWAY

Rather than driving to Maldon, consider steaming into the village the old-fashioned way, onboard a heritage steam train operated by the Victorian Goldfields Railway.

Start your trip in Castlemaine, where you'll hop on a train for the 45 minute journey to Maldon. You'll then have about 2.5 hours to spend at your leisure exploring Maldon, including time for lunch, perhaps in the beer garden of the Maldon Hotel. Then catch the return train back to Castlemaine.

Trips operate every Wednesday and Sunday (except during February), plus on Saturdays during school holidays and some public holidays. Well-behaved dogs are welcome to join you for free in the Excursion Class carriages. These historic wooden carriages have opening windows that make for an authentic experience.

SPEND THE AFTERNOON AT LAKE WENDOUREE

Lake Wendouree in Ballarat has long been a popular leisure spot, and it's a great destination to visit with your dog. Top of the list is the 6km Steve Moneghetti Track that loops around the lake. It's the perfect spot for an on-leash walk with your pup.

While walking along the lake, grab a dog treat from the kiosk at Pipers by the Lake (enquire if they have any dog-friendly ice-cream!), or make a booking for the Boatshed Restaurant with its dog-friendly deck overlooking the lake.

On the western side of the lake are the Ballarat Botanical Gardens, where on-leash dogs are also welcome. The gardens were designed and planted in the 1860s, so they contain many large mature trees. Another focus of the gardens is begonias, with a festival held every March.

HIKE UP MT BUNINYONG

For a more strenuous walk near Ballarat, head to Mount Buninyong Scenic Reserve, about a 20 minute drive south-east of the city. The reserve surrounds Mt Buninyong, a 745m high extinct volcanic mountain that is a landmark of the district.

There are multiple walking tracks in the reserve, with dogs on a leash allowed on all of them. One of the most popular trails is the Zig Zag Trail, which ascends from Blackberry Lane Reserve to the summit and lookout tower on top of the mountain. Just over 1km in each direction, you can also combine the track with the 2.6km Summit Loop.

Another great spot for bushwalking around Ballarat is Creswick Regional Park, about 20 minutes drive north of Ballarat. Leashed dogs are welcome throughout the park, with multiple short walks on offer.

MARVEL AT THE GREAT STUPA OF UNIVERSAL COMPASSION

One of the more unusual sights in the Goldfields region is the Great Stupa of Universal Compassion. The largest stupa in the western world, it's currently being constructed about 15 minutes west of Bendigo.

The stupa, also known as a pagoda, is based on the Gyantse Stupa in Tibet. It's surrounded by the Peace Park Gardens, containing many monuments from different faiths. With entry daily by donation, allow about 90 minutes to follow the self-guided tour through the gardens and visit the stupa.

During my visit, pets were welcome to join you both outside and inside the stupa. There's also plenty of dog-friendly tables at the on-site cafe.

Below: **The historic town of Maldon**
Opposite: **The Central Deborah Gold Mine**

How to get there

Ballarat is a 90 minute drive north-west of Melbourne, while Bendigo is less than 2 hours drive directly north.

When to visit

The Goldfields region is at its best during spring and autumn, when its many parks come alive and temperatures are generally mild.

Dog-friendly parks

Harcourt Dog Park, Strathdale

One of three fenced off-leash dog parks around Bendigo, this huge expanse of grass has plenty of room for dogs to run and play, along with a paved footpath traversing it. It even has its own dog toy box.

Pioneer Park, Wendouree

One of the best off-leash dog parks in Ballarat, this large park near the freeway is great for adventurous dogs. Mainly fenced, there are gravel walking paths and two ponds, along with water fountains and bins.

Top: Dog-friendly cafe in Maldon
Bottom: The Great Stupa of Universal Compassion

Dog-friendly dining

Dog-friendly accommodation

The Boardwalk,
Bendigo

At The Boardwalk, located on the edge of Lake Weeroona, Chino the resident labrador is ready to welcome four-legged guests, who can choose from their own dog menu. Open daily for breakfast and lunch. Enter with your dog from Nolan Street, and enjoy the 1.5km stroll around the lake before or after your meal.

Percy and Percy,
Bendigo

This cute former corner shop is open for breakfast and lunch, except on Sunday. There's plenty of dog-friendly seating out front and in the back courtyard, and I was personally delighted with the choice of three different hot chocolates.

Hop Temple,
Ballarat

This colourful laneway venue offers a choice of 17 rotating taps and over 200 craft beers, plus a casual dining menu including in-house smoked meats. Dogs are welcome in the laneway area; check out their calendar for dog events.

BIG4 Ballarat Windmill Holiday Park,
Cardigan

An impressively pet-friendly caravan park. Camp with your caravan on a fenced site in the dog-friendly zone or book the Dogwood cabin with its own dog run. There's also a pet-friendly billabong at the rear.

BIG4 Bendigo Marong Holiday Park,
Marong

About 15 minutes west of Bendigo, this award-winning park allows dogs year-round, both on sites and in two dog-friendly cabins; the deluxe one has its own fenced and gated deck. There's also a dog wash.

Hotel Vera,
Ballarat

Located in a 19th-century mansion in the heart of Ballarat, the hotel allows one pet in the pet-friendly Lonarch Suite. They'll be pampered with their own lounge, pet bed, pet shower and access to a private, secure courtyard.

Hargreaves Cottage,
Bendigo

This cute yet fully renovated two-bedroom cottage is centrally located, within walking distance to the city centre and many attractions. Up to two pets are allowed, with an enclosed yard and off-street parking.

Great Ocean Road

The Great Ocean Road is one of Victoria's best-known attractions. Starting west of Melbourne at the beachy coastal town of Torquay, the road twists and turns along this scenic stretch of coastline, past impressive landmarks.

Unfortunately, many of the region's landmarks lie within national parks, making them difficult to see with a dog. However, there's still plenty of fun things to do with your pup. Allow at least a couple of days to explore from one end to the other!

The start of the Great Ocean Road

STROLL ON A BEACH

Countless spectacular beaches line the Great Ocean Road, and are great spots to visit with your dog. Rules for dogs visiting these beaches vary. While beaches within national parks are generally off limits to dogs, selected beaches allow off-leash dogs all day long.

During summer many beaches limit when dogs have access. Most commonly, dogs are permitted on the beaches only early and late in the day. These restrictions last from December to March or Christmas to Easter, depending on the council. Check the local signs for exact details.

However, if you visit the Great Ocean Road with your dog outside these peak months, dogs are allowed off-leash on many more beaches all day long. This was the case when I visited Lorne in November, with Schnitzel allowed to run off-leash along most of the gorgeous main beach, except for one short section.

Note that the surf at many of the beaches along the Great Ocean Road is rough, with swimming not recommended, including for dogs.

Lorne Beach

SPOT A KOALA OR TWO

The Great Ocean Road is one of the best places in Australia to spot koalas in the wild. Both of the last two times that I've driven along the road, I've spotted multiple koalas, as some of their favourite spots are well-known by locals.

One of the easiest places to spot koalas is at Kennett River, south of Lorne. Park outside the suitably named Kafe Koala, then walk along the road behind the caravan park. Generally, the best way to spot a koala is by seeing where the other tourists are standing and taking photos!

Dogs are not restricted in this location, so your dog can join you. Always keep your dog on a leash and remove them from the area if they become excited and start barking at the koalas.

Another popular spot to see koalas is along the turn-off to Cape Otway. I also spotted some just outside Apollo Bay. Keep an eye out for tourists stopped along the road taking photos.

HIKE TO BEAUCHAMP FALLS

Many of the waterfalls along the Great Ocean Road are off limits to dogs, including the popular Erskine Falls and Sheoak Falls near Lorne. To visit a waterfall with your dog, head further inland to Beauchamp Falls Reserve, part of Otway Forest Park, where dogs are allowed on-leash.

The carpark and a campground are located off Aire Valley Road. Turn off the Great Ocean Road at Skenes Creek to access it – be prepared for a 50 minute drive along a narrow, windy road, including a final 3km stretch of unsealed road.

The 20m high falls are accessed by a 1.5km walking trail that passes through magnificent mountain ash forest. Note that the walk includes lots of steps, which may be difficult for small or older dogs, and are slippery when wet. Allow up to 90 minutes for the return walk.

Not far from Beauchamp Falls is Stevensons Falls, close to the town of Forrest. These falls are also dog-friendly and just a short, easy stroll from the day-use area.

CAMP AT JOHANNA BEACH

While dogs are generally not allowed in Great Otway National Park, which covers much of the eastern half of the Great Ocean Road, there are a handful of places that you can visit with your dog, including Johanna Beach, just west of Cape Otway.

A popular surf and fishing beach, this beach is also home to a beachside campground, where dogs are permitted. Just keep your dog on a leash both on the beach and in the campground.

Advance bookings are recommended, especially during the busy summer period. Facilities are basic, with no showers and only non-flushing toilets, but the camping fees are very cheap and the location second to none!

COUNT THE TWELVE APOSTLES

One of the highlights along the western stretch of the Great Ocean Road is stopping off at the many rock formations, including the Twelve Apostles, Loch Ard Gorge, The Arch, London Bridge and the Grotto. However, these spectacular sights are within Port Campbell National Park or another area that forbids dogs. So what can you do when you are roadtripping with your dog?

The easiest sight to visit when travelling with your dog is also the most famous, the Twelve Apostles. The adjacent carpark is located just outside the national park, so you can park there with your pup. There's only a sign forbidding you from taking dogs any further at the start of the walking path to the lookouts.

If you're not travelling solo, I recommend taking turns to head to the lookout.

Alternatively, if the weather is cold and gloomy, like it was for my visit, and your pup is fine being left alone, you could leave your dog in your vehicle – just never do this during warmer weather.

🐾 WALK ALONG THE BAY OF MARTYRS

The most dog-friendly attraction along the western section of the Great Ocean Road coastline is the Bay of Martyrs. Dogs are allowed to join you on the cliff-top walkway between Peterborough and the carpark at the far end of the Bay of Martyrs, part of Bay of Islands Coastal Park.

Park at either end and walk your dog along the scenic track, which is 2km in each direction, and enjoy the views of the rugged coves and beaches below. Allow up to 2 hours for the walk, and keep your dog on a leash the whole way.

📍 FOLLOW THE GOURMET TRAIL IN TIMBOON

Close to the Twelve Apostles, I highly recommend turning off the Great Ocean Road to follow part of the Twelve Apostles Gourmet Trail, including visiting the cute rural village of Timboon.

I visited Schulz Organic Creamery & Cafe and tasted their range of cheese for a small fee. Order some of their food and drinks and sit at the tables in their lush garden, with dogs welcome to join you. I enjoyed the nachos topped with their own quark.

In Timboon itself is Timboon Fine Ice Cream. Unfortunately, they didn't have any of their dog-friendly ice-cream available when I visited, but they generously gave me a mini-cup of vanilla ice-cream for Schnitzel to devour outside. He loved it, and I also loved my own ice-cream.

How to get there

It's at least a 90 minute drive from Melbourne to Torquay, the official start of the road. Apollo Bay is a further 2 hours south-west along the windy road.

When to visit

With dogs restricted from many beaches along the Great Ocean Road over summer, consider a visit during spring or autumn; the days are still warm, but dogs are allowed off-leash on the sand. Weekends outside school and public holidays are best, to avoid the worst of the crowds.

Above: **Timboon Fine Ice Cream** Opposite: **The Twelve Apostles**

 **Dog-friendly parks**

Stribling Reserve,
Lorne

Dogs are allowed off-leash, except during events when they need to be leashed, at this reserve a few blocks back from the main beach in Lorne.

Top: **Great Ocean Road Brewhouse**
Bottom: **Apollo Bay Fishermen's Co-Op**

Dog-friendly dining

Dog-friendly accommodation

Swingbridge Cafe,
Lorne

Open daily for breakfast and lunch, or just coffee. Dogs are welcome in the outdoor seating area. Cross the swing bridge and head north along the shore afterwards to the local off-leash dog beach in Lorne.

Apollo Bay Fishermen's Co-op,
Apollo Bay

I enjoyed a delicious traditional feed of fish and chips at this co-op at the harbour. Sitting at the outdoor tables, Schnitzel even helped with keeping the local seagulls at bay.

Great Ocean Road Brewhouse,
Apollo Bay

Well-behaved dogs on a leash are allowed in the outdoor courtyard, which is fully enclosed during the cooler months. There are plenty of craft beers on tap, plus a wide-ranging menu. Dogs are also welcome to join you in the Taste of the Region tasting room just behind the pub.

Countrywide Cottages,
Bambra

These popular pet-friendly cottages are a 25 minute drive inland from Lorne. Each of the two- and three-bedroom cottages has a private fenced yard, with dog beds, blankets, bowls and treats provided.

Marengo Family Caravan Park,
Marengo

Just a few kilometres south of Apollo Bay, this beachfront caravan park welcomes pets year-round, both on sites and in all cabins, for no extra fee. Dogs are also allowed on the adjacent foreshore during part of the day.

Gum Tree Caravan Park,
Port Fairy

A great spot to stay at the western end of the Great Ocean Road. We received a warm welcome at this caravan park that allows pets year-round. It has multiple pet-friendly cabin options, plus its own off-leash area and playground for pups.

03

South Australia

Adelaide/Tarndanya	130	Eyre Peninsula	149
Limestone Coast	136	Outback South Australia	154
Go houseboating on the Murray River	142	Drive across the Nullarbor	160
Riverland	144		

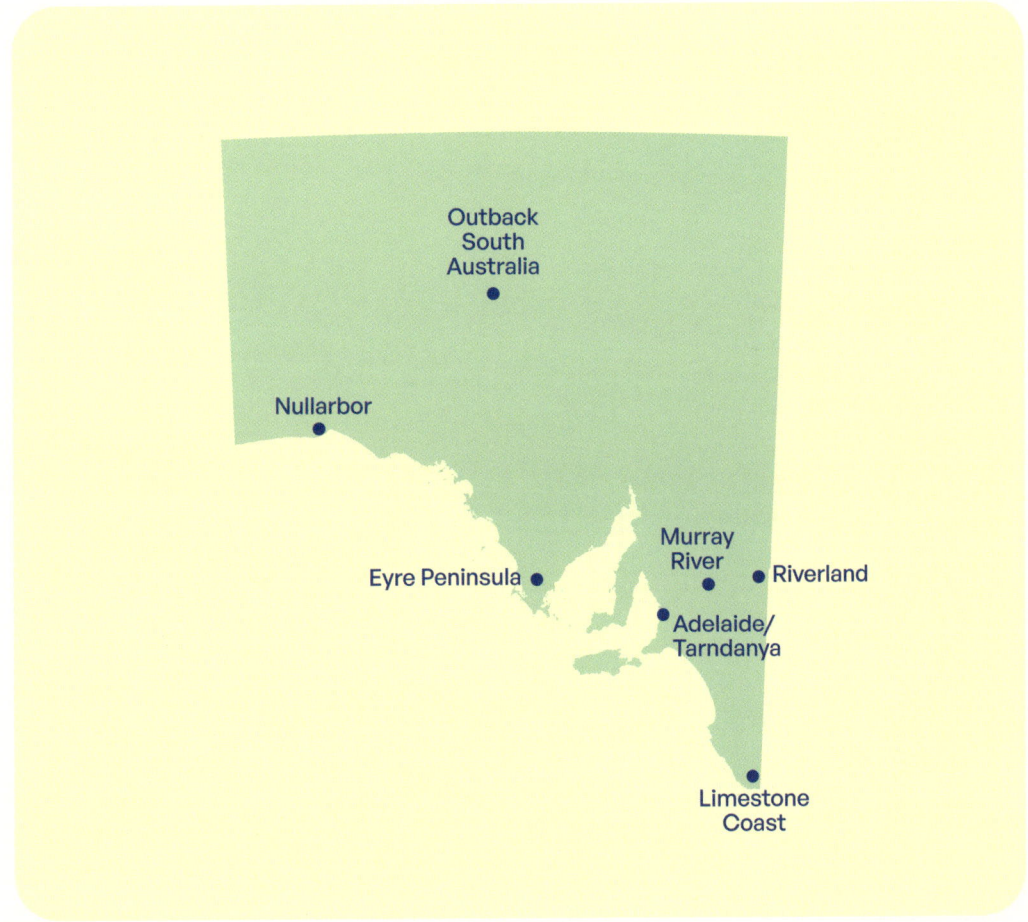

Adelaide/ Tarndanya

The capital city of South Australia, Adelaide combines the amenities of a large city with the relaxed ambience and compact size of a large town, surrounded by some of the country's most prestigious wine regions.

Nothing is ever that far away in Adelaide. And whether you're wanting to visit the beaches along the city's west, go hiking in a pet-friendly national park to the east or enjoy a day of wine tasting, you can do it all with your dog by your side!

Schnitzel at Himeji Garden in Adelaide

GO FOR A STROLL IN THE CITY

One of the best spots in Adelaide to enjoy a walk with your pup is along the banks of the River Torrens. Located on the northern side of the Adelaide city centre, between Rundle Mall and the Adelaide Oval, stroll through the open grassy parks with your pup and check out the famous Adelaide Oval sports ground from the outside.

If you detour south to the city streets, take a walk through Rundle Mall, the main shopping strip of the city. The mall is home to a number of sculptures, most famously *Mall's Balls*, but my favourite is the innocuously titled *A Day Out* – a group of life-size bronze pigs, including one scrambling up onto a bin. Make sure you keep your own dog on a leash and out of trouble!

VISIT HIMEJI GARDEN

On the opposite side of the Adelaide city centre, in the southern expanse of Adelaide Park Lands, is a secret gem – Himeji Garden. This Japanese-style garden was a gift from Adelaide's sister city in Japan, Himeji. Containing a picturesque pond and a Zen rock garden, it is a small but relaxing and beautiful spot to visit, with free entry.

Just like throughout the rest of Adelaide Park Lands, dogs are allowed in the garden, with only the usual rule of leashes being required. I recommend only visiting the gardens with quiet, well-behaved dogs, who can respect the peacefulness that other visitors are seeking.

HEAD TO A LOCAL BEACH

You don't need to travel far to enjoy a day at the beach with your dog when you're in Adelaide. Plenty of great beaches line the western edge of the city, including the popular Glenelg Beach, plus quieter options such as Henley Beach. These are two of my favourite spots in Adelaide. Both beaches feature wonderful white sand, plenty of dog-friendly outdoor dining and are beautifully placed to watch the sun set over Gulf St Vincent.

Even better, the rules for dogs on beaches in Adelaide are quite relaxed, especially compared to other Australian cities. On most beaches in Adelaide, the main restriction is that dogs need to be leashed between 10am and 8pm while daylight saving is in operation (October to March).

If you head to the beach in the morning or late evening during summer, or anytime during the day during winter, you're free to let your dog enjoy the sand and paddle in the water off-leash, except around playgrounds.

SPEND THE DAY TASTING WINE

It wouldn't be a trip to Adelaide without visiting some of the famous wine regions that surround it. The closest wine region to Adelaide is the Adelaide Hills, just 30 minutes to the east. Further afield are McLaren Vale, 45 minutes to the south; and the Barossa Valley, 60 minutes to the north. Both McLaren Vale and the Barossa Valley are renowned for their red wines.

Many cellar doors in these wine regions welcome dogs, at least in outside areas. It's best to make a booking in advance and inquire at the same time about the latest rules for dogs, or contact the local tourism associations for the latest listing of dog-friendly wineries. If the wineries you plan to visit have their own dogs, it's best if your dog is sociable.

One of the most dog-friendly wineries in the Barossa Valley is Levrier Wines. Your pup is likely to meet the resident wine dogs (so all visiting dogs need to be vaccinated). This winery has its own off-leash dog park complete with toys outside the cellar door, perfect for keeping your pup occupied while you make your way through the wines, or they can join you inside.

Some other pet-friendly cellar doors in the Barossa Valley include Langmeil Winery, St Hallett and the grounds of the historic Chateau Yaldara. These three cellar doors are each open seven days a week, but advance bookings are preferred. While visiting the Barossa, stop at Maggie Beer's Farmshop to stock up on jams and sauces or enjoy a platter overlooking the dam from the outdoor deck where dogs are welcome.

If you're heading south to the McLaren Vale wine region, try to visit Alpha Box & Dice. Well-behaved dogs are welcome at its cellar door, which has previously held annual Dog Day events. Open from Thursday to Monday, choose between two tasting options, with bookings recommended.

📍 TAKE A DAYTRIP TO HAHNDORF

The cute town of Hahndorf is just a 30 minute drive from Adelaide, and a wonderful destination to visit on a daytrip with your dog. With German roots going back to its founding in 1839, this town has previously been named the most dog-friendly town in all of South Australia.

I loved strolling with Schnitzel along the picturesque main street of Hahndorf, with many of its buildings constructed with typical Germanic timber-framing architecture. Some businesses are dog-friendly and will allow your pup inside, but always ask for permission.

It's also a must to have lunch at one of the many German restaurants in the town. Most restaurants have large outdoor dining areas out the front, great for enjoying a meal with your well-behaved pup by your side. Some of the best dog-friendly options include The Haus, Hahndorf Inn and the German Arms Hotel. Enjoy a lunch of hearty German cuisine, washed down with the local wine or a beer.

For something smaller but no less hearty, I recommend Wunderbar Hot Dogs. There's a range of German hotdogs on offer featuring kransky sausages and including a schnitzel option! I chose the German Dog with plenty of sauerkraut. Sit at the tables out front or enjoy a takeaway hot dog.

Just a short drive outside Hahndorf is Balhannah Dog Park. This huge dog park is

Below: **Historic Hahndorf** Opposite: **Underneath Glenelg beach pier**

the perfect place to let your dog off-leash, with a creek running along one side of it that's also great for doggy swims during the warmer months.

 ### GO HIKING IN THE HILLS

There are a large number of dog-friendly hiking options close to Adelaide, both on the outskirts of Adelaide and up in the Adelaide Hills.

On the south-eastern fringe of Adelaide is Belair National Park, one of South Australia's dog-friendly national parks and a great spot for hiking with your dog. Walks range from short, easy strolls through to longer hikes for experienced bushwalkers only.

One of the most popular walks is the challenging 6.5km Waterfall Hike that leads to the rock escarpments of the Upper and Lower waterfalls, or explore the easier 4.5km Microcarpa Loop. Keep your eye out for wildlife, including koalas, kangaroos and emus, and keep your dog on a leash at all times.

The nearby Brownhill Creek Recreation Park also allows dogs on a leash, as do the smaller Blackwoods Forest Recreation Park and Shepherds Hill Recreation Park. Close to Stirling in the Adelaide Hills is the Woorabinda Bushland Reserve, with 4km of walking tracks snaking through the bushlands surrounding Woorabinda Lake.

 ### HOP ONBOARD THE COCKLE TRAIN

An hour south of Adelaide is the town of Goolwa, the north-eastern terminus of the *Cockle Train*, which runs along the oldest steel-railed railway in Australia. The train makes regular 30 minute journeys between Goolwa and Victor Harbour, also stopping at Middleton and Port Elliot.

The timetable varies throughout the year, running daily at peak times but only two days per week during the off-peak season. Diesel locomotives are usually used, but on selected days a steam engine pulls the train. Buy your ticket on the day for a one-way or return journey, with four-legged passengers riding for free.

When to visit

Adelaide is at its best during summer, when the weather is warm and its beaches are tempting. However, the benefit of visiting during the cooler months is that dogs are generally allowed on the beaches all day long.

 # Dog-friendly parks

 # Dog-friendly dining

Pityarilla Dog Park,
Adelaide

Located on the southern side of the city, next to Glen Osmond Road, this dog park has two separate enclosed spaces for small and all-size dogs. Both areas are surrounded by high fences, plus there are double gates, water bubblers and a shelter.

Semapaw Park,
Semaphore Park

This dog park has two separate areas. As well as the main area with obstacles for active dogs, there's also a separate Sniff Space, designed as an off-lead adventure trail for timid or older dogs.

Bacchus Bar,
Henley Beach

This waterfront bar and restaurant are extra dog-friendly with leash-clips at the outdoor tables, water bowls and dog muffins on the menu. They're open for dinner from Thursday to Sunday, plus lunch on the weekend.

Malobo,
Henley Beach

I enjoyed coffee and drinks at this dog-friendly cafe right on Henley Square with beach views. The cafe is open all day long, with lots of options on its breakfast, lunch and dinner menus.

Malt Shovel Taphouse,
Adelaide

Part of the Adelaide Festival Centre and just across the footbridge from the Adelaide Oval, this brewpub is open until late, from Wednesday to Sunday. Dogs are welcome at the outdoor tables.

Fare and Square,
North Adelaide

Boasting that it has Adelaide's best dog menu, Fare and Square will have you choosing between Snoopy Eggs or Scooby Doo Stew for your pup. Or just order your pup a furchino, while you select from the all-day breakfast menu.

Dog-friendly accommodation

Mayfair Hotel,
Adelaide

Book your pet the Luxe Pets package at this luxury hotel in a renovated, heritage-listed building overlooking Rundle Mall. Up to two dogs or cats are permitted, up to 20kg each, with larger dogs permitted at the manager's discretion.

Adelaide Inn,
North Adelaide

Book a stay in one of the pet-friendly Deluxe Queen or Single rooms at this four-star hotel. Your dog will be provided with a large bed, bowls and access to a private courtyard, in return for a pet fee per night.

Brighton Beachfront Holiday Park,
Kingston Park

Pets are welcome year-round at this caravan park on the south-western edge of Adelaide. Choose between camping with your dog on one of the pet-friendly powered sites or staying in a pet-friendly cabin.

Dogs are allowed on Adelaide beaches

Limestone Coast

The south-eastern corner of South Australia is known as the Limestone Coast, thanks to the deposits of limestone that lie under much of the region, resulting in numerous caves and sinkholes, plus excellent soil for wine growing – all providing plenty of fun things to do with your pup.

Mount Gambier, the second largest city in South Australia, lies on the inland part of the region, while the coastline is dotted with a string of delightful small towns, including Robe and Kingston.

The vividly coloured Blue Lake over summer

WALK AROUND THE BLUE LAKE

The city of Mount Gambier is named after the volcano of the same name, which is surprisingly only dormant rather than extinct. The surrounding volcanic field is home to the youngest volcanoes in Australia, with Mt Gambier believed to have erupted as recently as 5000 years ago!

Mount Gambier is dotted with remnants of its recent volcanic past, from craters and lakes to sinkholes. The top attraction of the city is the iridescent Blue Lake, located in the old volcanic crater of Mt Gambier, and it's a great spot to visit with your dog.

Every year between November and March the lake turns a stunning deep turquoise blue. The colour of the lake changes almost overnight and remains brightly hued until late February or March, when it gradually changes back to a duller blue for the rest of the year. On a recent visit, I was lucky to view it just after it had turned turquoise blue.

Head to one of the many lookouts around the lake. There are multiple lookouts next to Bay Road, or follow John Watson Drive around the lake and stop at other viewing points. Even better, go for a walk around the lake with your dog. There's a 3.6km walking path that circles the entire lake, with dogs on a leash welcome to join you.

 ## GAZE INTO UMPHERSTON SINKHOLE

Another spectacular sight in Mount Gambier is the Umpherston Sinkhole. This sinkhole is located next to the Princes Highway on the eastern approach into the city centre. In 1886, a stunning, lush garden was created within the sinkhole that you can still descend into and explore.

Unfortunately, dogs are not permitted within the sinkhole, due to the wildlife that lives there. However, dogs are allowed to view it from above and explore the surrounding park, as long as they stay on a leash. I recommend taking turns to descend into the sinkhole if you're not travelling solo.

 ## HIKE A VOLCANO RIM

Another spectacular volcanic crater located not far outside Mount Gambier is Mt Schank, which also erupted about 5000 years ago. This volcano is a 15 minute drive south of town, and is surrounded by verdant farming country. Access is from Mountain Path Road.

There is a well-formed path up to the rim of the crater, with limestone slats to help you ascend. It's a tough climb, but if you're reasonably fit it should only take about 10 to 15 minutes. Dogs are welcome to join you, but need to stay on a leash.

Once you reach the top, you can just stop to catch your breath and take in the view from the rim of the crater, or choose to walk all the way around. This walking path is rather rough, but the views along the way are spectacular. Allow about an hour to complete the full 2.4km walk, including the ascent, rim walk and descent.

 ## TASTE WINE IN COONAWARRA

About 45 minutes drive north of the town of Mount Gambier lies Coonawarra, one of the premier red-wine regions in South Australia, with the locally grown cabernet sauvignon especially highly regarded.

Don't miss visiting some of the cellar doors in the region, with many welcoming your dog with you. Some of the dog-friendly wineries that are open daily include Balnaves of Coonawarra, Bellwether Wines, Majella Wines, Rymill Coonawarra and Wynns Coonawarra.

The trail up Mt Schank

Most wineries only allow dogs in outdoor areas, but a few may allow them inside the cellar door too. It's best to contact wineries in advance to confirm whether an appointment is required and ensure that your dog is welcome.

FOLLOW THE ROBE COASTAL WALK

The town of Robe lies right on the coast. An excellent way to explore its town centre, beaches and historical sites is by following the Robe Coastal Walk. The full 12km loop is still under construction, but some sections have already been completed.

The most interesting section of the coastal walk to follow is the western section, which visits the headland on the western edge of Robe, starting near the modern Robe Lighthouse, just off Adam Lindsay Gordon Drive.

The 3.5km trail loops around the headland and the town's foreshore. It passes the distinctive Robe Obelisk, the remains of the historic Robe Gaol, Robe Jetty, Lake Butler and the former Customs House (now a museum) before it terminates at Victoria Street. It's also possible to access each half of this trail from the end of Obelisk Road. Keep your dog on a leash and pack a water bowl for them.

Along the way, dogs are allowed off-leash at Lipson Park, adjacent to Lake Butler. Plus, just south of the start of the walk near the Robe Lighthouse. Dogs are also allowed off-leash on West Beach, with no time restrictions.

🐾 GO 4WDING ON THE BEACH

There are multiple beaches along the Limestone Coast where you can drive on the sand in a 4WD. While dogs aren't allowed at many of these beaches, head to the northern edge of Robe and the aptly named Long Beach.

Long Beach stretches for 12km from the edge of Robe to Boatswain Point. While the southernmost section between the first and second ramps is pedestrian only, vehicles are allowed access onto the sand north of the second ramp, just off the Esplanade. There's also a third ramp at the end of Steve Woolston Road.

Dogs are allowed off-leash north of the third ramp year-round, north to Boatswain Point Beach but excluding Guichen Bay Conservation Park. Between the second and third ramp, they are allowed off-leash, except between 9am and 8pm from December to the Easter long weekend.

Schnitzel at Umpherston Sinkhole

How to get there

Mount Gambier is located in the south-eastern corner of South Australia, less than 20km from the Victorian border. It's about a 5 hour drive from Adelaide. Robe is 90 minutes to the north-west of Mount Gambier, on the coast.

When to visit

For the best chance of sunny and warm weather, ideal for visiting the beaches, head to the Limestone Coast during summer. Note however that pet restrictions apply in many caravan parks during peak periods.

 ## Dog-friendly parks

 ## Dog-friendly dining

Hastings Cunningham Reserve,
Mount Gambier

This fenced dog park on Shepherdson Road has two areas. One is mainly for larger dogs, while the other is exclusively for small dogs. There's also a variety of obstacles for your pup to enjoy.

Lipson Park,
Robe

Dogs are allowed off-leash in this park adjacent to Lake Butler, with benches and poo bags provided. Just be aware that it isn't fenced and is next to a road.

San Piero Coffee Bar,
Mount Gambier

Open early each morning from Monday to Saturday, grab a coffee for yourself and a puppycino for your pup. The egg and bacon brioche rolls are highly recommended.

Drift @ Robe,
Robe

Make sure you head to this popular brunch spot in Robe early during busy summer days. Open daily from breakfast to lunch, it has a huge dog-friendly outdoor dining area.

Robe Town Brewery,
Robe

The only wood-fired brewery in Australia, this brewery is open during the afternoon from Tuesday to Sunday, plus later on Friday nights. Dogs are welcome inside and out, with burgers available on Friday nights and a food van on weekends.

Dog-friendly accommodation

Pine Country Caravan Park,
Moorak

This extra pet-friendly caravan park is just outside Mount Gambier. It welcomes pets year-round on all camping sites, plus in two dog-friendly cabins with their own yards. There's also a large off-leash dog park on-site.

Coonawarra Bush Holiday Park,
Comaum

Schnitzel and I enjoyed a stay in one of the glamping tents at this rustic park just north of Penola. Pets are welcome in the glamping tents, plus in the four ensuite cabins, as long as they have their own bed. There are also caravan and camping sites.

Lakeview Motel & Apartments,
Robe

Dogs are welcome in a number of the spacious rooms, ranging from standard to executive to family, at this motel with gorgeous views overlooking Dunn Lake.

Lakeside Tourist Park,
Robe

This award-winning park allows pets outside the peak Christmas and Easter long weekend periods. As well as on sites, pets are also allowed in a single pet-friendly cabin which needs to be booked directly.

Top: **Coonawarra Bush Holiday Park**
Bottom: **Umpherston Sinkhole**

LIMESTONE COAST

Go houseboating on the Murray River

For a very different kind of holiday with your dog in South Australia, why don't you consider hiring a houseboat? Spend your days floating on the meandering Murray and relaxing on deck, docking occasionally to visit a cafe or winery. Then moor for the night next to the bank, stars twinkling overhead.

You don't need a licence to drive a houseboat and there's also no need to leave your pet behind, with many of the houseboat companies that operate along the 650km stretch of the Murray River in South Australia offering pet-friendly houseboats for hire.

In the Murraylands region, covering the lower stretch of the Murray, just 80 minutes east of Adelaide, contact White Houseboats in Mannum. They have five large, luxury houseboats that are pet-friendly. Alternatively, Griffens Marina Houseboats in Blanchetown and Foxtale Houseboats in Morgan both have dog-friendly houseboats. If you're not hiring a boat for a large group, consider one of Griffens Marina's smaller four-berth boats.

Further upstream in the Riverlands region, there are plenty more dog-friendly houseboats to choose from. Contact Riverfun Houseboats in Paringa who have a wide range of houseboats of various sizes, many that allow pets onboard. Pet-friendly houseboats are also available from Wilkadene Houseboats, Liba Liba Houseboats and Renmark Houseboats. Contact them directly to find out which of their boats are pet-friendly, and their latest rules.

Another cute option, although not exactly a standard houseboat, are the boats for hire from River Wren Houseboats at Murray Bridge, conveniently close to Adelaide. They have a fleet of six small riverboats that are just the right size for a couple and one or two small dogs or a single large dog.

Before making a booking, speak directly to the houseboat company about their rules for dogs onboard. Some companies prefer dogs to remain out on the deck on their boats, while others simply request you keep them off the furniture and return the boat free of pet hair. Bring along everything you need for your dog, including a bed and bowls, plus plenty of old towels to dry off your pup when they inevitably have a swim in the river.

Be aware when spending the night on the river that noise travels further on water, including the sound of barking. Always be considerate to other boats in the area! Also keep your dog restrained overnight, so there aren't any unexpected midnight accidents.

When staying on a houseboat with your dog, a common question is about where they do their business. Unless your dog is trained to use puppy pee pads, it's best to go ashore regularly with them, so that they can do their business on dry land, always keeping your dog leashed.

If houseboating along the section of the Murray River around Renmark, keep in mind that some parts of the adjacent Murray River National Park are dog-friendly (*see* p. 145), including the Paringa Paddock section and Lyrup Flats between Renmark and Berri.

Pets are welcome onboard some houseboats

GO HOUSEBOATING ON THE MURRAY RIVER

Riverland

On the eastern edge of South Australia lies the fertile Riverland region, where the mighty Murray River crosses the Victorian border and meanders past the small country towns of Renmark and Berri.

A popular fruit- and wine-growing region, it's also a great destination for a relaxing stay with your dog. Spend your days exploring scenic stretches of the river, the remains of early European settler sites and even one of South Australia's dog-friendly national parks.

Below: **Silo art in Waikerie** Opposite: The view from Heading Cliff Lookout

📍 HEAD TO A RIVER LOOKOUT

When visiting the Riverland region, make sure you visit one of the terrific lookouts located along the Murray River that give you a great perspective of this mighty river – the longest in Australia.

One of the best lookouts close to Renmark is the Heading Cliff Lookout, with its richly hued limestone cliffs that tower above the water and reflect the blazing sun. It's only a 15 minute drive north of Renmark, along a sealed road.

Note that there are signs about the usage of baits in the surrounding nature reserve. I carried Schnitzel to the metal lookout structure, just a short walk from the carpark. Alternatively, keep your dog on a short leash and possibly use a muzzle.

Another great lookout to visit is at Big Bend, the largest bend along the entire Murray River. Big Bend Lookout is located south of the towns of Swan Reach and Blanchetown, on the eastern bank of the river. Take in the view of the long bend and the adjacent floodplain from high up on the riverside cliff.

📍 VISIT A DOG-FRIENDLY NATIONAL PARK

While most national parks in Australia strictly prohibit dogs, that's not the case with a handful of national parks in South Australia, including parts of Murray River National Park around Renmark and Berri. A number of sections of the national park allows dogs: Paringa Paddock, Lyrup Flats, Kingston-on-Murray and the old Rodeo Grounds area at Katarapko. Note that dogs are prohibited from the Gurra Gurra and Bulyong Island sections.

Paringa Paddock is a great spot near Renmark to enjoy a long walk with your energetic dog. Located between Renmark and Paringa, on the southern side of the highway, the park has walks ranging from 4.3km to 7.5km long. The best spot to park and access the walks is on the northern side of the highway, near the caravan park, where there's a tunnel under the highway.

While in the area, I also recommend walking along the short boardwalk on the Murray River side of the carpark. It's a tranquil spot filled with towering reeds that's popular for photography and spotting birdlife.

Lyrup Flats lies between Renmark and Berri, on the northern side of the river from the small town of Lyrup. There are multiple campsites (*see* p. 148) and day-use areas.

Kingston-on-Murray is a wetlands area with a newly developed network of trails adjacent to the town of the same name, while the Katarapko section of the park is south-west of Berri – dogs are only allowed here in the old Rodeo Grounds area.

Top: **Beer tasting at Woolshed Brewery**
Bottom: **The boardwalk near Paringa Paddock**

While visiting Murray River National Park, make sure your dog is restrained on a leash no longer than 3m long, unless they are confined within a motor vehicle, trailer or vessel.

DISCOVER MUSEUMS AND HISTORICAL SITES

The Erawirung People are the Traditional Owners of this region, however in the mid-19th century European settlers arrived in the area, attracted by the fertile soil and plentiful water. There are plenty of small museums and sites to visit that delve into this history, and dogs are welcome to join you at many of them.

In Renmark itself, take a stroll along its beautiful waterfront area. The *PS Industry*, a historic paddlesteamer, is normally moored out the back of the visitors centre. After dark this stretch is also known as 'Possum Parade', probably best skipped if you're visiting with a dog!

Not far from Berri is the Loxton Historical Village, a 20 minute drive south on the southern bank of the Murray River. Over 45 re-created buildings and exhibits along the banks of the Murray tell the story of the region's early European settlers. Pet dogs are welcome to visit with permission, so reach out and see if your dog is allowed. Plan to spend the whole day and take a picnic lunch to enjoy on the grounds.

Alternatively, just outside Renmark is the Paringa Community Museum. This small volunteer-run museum has a collection of old machinery, and on-leash dogs are welcome to join you on a visit. The museum is open on Monday, Wednesday and Friday, with just a small entry fee.

🎨 VIEW SOME SILO ART

Some beautiful examples of silo art stand tall in the Riverland region, with dogs generally allowed in the viewing areas. A short drive from Renmark are the silos in Paringa, just east across the Murray River. Both sides of the two silos are painted with scenes illustrating the local Murray River lifestyle.

Further west in Waikerie, a 50 minute drive west of Renmark towards Adelaide, is another pair of silos that shouldn't be missed. I was delighted by the colourful regent parrot on one of the silos.

🍷 DROP INTO A RIVERLAND WINERY

While the Riverland region may not have the same prestige as some of the other wine-growing regions in the state, there's certainly plenty of wine grown in the region.

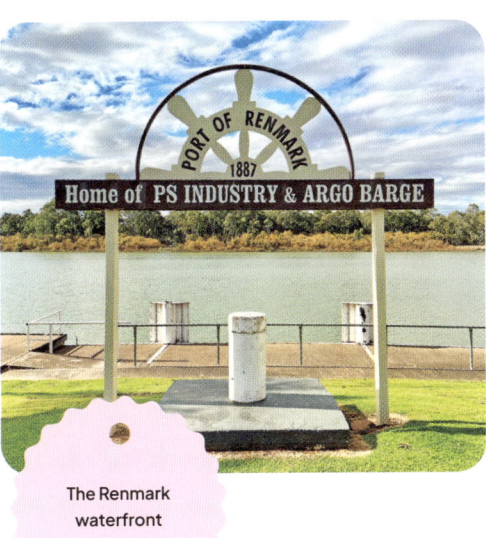

The Renmark waterfront

Berri Estates, just outside Glossop, is the largest winery in the Southern Hemisphere. It's possible to drop in and buy some wine (even a cask) at their cellar door.

But for a dog-friendly experience I recommend heading to Caudo Vineyard. West of Waikerie, this riverside winery is even accessible by boat. Book a riverbank picnic table to enjoy the menu which focuses on local produce, accompanied by a glass of their wine or their own range of sangrias. Alternatively, make a booking for a wine tasting from Tuesday to Friday. Pets are welcome.

🍺 ENJOY A BEER AT THE WOOLSHED BREWERY

If you'd prefer to spend a sunny afternoon sipping on beer rather than wine, head to the Woolshed Brewery. This popular brewery is a 15 minute drive to the north of Renmark.

The brewery occupies a beautiful spot next to the river, with plenty of outdoor tables underneath shady trees and looking out over the water. There are even two resident brewery dogs for your pup to make friends with. It's the perfect spot to while away an afternoon. The brewery is open from Wednesday to Sunday.

How to get there

Berri is a 3 hour drive north-east of Adelaide. Renmark is just a 15 minute drive further down the road from Berri.

When to visit

The Riverland enjoys sunny, warm days year-round. It can get very hot during summer; spring or autumn are best.

 ## Dog-friendly parks

 ## Dog-friendly accommodation

Renmark Off-Leash Dog Park,
Renmark

Located on the corner of Paringa and Seventeenth streets, this park is fully fenced, with two areas: one for puppies and small dogs, and a larger area for other dogs. Drinking water, benches and even some pipes to explore are provided.

Berri Off-Leash Dog Park,
Berri

Part of the Colin Jennings Apex Park beside the highway, this park is fully fenced and provides a water bowl, but doesn't have a separate area for small dogs.

Riverbend Caravan Park,
Renmark

One of the most welcoming dog-friendly accommodation options in the area, this park on the banks of the Murray welcomes pets year-round, on all sites. It also has two pet-friendly cabins, each with its own yard.

Waikerie Holiday Park,
Waikerie

Dogs are welcome at this caravan park, where there are plenty of poo-bag dispensers around the park and a pet-friendly cabin that can accommodate up to four guests and two pets, and boasts its own fenced area.

Lyrup Flats Campground,
Monash

Camp with your dog in this dog-friendly national park campground. There's a variety of sites available, many suitable for multi-family groups. When booking online, access conditions and distance to toilets are listed for each site.

 ## Dog-friendly dining

Cinnamon Grove,
Renmark

This cafe in a beautiful garden setting loves welcoming four-legged friends. Open daily from Thursday to Monday; just ask for permission before letting your pup off leash!

River Jacks Cafe,
Berri

Located right on the waterfront, this cafe has plenty of dog-friendly outdoor tables. It's open daily for both breakfast and lunch.

Eyre Peninsula

The Eyre Peninsula is a huge region and the largest peninsula in South Australia, lying between Port Augusta and the Nullarbor Plain. The peninsula is famous for its stunning remote beaches (which you can often enjoy alone with your dog), plentiful seafood and many wildlife experiences.

Whether visiting the region with your dog on a short getaway from Adelaide or on a Big Lap of Australia, spend your days slowly exploring the coastal towns dotted up and down the east and west coasts.

Farmland meets sand dunes on the Eyre Peninsula

🌊 EXPLORE REMOTE BEACHES

The beautiful beaches of the Eyre Peninsula are a major highlight for most visitors, and the same applies when visiting with a dog. Many beaches allow dogs on them, with both on-leash and off-leash options.

The rules for dogs on Eyre Peninsula beaches differ from section to section, with many small local government areas making it difficult to find out the rules. However, based on my observations, it's rare for dogs to be outright prohibited from beaches, except for in Lincoln National Park, Coffin Bay National Park and some other conservation areas.

On the east coast of the Eyre Peninsula, dogs are allowed off-leash during the early morning and late evening on the beach at Tumby Bay and the Port Lincoln Foreshore, plus on-leash at both beaches during the day. Check the signs for the exact hours.

The west coast beaches tend to be more dog-friendly. Two of the most spectacular beaches where dogs are allowed off-leash all day long are Farm Beach and Greenly Beach. Just check the conditions of the unsealed access roads first, if you don't have a 4WD.

Some more accessible off-leash beaches include Long Beach near Coffin Bay, the beach just north of the jetty at Elliston and the beach at Sceale Bay.

Note though, that even if dogs are allowed off-leash on the beach, you should keep an eye out for nesting seabirds. If any are around, keep your dog leashed.

🌊 CAMP NEXT TO THE BEACH

There are countless dog-friendly beach campsites dotted all along the Eyre Peninsula, many of them run by local councils. Spend a night or an entire week, depending on the rules, relaxing next to the beach at the campsite of your choice.

Most of the campsites only have basic facilities, with either no fee or a small fee per vehicle. While some sites are accessible by 2WD, others require 4WD access or a tolerance for rough roads, so double-check the access conditions in advance. Some sites may also require you to be fully self-contained, such as the popular Perlubie Beach campground.

Right: **Clifftop sculptures at Elliston**
Opposite: **Schnitzel at Murphy's Haystacks**

Schnitzel and I spent the night at Walkers Rocks Campground, about 12km north of Elliston on the western side of the peninsula, accessed by a 3km unsealed road that is generally in good condition. There's a beautiful beach with great fishing behind the campground, along with clean toilets and a cold shower. A small nightly fee is charged.

We also camped for the night at Fitzgerald Bay, north along the coast from Whyalla. This free campsite with flushing toilet facilities is also beachfront – Schnitzel loved sniffing around in the sand. The access road is sealed except for the final few hundred metres.

FOLLOW THE OYSTER WALK AT COFFIN BAY

Coffin Bay is one of the prettiest spots on the Eyre Peninsula. Its calm waters are home to some of the best oyster farms in Australia. While I doubt you're going to share any oysters with your dog, they would love a stroll with you along the Oyster Walk.

This walking path wraps around the waterfront of the bay, clocking up an impressive 12km, although you can just walk part of it. Dogs are allowed on a leash along most of the walk, except the eastern section in Kellidie Bay Conservation Park.

Along the way, I recommend stopping and enjoying some of the locally grown oysters at the waterfront Oyster HQ (*see* p. 153).

AMBLE ALONG A MANGROVE BOARDWALK

Along the eastern side of the Eyre Peninsula lie a number of stretches of impressive mangroves. The best spot to view the mangroves is at Arno Bay, where local volunteers have constructed the award-winning Arno Bay Estuary Boardwalk.

Head to the southern side of town, or walk along the path past the caravan park, then choose whether to first walk the Creek Mouth Boardwalk or Crab Flat Loop. The former is a 600m long boardwalk to the creek mouth and beach, while the latter is a 640m loop. Leashed dogs are permitted along both boardwalks, plus on the beach.

CHECK OUT MURPHY'S HAYSTACKS

Another interesting natural formation on the Eyre Peninsula is Murphy's Haystacks. These distinctive pinkish rock outcrops are actually granite inselbergs, formed when the dune sand above was eroded over thousands of years.

The Haystacks are located on private land, not far off the highway, about 40km south of Streaky Bay. Public access is provided in return for a small donation per adult or family, with no prohibition on dogs. There's a short walking track wandering in between the Haystacks.

🍴 EXPLORE THE MURALS OF TUMBY BAY

In recent years the town of Tumby Bay on the eastern side of the Eyre Peninsula has run the annual Colour Tumby Festival in March, which has left the town with many impressive murals adorning its walls, some painted by internationally renowned artists.

Walk through the streets with your dog on-leash. Most artworks are around North Terrace and Mortlock Street. Check the latest festival guide for a map. One of my favourite works is the mural by Adnate and Vera Richards at the Yacht Club, exploring the First Nations heritage of the area.

While you're in Tumby Bay, also stop at the grain silos just off the highway, and view the beautiful mural created by Ron, celebrating the joy of swimming off the local jetty. Other impressive murals on the Eyre Peninsula can be seen at Kimba and Cowell, although the latter is best viewed from the sports grounds where dogs are not allowed.

📍 BE AWED BY TALIA CAVES

On the western side of the peninsula, not far south of the town of Venus Bay, detour towards the coastline to view the spectacular Talia Caves. These caves consist of two formations: the large cavern known as the Woolshed, accessed along a wooden walkway; and the Tub, a large crater in the cliff with a tunnel connecting it to the sea. There's no restriction on dogs joining you.

The unsealed access road to Talia Caves is notorious for being rough. Although not strictly 4WD-only, your vehicle needs to be up to the challenge of a corrugated road. The best time of year to visit the spot is during the warmer months, when you can also enjoy a dip in the gorgeous rockpools adjacent to the caves.

Stunning coastal views

How to get there

It's nearly a 400km drive from Adelaide to Whyalla, the gateway to the Eyre Peninsula. Distances between towns on the peninsula are huge, with Port Lincoln around a 270km drive south, and Ceduna a 450km drive west, of Whyalla.

When to visit

Late summer and early autumn are beautiful times to visit the Eyre Peninsula, with the beaches at their best. I've visited the Eyre Peninsula twice in June and, while I've had some beautiful sunny weather at times, the water has been freezing cold!

Dog-friendly parks

Dog-friendly dining

Whyalla Dog Park,
Whyalla Norrie

This large fenced area is mainly open space, with some agility equipment, water fountains and undercover seating. There's plenty of room for multiple dogs, plus a smaller area for small or elderly dogs.

Oyster HQ,
Coffin Bay

This waterfront oyster restaurant and bar are open daily, until early evening. I enjoyed a wonderful sunset with freshly shucked oysters and wine. Dogs are welcome on the outside deck. Bookings are recommended.

The Fresh Fish Place,
Port Lincoln

Open all day long, Monday to Friday, plus until early afternoon on Saturday. The extensive menu of locally caught seafood is available for both dine-in and takeaway. There are only a few dog-friendly outdoor tables, so consider enjoying a picnic near the waterfront.

Dog-friendly accommodation

Shelly Beach Caravan Park,
Ceduna

Schnitzel and I enjoyed our stay at this beachfront caravan park south of Ceduna. Pets are allowed on sites plus in selected pet-friendly cabins. Don't miss the scenic dune walking track.

Whyalla Caravan & Tourist Park,
Mullaquana

This caravan park has a fabulous off-leash dog park on-site, with agility equipment and a patch of grass. Dogs are allowed on sites, plus in selected cabins.

Beer Garden Brewing,
Port Lincoln

Pull up a seat in the dog-friendly beer garden and enjoy one of the tasting paddles alongside a wood-fired pizza. Note that it is usually only open Thursday to Sunday.

EYRE PENINSULA

Outback South Australia

Pack your pup in the car or caravan and head north of Adelaide past the edges of the state's farming land to the rocky outcrops of the majestic Flinders Ranges, passing ghost towns along the way. Or head even further to the remote north of the state and the isolated opal mining town of Coober Pedy to experience the mythical Outback South Australia.

The Flinders Ranges from the west

DRIVE THROUGH THE FLINDERS RANGES

The beautiful Flinders Ranges region in outback South Australia is more than just the national park of the same name surrounding Wilpena Pound. For a stunning day out, I recommend driving north from the gateway town of Hawker to the old mining hamlet of Blinman.

While the fully sealed 110km long highway passes through some clearly signposted sections of Ikara–Flinders Ranges National Park, skip stopping inside the park with your dog and instead stop at some of the beautiful lookouts just outside the park, with glorious views of the rugged ranges.

Some of the best views are from Arkaba Lookout, Elder Range Lookout, Rawnsley Lookout and Hucks Hill Lookout – I stopped at each with Schnitzel. All these lookouts are just off the road – keep an eye out for the signs.

Another lookout further off the highway, along an unsealed access road, is Stokes Hill Lookout. Also consider following the gravel access road to the Great Wall of China, a scenic rock formation just south of Blinman.

Rather than returning by the same route, consider following the Parachilna Gorge Scenic Drive from Blinman over to Parachilna. It takes you through some spectacular rugged landscapes. You can even stay at the popular free campsites along the way – perfect for a peaceful outback stay with just your pup.

While the 32km long road is unsealed, if it's been recently graded it's fine for 2WD vehicles. This was the case when I visited. Just take your time! Ask about the current road conditions at the Mine Booking Office in Blinman.

At the end of the drive, you'll arrive at Parachilna, home to the Prairie Hotel with its famous 'feral food' menu and an on-site brewery. The hotel is open from Wednesday to Sunday for lunch, except for a few months over summer. Pet dogs are welcome to join you when you're dining or enjoying a drink outside or on the verandah. From Parachilna, it's 92km back to Hawker along the sealed Outback Highway.

STAY AT AN OUTBACK STATION

There are multiple sheep stations around the Flinders Ranges that welcome campers and are generally also dog-friendly. The level of facilities on offer varies. Some also have cabin and lodge accommodation, although generally these aren't pet-friendly.

One popular dog-friendly station is Rawnsley Park Station, about 35km north of Hawker on the road to Wilpena Pound. As well as pet dogs being permitted on the powered and unpowered sites in the caravan park, pets are also allowed in their standard three-bedroom holiday units and two pet-friendly cabins. And if you'd like to visit the nearby national park, you can leave your dog in a shaded run for a fee.

Another pet-friendly station nearby is Willow Springs, which offers paid private, unpowered bush-camping sites, plus the pet-friendly Jillaroo's Hut.

WATCH THE QUORN SILO LIGHT SHOW

While there are many silos across Australia that have been painted with magnificent murals in recent years, for something different head to Quorn in the southern Flinders Ranges to experience the nightly silo light show.

Thanks to heritage rules preventing the silos from being painted, instead a light show is projected onto the silos every night shortly after sunset, celebrating the Flinders Ranges, the Pichi Richi Railway and other local stories. The main show lasts for 60 minutes and is followed by another 90 minutes of local artwork projections.

Bring your own chair and dog, and find a spot in the viewing area next to the visitor information centre. Or watch from the comfort of your own car, tuning to the listed radio frequency to hear the narration.

UNLOCK HISTORIC BURRA

The town of Burra is fascinating to visit with your dog when driving north to the Flinders Ranges. Once the home of the extensive Burra Copper Mine – the largest metal mine in Australia at the time – the town is now one of the best preserved Victorian-era towns in Australia, plus home to many significant mining remains.

Top of the sights to see in Burra is the open air museum located at the site of the former open-cut Burra Mine. To visit this and other historical sites around town, buy the Burra Heritage Passport from the information centre in Burra. In return, you'll be lent a key for two days that will provide you with access to eleven locked sites.

As well as the former mine, you can also visit the Redruth Gaol, the cellars of the Unicorn Brewery, miners' dugouts and the former police lockup. Dogs are welcome to join you on your explorations, and are permitted inside some buildings.

Just north of Burra, keep an eye out for a famous sight just off the road. The derelict Cobb & Co Coach House Hotel was made famous on the cover of Midnight Oil's *Diesel & Dust* album and is a picturesque sight.

HEAD UNDERGROUND AT AN OPAL MINE

The outback town of Coober Pedy owes its existence to opal mining – it's been dubbed the opal capital of the world. Whether you're just stopping in Coober Pedy for the night or a couple of days, don't miss visiting an opal mining museum and finding out more about these precious gems and the mines.

Tom's Opal Mine is a former mine that operated during the 1980s and '90s. It has now been turned into a museum. Dogs of all sizes are welcome at the mine, whether you choose the self-guided option or to join a guided tour. Afterwards, don't miss the chance to 'noodle' for opals on the dirt heaps outside, with help from your pup of course.

Coober Pedy is also home to many quirky attractions around town, from the *Big Miner* sculpture to a concrete UFO to the Big Winch – perfect for selfies. At sunset head up to the Big Winch Lookout next to the 8m tall Big Winch. Dogs are welcome to join you walking up to the lookout, but are not allowed at the adjacent cafe.

SPEND A NIGHT UNDERGROUND

It wouldn't be a true experience of Coober Pedy without spending the night underground. The original inhabitants of the town built underground houses or 'dugouts' to escape the brutal summer heat in the days before air-conditioning, but it's a peaceful experience any time of year.

There's a wide range of underground accommodation options, including many that allow pets, from underground motel rooms to an underground camping area. There's also a number of holiday rentals in underground homes, some that allow pets to join you.

To learn more about underground life, take a tour at Faye's Underground House, an original underground home in Coober Pedy. Tours cost just a small fee and pets are welcome to come along.

EXPLORE THE BREAKAWAYS

One of the most beautiful attractions around Coober Pedy is the Breakaways, a series of low colourful hills to the north of town. Situated within the Kanku–Breakaways Conservation Park, which is owned by the Antankirinja Matu-Yankunytjatjara People, pets are welcome in the park, as long as they remain leashed.

Buy a permit for your vehicle in advance from the District Council of Coober Pedy website (or use the computers at the information centre), then take Kempe Road out of town. It's a 70km loop drive, and you'll pass by Moon Plain and a section of the 2150km long Dog Fence (used to keep dingoes and wild dogs out of southern Australia), as well as two lookout points.

Note that the unsealed road used to access the park should not be driven on after rain – so skip this attraction if there has been recent rain or double-check at the information centre. At the park, keep to the formed walking trails.

Below: Outback art in Cradock Opposite: A Flinder Ranges lookout

How to get there

Hawker, the gateway to the Flinders Ranges, is almost a 400km drive north of Adelaide, or 100km north-east of Port Augusta. Coober Pedy is 850km north of Adelaide, including a long and empty 540km drive north-west of Port Augusta.

When to visit

Skip outback South Australia during summer – the temperatures can be scorching, with many attractions also closed, particularly in Coober Pedy. The Flinders Ranges are at their best during autumn or spring, when the weather is great for exploring on four paws.

 ## Dog-friendly parks

 ## Dog-friendly accommodation

Hawker Dog Park,
Hawker

Hawker is home to a fenced dog park, just opposite the local caravan park. There are two fenced areas – take your pick.

Burra Dog Park,
Burra

The local dog park on Smelts Road is home to two fully fenced off-leash areas, where there are also drinking water and shelters.

 ## Dog-friendly dining

Flinders Food Co,
Hawker

This popular cafe serves excellent coffee, including takeaways, or take a seat at one of the dog-friendly tables out the front. Open daily for breakfast and lunch except on Monday; the food is also highly rated.

Downunder Gallery and Cafe,
Coober Pedy

One of the most highly praised cafes around Coober Pedy. Dogs are welcome out the front in the outdoor seating area. The cafe is open from Monday to Saturday for breakfast and lunch.

Comfort Inn Coober Pedy Experience,
Coober Pedy

All the rooms at this small hotel are located underground, with selected rooms designated as pet-friendly, with no additional charge. Let the management know in advance you'll be bringing a pet.

Riba's Underground Camping,
Coober Pedy

One of the only places in the world you can camp underground, this campground is a few kilometres south of Coober Pedy. Note that only tents are allowed in the underground campsite, but there are also above ground campsites for caravans and campervans, both powered and unpowered.

The Big Winch Lookout in Coober Pedy

The Prairie Hotel in Parachilna

Drive across the Nullarbor

To break up your journey across the Nullarbor, from South Australia to Western Australia, I recommend stopping off at these attractions along the way, both to stretch everyone's legs and to stop boredom from taking over.

Windmill Museum

Penong, 75km west of Ceduna, has long been called the windmill capital of Australia. It's now home to an outdoor museum showcasing many historical examples of windmills, including a huge Comet, the largest windmill in Australia. It's free to visit, but donations are welcome.

Camel, kangaroo and wombat sign

There are multiple classic road-sign photo ops along the Nullarbor – don't miss taking a selfie with your pup at them! The first camel, kangaroo and wombat sign is just after Yalata Roadhouse, but there's a few other locations along the South Australian part of the drive.

Nullarbor Plain sign

The official Nullarbor Plain is only along one section of the drive. When driving west, you'll find the sign marking its eastern edge just before the turn-off to the Head of Bight Visitors Centre, about 265km west of Ceduna. If driving in the opposite direction, the sign is just before the Nullarbor Roadhouse.

Head of Bight Visitors Centre

This centre is home to multiple whale-watching platforms, high on the cliffs above the Head of Bight. If you visit during the whale-watching season between June and October, spotting whales is virtually guaranteed, with a cheaper entry fee during

There's a certain romance about driving across the Nullarbor, the long 1200km stretch of highway between Ceduna in South Australia and Norseman in Western Australia. On the other hand, it's a rather long, boring, straight drive, and if you're completing a Big Lap around Australia or visiting southern Western Australia with your dog, there's really no way to avoid it.

the rest of the year. While dogs aren't allowed inside the centre or at the platforms, it's okay for dogs to remain in the carpark on a leash.

Bunda Cliffs

Between the Head of Bight Visitors Centre and the South Australian border is a beautiful stretch of cliffs, the 200km long Bunda Cliffs. There are three signposted lookout points, plus many more unofficial ones. The best lookout to stop at during the morning is the middle one, while I found the eastern lookout best in the afternoon.

Old Telegraph Station ruins

The small town of Eucla in Western Australia (with a population of 37) is the only proper town along the Nullarbor. It was established as a Telegraph Station in 1877 – once the busiest station outside the state capitals. These days the ruins of the station lie 4km south of the modern town, partially buried by sand dunes. It's a picturesque spot to visit.

Madura Pass Lookout

The Nullarbor drive is mainly but not entirely flat, with one of the most significant changes in elevation occurring at Madura Pass, about 180km west of Eucla. At the top of the pass, pull off to the lookout and take in the views across the Roe Plains below.

Caiguna Blowhole

The entire Nullarbor is situated on a limestone plateau, dotted with caves and blowholes. The easiest blowhole to visit is the Caiguna Blowhole, 5km west of the Caiguna Roadhouse. Stop for a moment and feel the air moving out of this opening from the caves below.

An iconic photo stop on the Nullarbor

90 Mile Straight sign

The longest straight section along the Nullarbor, in fact anywhere in Australia, is the 90 Mile Straight – 146.6km long without any bend. Starting just west of Caiguna Roadhouse, the other end is marked with a sign 20km east of Balladonia Roadhouse.

04

Western Australia

Perth/Boorloo	164
Esperance/Kepa Kurl	170
Try to catch Wave Rock	176
Albany/Kinjarling	178
Margaret River	184
Feed the dolphins at Monkey Mia	190
Ningaloo Coast	192
Broome/Rubibi	197
Chill out at Lake Argyle	204

Perth/ Boorloo

The Western Australian capital of Perth is one of the most remote cities in the world, however, it's still very welcoming to dogs. There's plenty to do, no matter if you're a local or have just completed the long drive across the Nullarbor.

And since you've come all this way, you should spend some time in the port city of Fremantle or 'Freo'. Arguably the most dog-friendly part of Perth, it mixes historical charms with beachfront breweries and restaurants, and of course plenty of dog-friendly beaches.

Exploring Kings Park

STROLL AROUND KINGS PARK

Right on the doorstep of Perth city centre is the massive Kings Park. At over 400 hectares, it's no wonder this is such a popular destination. With views of the city and Swan River, the park contains the Western Australian Botanic Garden, as well as sections of natural bushland.

Leashed dogs are allowed throughout most of Kings Park. The main exceptions are the elevated section of the Federation Walkway and the Naturescape Park, plus during selected organised events.

Pick a section and head for a walk – I enjoyed a stroll around Roe Gardens with Schnitzel. The Water Garden Pavilion is another popular spot. It's also a delightful place for a picnic – just make sure your pup doesn't try to taste someone else's picnic!

FROLIC ON A WEST COAST BEACH

Perth is blessed with many beautiful ocean beaches, perfect for swimming nearly year-round, taking a walk along the sand or just enjoying the spectacular west coast sunsets. During your visit to Perth, it's a must to catch at least one of these sunsets at the beach with your pup by your side.

Luckily, there's plenty of dog-friendly beaches along this coastal strip – it seems that nearly every second beach along the coast is dog-friendly, far more than in the east coast cities of Australia.

One of the most popular off-leash dog beaches is the long dune-lined expanse of Leighton Dog Beach, also known as Mosman Beach. Dogs are permitted off-leash along a huge stretch of coastline, from South Cottesloe to the railway overpass.

Another popular off-leash dog beach is South Fremantle Dog Beach. Not far south of Freo, this beach was very popular on the Saturday morning Schnitzel and I visited. Alternatively, head further south to North Coogee Beach, which is also dog-friendly, but quieter.

If you'd prefer to head north of the city, check out the sparkling waters of Hillarys Dog Beach. Dogs are allowed off-leash on the beach year-round. Dogs are also allowed off-leash (except during the mornings from Monday to Saturday when they need to be kept leashed) on Hillarys Horse Beach, immediately to the north.

EXPLORE HISTORIC FREMANTLE

Traditionally considered a separate city to Perth, the port city of Fremantle or 'Freo' is just a 30 minute drive away. During my visit to Perth with Schnitzel, I spent quite a bit of time in Fremantle, home to many off-leash dog areas and sidewalk cafes.

Fremantle is renowned as having the most intact 19th century port city townscape anywhere in the world. I recommend taking a walk with your dog down High Street and through the West End to admire the many historic buildings.

While dogs aren't allowed inside Fremantle Prison or the Fremantle Markets, they're welcome to visit the Fremantle Round House. Built between 1830 and 1831 as the first civil gaol in the colony, these days the Round House is the state's oldest building, with entry to the basic interior by gold coin donation. Try to time your visit for the 1pm cannon firing, but keep your distance to protect your dog's sensitive ears.

A far more modern addition to the Fremantle waterfront is the statue of Bon Scott, the former lead singer of Australian rock band AC/DC and one of

Freo's favourite sons. Make sure you and your pup get a selfie or two with the statue!

TASTE THE BEERS AT LITTLE CREATURES

The Fremantle waterfront is home to the ever-popular Little Creatures Brewery. Established in 2000 with the aim of brewing an American-style IPA locally, the beers are still brewed on-site. The building was originally constructed to house America's Cup yachts.

The beer garden outside the front of the brewhouse is dog-friendly, with well-behaved leashed dogs welcome. I recommend pulling up a seat and ordering a tasting tray, featuring the full range of beers, including some special brews only served on-site. There's plenty of food options on offer, including a range of wood-fired pizzas.

HEAD TO THE SWAN VALLEY

On the eastern fringes of Perth is the Swan Valley, Western Australia's oldest wine region. Vineyards have been planted here since 1829.

With a wide variety of cellar doors, breweries, distilleries and local produce stores, there's plenty of dog-friendly options, no matter your preferred tipple. Also don't miss out on enjoying lunch at one of the many on-site restaurants. One winery that is particularly popular with dog owners is Ugly Duckling Wines. This boutique winery is open daily for tastings, with cheese platters on offer too.

While visiting the Swan Valley, make time to wander through the village of Guildford. Established in 1829 and one of only three towns in Perth on the National Trust register, it's well known for its colonial architecture.

GO HIKING AT NOBLE FALLS

For a delightful but easy bushwalk with your dog, head to Noble Falls. The falls are located just east of the country town of Gidgegannup, about a 50 minute drive east of the city centre. Park up at the Noble Falls carpark, opposite the tavern of the same name.

The falls are at their best during winter, when rainfall is highest, or else visit during the springtime to enjoy the beautiful wildflower displays. Allow about 75 minutes for the 3.5km walk, or else there is a shorter 1.3km option.

Left: **Beach-time in Perth/Boorloo** Opposite: **The Fremantle foreshore**

Best of all, dogs are allowed off-leash, as long as they remain under your full control. And if you don't pack your own picnic lunch, you can enjoy lunch (or just a beer) afterwards at the Noble Falls Tavern, in the dog-friendly beer garden or on the deck.

If you'd prefer not to drive so far for a hike with your dog, head instead to Ashfield Flats in Bassendean, a 20 minute drive east of the city. This urban bushland reserve is the largest remaining river flat in the Perth metropolitan area, and is popular with dog owners and walkers.

RIDE ON A HISTORIC STEAM TRAIN

About a 75 minute drive south of Perth is Dwellingup, home to the Hotham Valley Railway. The railway operates two train excursions that welcome dogs of all sizes onboard.

From May to October, hop aboard a steam locomotive, the *Steam Ranger*. This 2 hour excursion travels along the state's steepest and most spectacular section of railway. Trains depart on Sunday, plus Wednesday during school holidays.

Alternatively, the *Dwellingup Forest Train* operates year-round. Enjoy a 2 hour trip travelling 8km east to Etmilyn, including a walk through the forest. There are departures on Saturday, Sunday, selected public holidays and Wednesday during school holidays when the *Steam Ranger* isn't scheduled.

When to visit

Head to Perth during spring or autumn. The days will still be warm with plenty of sunshine, but you'll avoid the scorching days of summer and the rainy days of winter.

Dog-friendly parks

Ozone Dog Agility Park,
East Perth

While small in size (and best for smaller dogs), this park is conveniently located in the centre of Perth. It is fully fenced and has an excellent obstacle course.

Riverside Gardens,
Bayswater

Located on the banks of the Swan River, this large reserve has two off-leash areas and a dog swimming beach. On the weekends, look out for the coffee van and food truck.

Dog-friendly dining

Slate Cafe,
Bennett Springs

One of the most pet-friendly spots in Perth, this cafe not only has a large grassed outdoor area where dogs are welcome to join you, but also a fenced dog playground. Regular breed-specific play dates are held every Sunday.

Union Kitchen,
Mindarie

Open daily for breakfast and lunch, with a long and diverse menu. Your pup can also choose from their own menu, featuring Mutt Shakes, a Dogs Bark-fest and Pupsicles.

Bathers Beach House,
Fremantle

Dine on seafood or enjoy a cocktail at the Fremantle waterfront while watching the sunset. Dogs are welcome at the outdoor tables of this restaurant, open daily for lunch and dinner.

Beer tasting tray at Little Creatures

Dog-friendly accommodation

QT Perth,
Perth

Enjoy a stylish stay at this city hotel, with one dog up to 20kg permitted per room. Your dog will be provided with their own bed and a dog-friendly minibar as part of the Pup Yeah! package.

Banksia Tourist Park,
Hazelmere

This park near the Swan Valley has a variety of pet-friendly cabins, ranging from budget to deluxe, as well as pet-friendly caravan and camping sites.

Fremantle Village,
South Fremantle

I enjoyed our stay in the campervan area of this caravan park just south of Fremantle. Pets are allowed on sites only, and must be registered with the office. It's a short walk to the off-leash North Coogee Beach.

Mosaic wall at South Fremantle Dog Beach

PERTH/BOORLOO

Esperance/ Kepa Kurl

The remote town of Esperance on the southern coast of Western Australia is deservedly famous for its beautiful white sandy beaches. The most famous beach in the area is Lucky Bay, thanks to its amazingly white sand and the many images of kangaroos lounging on its sand. While this beach is off-limits to four-legged visitors because it's in Cape Le Grand National Park, there's still plenty of dog-friendly beaches that you can visit, many of them off-leash. Start dreaming of the perfect beach holiday with your pup.

Lighthouse sculpture along the foreshore

VISIT THE BEAUTIFUL BEACHES

Dogs are welcome to join you in visiting most of the beaches around Esperance. Each beach features the stunning white sand that the region is renowned for, plus many have calm waters due to the surrounding bays.

Other than the beaches in nearby national parks, such as Lucky Bay, the only other stretch of sand where dogs are prohibited is the western end of Twilight Beach, near the Surf Life Saving Club. Many of the other beaches are off-leash all day long, but some have restricted hours. If in doubt, check the beach for signs or ask a local.

The best way to visit the beaches of Esperance with your dog is by driving along the Great Ocean Drive. This tourist drive follows the magnificent coastline west of the town, before looping back. It's only 40km long and could be completed in just over an hour, but it's easy and fun to spend the whole day visiting the beaches along the way.

Some of the dog-friendly beaches along the route include West Beach, Blue Haven (one of my favourites despite the stairs), Salmon Beach, Fourth Beach, Ten Mile Lagoon and Eleven Mile Beach. There are carparks beside each beach, as well as varying facilities. Out of these, only West Beach has restricted off-leash hours: dogs are only allowed off-leash from 5am to 8am, then 4pm to 8pm; they need to be leashed during the rest of the day.

If you'd prefer more time to take in the view, follow the Great Ocean Walk. This shared cycle–pedestrian pathway runs parallel to the drive as far as Twilight Beach. It's 12km long in total from the town centre, or 8km if you start at West Beach. It's also easy to just walk a shorter section, thanks to the many carparks along the route.

Just before you reach the far end of Twilight Beach, there's a side route on the walk. Take the 4.5km pathway through bushland to Pink Lake Lookout – just don't expect to see a pink lake at the other end! While Pink Lake on the edge of Esperance is a pretty spot, it stopped being pink about 20 years ago due to decreased salt content.

There are also dog-friendly beaches to the east of Esperance. Head to Bandy Creek Beach, on the eastern side of Bandy Creek Fishing Boat Harbour, or continue on to the westernmost part of Wylie Bay, at the end of Wylie Bay Road.

Schnitzel at West Beach

Below: **Whale Tail Sculpture on the foreshore** Opposite: **Flight of beers at Lucky Bay Brewing**

 HEAD TO LUCKY BAY BREWING

While dogs aren't permitted at Lucky Bay, the local brewery named after this popular spot is certainly dog-friendly! Lucky Bay Brewing has plenty of outdoor tables, both under shelter and scattered on the lawn, where your pup is welcome to join you. I was even asked if Schnitzel wanted his own drink (of water, of course).

The brewery is situated just outside town on Bandy Creek Road and is a proudly local operation, using locally grown barley directly purchased from farmers. With a long list of beers on tap, I recommend starting with one of the tasting paddles. They also stock a range of Western Australian–sourced wines.

If you're feeling peckish, the list of wood-fired pizzas is nearly as long as the list of beers. During selected hours there are also additional food options, such as cheese boards, tacos and lamb skewers. Double-check the opening hours and kitchen hours in advance.

 GET UP CLOSE TO A WIND FARM

Esperance has long been a pioneer in wind power, both due to the town having its own power grid and its frequently windy weather. The town was home to both the first research wind farm and the first commercial wind farm in Australia.

It's possible to visit the Salmon Beach Wind Farm as a side trip while driving along the Great Ocean Drive, with no restrictions on pets joining you.

Although this research wind farm has now been decommissioned, with only one out of its six turbines remaining, it's still worthwhile exploring. Follow the short walking trail with multiple information panels along the path.

STROLL ALONG THE FORESHORE

While the beaches outside Esperance get all the attention, there's also a beautiful foreshore right next to the town centre. And the best way to explore it, including with your dog, is by going for a stroll.

Starting from the Taylor Street Jetty, near the Southern Ports area (which is off limits to the public), it's possible to keep walking for nearly 5km to the far end of Castletown Quays Beach on the foreshore path. Along the way you'll pass stretches of beaches, multiple jetties and parks dotted with picnic tables and other amenities.

One section of the beach you'll pass is off-leash for part of the day. On the eastern side of Tanker Jetty, until Straker Street in Castletown, dogs are allowed off-leash between 5am and 8am, and 4pm and 8pm. The rest of the day they need to be on-leash.

There are plenty of cafes, restaurants and even food trucks along the way to break up your walk. Also keep an eye out for the *Whale Tail* sculpture in the James Street Precinct and the *Lighthouse* sculpture near Taylor Street Jetty.

 GO HIKING AT ROTARY LOOKOUT

On the southern side of Esperance, near the start of the Great Ocean Drive, follow the signs for 'Dempster Head and Lookout' to reach the Rotary Lookout. As well as a great vantage point to view the surrounding bays (especially during whale-watching season), the lookout is also the starting point of a number of dog-friendly walks.

Choose from four short walks; all allow on-leash dogs. If you have limited time, follow the 800m Rotary Walk that loops around the top of the headland. If it's close to sunset, add on the extension to Taananeditj Summit, a popular sunset viewpoint.

However, the most adventurous walk from the lookout is the 1.3km hike to Lovers Cove, a secluded pretty beach with no road access. Allow 30 minutes each way. Just keep in mind the final stretch over granite is slippery during wet weather.

How to get there

Esperance is an 8 hour drive south-east of Perth. If you're taking the more coastal route, allow about 12 hours over multiple days. Alternatively, it's a popular initial destination in Western Australia after crossing the Nullarbor. Simply turn south at Norseman and drive for 2 hours towards the coast.

When to visit

Esperance is most popular during summer. During winter the water is too cold for swimming and many days are rainy or at least cloudy, although you may spot whales in the water.

 ## Dog-friendly parks

 ## Dog-friendly dining

Wildcherry Dog Park,
Castletown

This fenced dog park is located next to Wildcherry Avenue. As well as separate fenced areas for small and large dogs, it features seating, shelters, water, natural agility equipment and a sand pit.

Taylor Street Quarters,
Esperance

Overlooking the water near Taylor Street Jetty, this restaurant is open from 10am to late, Tuesday to Sunday. It's a great spot to enjoy a coffee, glass of wine or a cocktail. The outdoor tables are dog-friendly, with water bowls provided.

Coffee Cat,
Esperance

Previously just a van in the carpark, the Coffee Cat is now established in a more permanent container at the Tanker Jetty Precinct. Grab a coffee and snack while strolling along the waterfront on weekday mornings.

Bottom: **Excited to head into Lucky Bay Brewing**
Opposite: **Ten Mile Lagoon is a dog-friendly beach**

WESTERN AUSTRALIA

Dog-friendly accommodation

RAC Esperance Holiday Park, Castletown

This large, recently renovated park is close to the beach on the northern side of town. Pets are welcome year-round. Up to two pets are allowed on all campsites, plus in the pet-friendly two-bedroom cabins. There's even a dog wash on-site – just the thing after spending the day at the local beaches!

Esperance Bay Holiday Park, Esperance

This caravan park is also pet-friendly year-round. It's just a short stroll from the town centre and Taylor Street Jetty area, with pets permitted on both powered and unpowered sites, but not inside cabins.

EcoValley Retreat, Pink Lake

This child-free retreat near Pink Lake has two self-contained units suitable for couples and their dogs. The dog-loving owners allow dogs off-leash on the property.

Try to catch Wave Rock

Wave Rock is a magnificent granite formation shaped like a wave, part of the larger Hyden inselberg. Located hundreds of kilometres from the coast (and any kind of water), the rock is about a 4 hour drive east of Perth in the wheatbelt region of Western Australia, near the small town of Hyden.

The most surprising thing about Wave Rock, apart from the fact that it wasn't actually formed by water, is that it's not located in a national park. Managed by the local council, your dog is welcome to join you in visiting this impressive natural formation.

Adjacent to the rock is the Wave Rock Caravan Park, the easiest place to camp when visiting Wave Rock. Pets are permitted on both powered and unpowered sites, plus there is at least one pet-friendly cabin – make sure you book well in advance! Alternatively, inquire whether any pet-friendly cottages are available at the nearby Wave Rock Resort.

It's less than a 5 minute walk from the caravan park to Wave Rock. Note that if you aren't staying at the caravan park, a vehicle entry fee applies. At 15m high and 110m long, the granite cliff is even more impressive in real life, and the perfect spot for selfies with your pup – I took plenty with Schnitzel!

After checking out the rock, continue exploring by following one of the walking tracks that crisscrosses the area. Leashed dogs are allowed on all the walks, except for the section of the Hyden Rock Walk that ascends up onto the larger inselberg and passes through the local water catchment area.

One of the most popular walks is the 1.7km loop to Hippo's Yawn and back. I thought this equally intriguing rock formation really does look like the gaping mouth of a hippo! The walk is well formed and flat, with interpretive panels along the way. There's also a carpark next to Hippo's Yawn, if you'd prefer to drive.

For a longer walk, I recommend the Wave Rock Walk Circuit. As well as visiting Hippo's Yawn, this 3.6km loop also takes in the salt-lake landscape to the north, with multiple boardwalks passing over the swampy areas. Along the way you'll also pass the salt swimming pond, with entry included if you're staying at the caravan park. The cool waters are an inviting spot for a swim, with no prohibition on dogs in the surrounding area, although they need to stay out of the pool.

About 16km north of Wave Rock is another granite outcrop known as The Humps. The Humps are located in a separate reserve, with no entry fee or prohibition against dogs. The road to the reserve is largely sealed, although the final 1.5km section is unsealed, but still suitable for 2WDs.

The highlight of a visit to The Humps is Mulka's Cave, one of the most significant Noongar rock-art sites in southern Western Australia. Over 450 handprints and images are dimly visible over the walls of two chambers. I recommend leaving your pup outside. There are also two walking trails: the 1.7km Kalari Trail ascends to the top of The Humps, while the 1.2km Gnamma Trail focuses on the Noongar perspective of the surrounding landscape.

A birds-eye perspective of Wave Rock

Albany/ Kinjarling

The largest city on the southern coast of Western Australia, Albany has a long and winding history, with the Menang Noongar People having lived on this land for over 25,000 years. It was also the first colonial settlement in the state, predating Perth, and home to an important whaling station.

You can explore many of Albany's historical sites with your pup. But the chief dog-friendly attraction is its beautiful natural setting on King George Sound.

Whalers Cove Beach

Memorial at Albany Heritage Park

📍 EXPLORE THE HISTORIC PRECINCT

Albany's main historic precinct is located close to its waterfront, on the western edge of the city's current centre. Don't miss exploring this area on foot with your dog. Make sure you check out the exterior of the sandstone Albany Convict Gaol, built in 1852. Not far away is the Patrick Taylor Cottage, the oldest surviving post-colonial dwelling in the state, built in 1832.

However, the most interesting sight to see in the precinct is the *Brig Amity*. This replica two-masted sailing ship was built in the 1970s, a copy of the ship that carried the first European settlers from Sydney to the new colony of Cape George Sound, as the Europeans had then named it, now Albany.

Admire the brig from the outside with your dog. For humans, it's also possible to venture onto the deck, and for a small fee a short audio tour of the lower deck is offered – if travelling with others, perhaps take it in turns to experience it.

📍 HEAD TO ALBANY HERITAGE PARK

On the headland on the other side of the city centre is the National Anzac Centre and Albany Heritage Park. While the museum naturally doesn't allow dogs inside, on-leash dogs are allowed throughout the remainder of the park.

Close to the National Anzac Centre is the Convoy Walk, leading up to Convoy Lookout. Many of the ships full of soldiers sailing to Gallipoli during World War I assembled in King George Sound, and a diagram shows what the formation looked like – I found it intriguing to imagine. There's also the remains of the fortifications that stood here, plus examples of old heavy guns.

At the other end of Albany Heritage Park, leave your vehicle at the bottom of the Avenue of Honour and walk with your pup up the stairs to the impressive, hill-top Desert Mounted Corps Memorial. Also check out Padre White Lookout nearby.

VISIT THE BEACHES OF FRENCHMAN BAY

The beaches at Frenchman Bay are some of the most beautiful beaches I've seen anywhere, and it's great that they're dog-friendly. Dogs are allowed off-leash on most beaches in the area outside Torndirrup National Park. Don't miss heading out to the bay, a 25 minute drive from the centre of Albany, for an afternoon or the day.

My favourite beach along Frenchman Bay is Whalers Cove, also known as Fisheries Beach. It's tucked in behind Uredale Point and on the sunny winter afternoon I visited, Schnitzel and I had it entirely to ourselves.

Another beach along the bay is Frenchman Bay Beach, close to the Historic Whaling Station. While dogs are unsurprisingly not allowed inside the popular tourist attraction, they are allowed on-leash at the start of the beach, plus off-leash after the boat ramp. Another off-leash beach to check out nearby is Goode Beach.

Closer to Albany, there are also some off-leash beaches around town. Head to Middletown Beach, with dogs allowed off-leash on the long stretch between the end of Flinders Parade and Firth Street in Emu Point. Dogs are also allowed off-leash on the small beach next to the marina in Emu Point, between Hunter and Swarbrick streets.

HIKE THE UREDALE POINT HERITAGE TRAIL

For a dog-friendly bushwalk near Albany, head to Whalers Cove and the start of the Uredale Point Heritage Trail. This 5km loop is recommended for those with some bushwalking experience and takes about 2 hours to complete.

As well as the cairn marking the spot where Captain George Vancouver claimed the area for Britain in 1791 (the point was formerly known as Point Possession), there are some spectacular views of King George Sound along the way. Dogs should be kept on a leash on the trail.

WATCH FOR WHALES

Whaling was once a major industry in Albany, until the closure of the whaling station in 1978. Luckily, the focus is now on peacefully watching the whales during their annual migration, whether on boat trips or from the shore, with whales most likely seen between June and October.

One of the best places to spot whales with your dog is from Convoy Lookout in Albany Heritage Park. Alternatively, head to Marine Drive, which loops around the headland underneath the park. There are multiple lookouts along the drive, as well as a cycle–pedestrian path that runs roughly parallel to it. Dogs on a leash are welcome on the path.

TASTE THE FLAVOURS OF THE TOWN OF DENMARK

One of the best daytrips from Albany is to the small town of Denmark, about a 45 minute drive west. It's a must-visit for all foodies. And as part of the Great Southern wine region, it's home to many cellar doors.

Many of the cellar doors in Denmark are dog-friendly. My favourite dog-friendly winery in the region is Singlefile Wines. This winery is famous for both its chardonnay and its Coco d'Vino tasting, which combines specially crafted chocolates with a tasting of three wines. On the rainy winter morning I visited, it was lovely to relax inside with the

Coco d'Vino tasting, in front of an open fire and with Schnitzel by my side.

I also recommend a visit to Denmark Farmhouse Cheese, co-located with Duckett's Mill Wines on the Scotsdale Road Tourist Drive. While dogs aren't allowed inside the shop, they are allowed in the outside area. Don't miss stocking up on the handmade local cheeses, at surprisingly affordable prices.

To buy more local products, head to the Denmark Good Food Factory, 18km west of town. On-site is the Elephant Rocks Cider Company. There's also an extensive range of sauces, toffee and more for sale, plus a burger bar. Dogs are welcome to join you in the outdoor area.

Two more destinations I recommend around Denmark are the Boston Brewing Co., just east of town, and Mrs Jones Cafe. At the former, sample from the range of craft beers on tap. It's also a popular spot for lunch and dinner, with plenty of outdoor tables, perfect for enjoying sunny days and evenings with your pooch. Meanwhile, Mrs Jones Cafe serves arguably the best coffee in town.

Note that the popular Greens Pool and Elephant Rocks just outside of Denmark are not dog-friendly, as they are located in a national park. For a dog-friendly beach, head instead to Prawn Rock Dog Beach. I also recommend heading inland to Harewood Forest, where there's a 2.8km dog-friendly walking track through the forest.

The Desert Mounted Corps Memorial at Albany Heritage Park

How to get there

Albany is a 420km drive south of Perth, if taking the direct highway, or 480km west of Esperance.

When to visit

The best time to visit Albany depends on what you plan to do. While it's generally best to avoid the rainy winter months, particularly if you're heading to the beach, these months are the best time of year for whale-watching.

 ## Dog-friendly parks

Foundation Park, Albany

Dogs are allowed off-leash at this unfenced park close to the town centre and the historic precinct.

Bovell Square, Emu Point

If visiting Emu Point with your dog, head to Bovell Square for some off-leash exercise time.

Top: **Coco d'Vino** tasting at Singlefile Wines Bottom: Schnitzel at the *Brig Amity*

Dog-friendly dining

Kate's Place,
Albany

This cafe on Stirling Terrace is open daily for breakfast and lunch, with dogs welcome to join you at the outdoor tables.

Earl of Spencer Historic Inn,
Albany

Grab a table in the dog-friendly beer garden of this 19th-century inn, open from Tuesday to Saturday for lunch and dinner.

Ocean & Paddock,
Middleton Beach

While this award-winning fish cafe has no outdoor tables, I recommend ordering a takeaway meal like I did, then heading to a nearby dog-friendly park to enjoy it.

Dog-friendly accommodation

Emu Beach Chalets,
Emu Point

Take your pick from a variety of one- to three-bedroom cottages, located just behind the off-leash dog beach at Emu Point. Pets are permitted inside, just not on beds or furniture; an additional fee and bond applies.

ibis Styles Albany,
Albany

Selected ground-floor rooms at this four-star hotel are pet-friendly. Phone directly to make a booking.

Tasman Holiday Parks – Albany,
Centennial Park

Pets are allowed on sites at this caravan park with great facilities, plus there are three pet-friendly one-bedroom chalets, with pets permitted for an extra cleaning charge.

Cosy Corner Campground,
Kronkup

This cheap campground is a 25 minute drive west of Albany, next to an off-leash beach. The final 500m of the access road is unsealed but still accessible for 2WDs, and I enjoyed the secluded sites.

Margaret River

Depending on who you speak to, the Margaret River region is best known either for its world-class wineries or its incredible surfing beaches. Lap up both when you visit the region with your dog, whether just for a weekend break or for a longer stay.

After you check out the best surfing breaks with your pup by your side, let them off-leash to hit the sand and water at the local dog beaches. Then visit the region's delightfully dog-friendly wineries and craft breweries to wind down and really relax.

Off-leash walk along Yallingup beach

🍷 TASTE WORLD-CLASS WINES

Margaret River is renowned as one of the top wine-growing regions in Australia. Countless cellar doors are open to the public throughout the region, often open daily, with many of them also welcoming dogs.

I recommend dropping by the visitor centre in Margaret River for the latest list of pet-friendly wineries, or contacting wineries directly to ask whether they allow dogs. Keep in mind that some cellar doors only allow dogs outside, but conduct their tastings inside, so double-check in advance.

One of the most dog-friendly wineries I visited was Swings & Roundabouts. This winery has a beautiful outdoor area, including its distinctive swing seats, perfect for enjoying a glass of wine or a meal on a sunny day. Your dog will enjoy the cute dog-drinking station outside. Dogs are also allowed in the semi-enclosed dining area.

Two more excellent dog-friendly wineries to visit are the award-winning Stella Bella Wines, which also welcomes dogs inside and is terrific for BYO picnics; and Woody Nook Winery in Wilyabrup, also home to the Nookery Cafe.

If you're interested in taking a winery tour with your pup, contact Grape Escape South West Tours to find out about their private Pawesome Tours.

… OR RELAX WITH A LOCAL BEER

If you'd prefer to relax with an ale instead of a glass of wine, there are a growing number of breweries dotted throughout the Margaret River region. And even better, nearly all of the breweries are dog-friendly, including some that allow dogs inside (generally if they don't have a kitchen).

My favourite dog-friendly brewery during my recent visit was Wild Hop Brewery in Yallingup. Dogs are permitted on the deck at the brewery, including the enclosed section, plus on the grass. The deck is the perfect spot to enjoy some afternoon sunshine while looking out over the dam, with the staff warmly welcoming Schnitzel. Choose your own tasting paddle from the ten taps of batch-brewed beer on offer.

Another dog-friendly brewery option is Beerfarm in Metricup. This brewery is dog-friendly both inside and out, plus there's a designated off-leash area. Accompany a tasting of the beer with some of their own smoked meats.

CHECK OUT THE SURF

The Margaret River region is also famous for its surf, with an event on the World Surfing Tour held in the region each year. While visiting the region, be sure to check out some of its renowned surfing breaks.

One of the most famous surfing spots is the suitably named Surfer Point in Prevelly, immediately west of the town of Margaret River. Head to the lookout and check out the action on the waves down below, with dogs on a leash allowed to join you. The point is also a great spot to watch the sunset, and on busy days food vans often pull up late in the afternoon.

Close to Surfer Point is Prevelly Beach, one of the best off-leash beaches in the region, with the chance for your dog to have a paddle in the waves – just be cautious when the surf is up! Dogs are allowed off-leash on the northern section of the beach, north of the Georgette Way beach access footpath. Dogs are also allowed off-leash (except in the playground) in Riflebutts Reserve behind the dunes.

Surfer's Point in Prevelly

Other off-leash surf beaches in the region include Gracetown Dog Beach (accessed from the dirt access road just before Percy Street), the northern part of Yallingup Beach (north of the Dawson Drive beach access path) and a long section of foreshore at Augusta, alongside Albany Terrace between the river mouth and the caravan park.

If your pup isn't a fan of the surf, head to Dunsborough and the calm waters of Geographe Bay. Dogs are allowed off-leash along much of the Dunsborough Foreshore. Or drive further north to Eagle Bay, one of the most beautiful off-leash spots with its white sand meeting crystal-clear waters. Dogs are allowed off-leash year-round on the beach in between the public access way and 450m north of Jingarmup Brook.

WANDER THROUGH COWARAMUP

While the town of Margaret River is quite chic, with a strip of upmarket restaurants, cafes and boutiques, I found that the town of Cowaramup to the north retains its country charm, and is another delightful spot to visit along with your pup.

Wander along the main street, stopping in at some of its excellent food stores selling products ranging from handmade chocolate to preserves to locally roasted coffee. While pet dogs are generally not allowed inside, there are often water bowls outside.

While in Cowaramup, try spotting some of the local sculptures of cows. They were added partially in reference to the town's name, plus as a nod to the significant milk production of the surrounding district.

There are also some beautiful murals to check out, including the bird wings at the Cowaramup Agencies building.

📍 DRIVE THROUGH THE TALL FORESTS

The Margaret River region contains many magnificent forests of tall jarrahs, karris and marris, many of them contained within Leeuwin–Naturaliste National Park, including one of the most beautiful stands of towering karris, Boranup Forest.

While it's not possible to visit the sights within the national park with your pup, it is possible to take a scenic drive with your pup through the national park and Boranup Forest. Head south from Margaret River along Caves Road towards Augusta. Just don't stop inside the national park boundaries with your dog.

How to get there

Margaret River is a leisurely 3 hour drive south of Perth – too far for a daytrip but perfect for a weekend away. The entire region stretches for over 100km between Dunsborough in the north and Augusta in the south.

When to visit

The most popular time to visit Margaret River is during the long days of summer. If your focus is on wine-tasting and exploring, consider spring or autumn.

The Boranup Forest

 ## Dog-friendly parks

 ## Dog-friendly dining

Brookfield Reserve,
Margaret River

Let your dog enjoy some off-leash time at this fenced dog park on the corner of Bottlebrush Drive and Leschenaultia Avenue.

The Berry Farm,
Rosa Glen

Stars of the menu here are the Berry Farm's own jams, chutneys and other preserved goodies – I highly recommend the scones with delightfully thick strawberry jam. There's plenty of dog-friendly outdoor tables, along with water bowls. Also ask about the homemade dog treats.

Olio Bello,
Cowaramup

A producer of fine organic olive oils, their menu is mainly Italian cuisine, featuring its own olive oil and a range of farm produce. Make sure you book an outdoor table, with dogs permitted both in the outdoor garden seating area and on the deck. Dog water bowls are provided.

Yardbyrd,
Witchcliffe

This highly rated cafe is open daily for breakfast and lunch, with a reasonably priced menu. It has a relaxing outdoor area and plenty of bowls for four-legged guests.

Scones at The Berry Farm

# Dog-friendly accommodation

Southern Stars Park,
Anniebrook

This caravan park near Dunsborough is one of the best pet-friendly (and friendliest!) parks in Western Australia. As well as fenced powered and unpowered sites, there is an enclosed off-leash area for all canine guests, that Schnitzel loved.

Petra Olive Oil Estate,
Yallingup

Book a stay at one of the five dog-friendly luxury chalets on the estate. Generally, only one adult dog is permitted per chalet, with an additional charge per night.

Yallingup Lodge & Spa Retreat,
Yallingup

Enjoy a luxury stay at this spa retreat with your pup. Choose between staying in the pet-friendly glamping tent or the special Pet Suite with its own private garden and king-size spa.

Karridale Cottages,
Karridale

These rustic two-bedroom cottages and studios between Margaret River and Augusta are dog-friendly, with dogs allowed inside. There's a dog exercise area, plus a bushwalk through the property.

Swings & Roundabouts winery

Feed the dolphins at Monkey Mia

The resort town of Monkey Mia is located on the shores of Shark Bay, which is the westernmost point of Western Australia and a World Heritage–listed site, thanks to its unique flora and fauna. Monkey Mia in particular is famous for its resident dolphins, who are handfed on the beach each morning. I dreamed of visiting this spot when I was a little girl fascinated by dolphins!

The daily feedings still take place, with up to three feedings between 7.45am and 12pm. The most popular session is at 7.45am, with many guests of the adjacent resort waiting to be led onto the beach by the local program volunteers. There is no guarantee that all three sessions will happen – only two occurred each day during my visit. An entry fee applies to cover the dolphin experience.

Unsurprisingly, dogs are prohibited from the dolphin experience area on the beach, but it is fine to stand and watch with your dog from either the jetty or the boardwalk behind the beach. Schnitzel had no idea what the fuss was about! Dogs on a leash are also allowed to walk along the rest of the Monkey Mia beach with you.

A key reason for the World Heritage listing of Shark Bay is its large population of dugongs. The best way to spot a dugong is to go on the morning wildlife cruises run by Perfect Nature Cruises, departing each morning from the wharf at Monkey Mia. Best of all, it's possible to bring your well-behaved dog on the cruise.

During the 2.5 hour cruise, as well as dugongs, you'll likely spot dolphins, turtles and the diverse birdlife of the region, including diving cormorants. Fewer dugongs are spotted during winter, when the nearby waters become too cold. But on the day of my cruise in June, I was lucky enough to spot a mother dugong and her calf.

There's no additional charge for pet dogs on the cruise, with advance bookings recommended. It's best to bring along a water bottle and portable bowl for your pup to stay hydrated. Alternatively, if you'd prefer a shorter cruise on Shark Bay, there's also a 1.5 hour sunset cruise – a more laidback, leisurely option.

You can also view the local marine life up-close on a visit to the Ocean Park Aquarium, located on the other side of the peninsula, south of Denham. Be guided around the aquarium to see the turtles, sharks, stingrays and stonefish on a 1 hour tour. Leashed dogs are welcome to join you. There's also an hourly shark feeding.

It's possible to stay at Monkey Mia along with your dog, at the RAC Monkey Mia Dolphin Resort, as long as you have your own campervan, caravan or tent. Pets are allowed on powered and unpowered sites, but not inside the resort rooms and villas. Pets are welcome at the outdoor tables at the on-site Boughshed Restaurant and in the beer garden at the Monkey Bar.

Alternatively, stay on the other side of the peninsula in the nearby town of Denham. There are three caravan parks in Denham, all allowing dogs on sites. You can dine with your dog at both the Shark Bay Hotel and the Waterfront Hotel, with dogs allowed in the beer garden at the former and on the balcony at the latter. There are also off-leash dog beaches at either end of the main promenade.

Top: **Schnitzel on Perfect Nature Cruises**
Bottom: **Monkey Mia's famous dolphins**

FEED THE DOLPHINS AT MONKEY MIA

Ningaloo Coast

While the Great Barrier Reef gets most of the attention, an equally world-class coral reef lies just off the coast of Western Australia: the Ningaloo Reef. With the reef just metres off the shore in places, it's an easy spot for snorkelling, and there are some dog-friendly swimming spots.

Make a beeline for the main town of Exmouth or the smaller outpost of Coral Bay. Or stay at one of the many sheep or cattle stations that dot the southern section of the Ningaloo Coast; many also welcome pet dogs.

Snorkelling at Ningaloo Reef

EXPLORE CORAL BAY

When visiting the Ningaloo Reef, most people stay at the larger town of Exmouth. The small outpost of Coral Bay only has a single dog-friendly caravan park, which is often booked out, but it's well-worth making the 90 minute drive to the town for a daytrip. While the best snorkelling spots close to Exmouth are off limits to dogs because they're inside the national park, the same doesn't apply at Coral Bay.

Unsurprisingly, dogs aren't permitted on Bills Bay, the main beach at Coral Bay, with multiple signs to remind you. However, they are allowed in the grassed park behind the beach and in the adjacent carpark. If you're not travelling solo, take turns looking after your pup, while the others enjoy a snorkel off the beach in the sparkling blue water.

Alternatively, the beaches south of Purdy Point at the southern edge of Bills Bay are dog-friendly. The main dog beach in Coral Bay is Paradise Beach, between Purdy Point and the local boat ramp. It's accessible by an un-signposted 4WD track, or walk around the rocky point at low tide.

Two other options are the small beach next to the boat ramp, or Five Finger Reef. The turn-off for Five Finger Reef is just before the boat ramp, but it's a 4WD only track. I wish I could have visited, as I've heard great reviews about the snorkelling! Always check for any new signs regarding access rules for dogs.

RELAX AT BUNDEGI BEACH

The best snorkelling beaches close to Exmouth are all located in Cape Range National Park, which prohibits dogs. Many of the beaches on the other side of the North

The OTC Satellite Dish in Carnarvon

West Cape before the park boundary are also out of bounds to dogs due to turtles laying eggs on the beaches.

My pick of the few dog-friendly beaches close to town is Bundegi Beach, a 10 minute drive north of Exmouth, near the tip of the cape. Located just inside Exmouth Gulf, the beach is still beautifully sandy and offers crystal-clear waters for swimming. Best of all, dogs are allowed off-leash on the beach.

Dogs are also allowed off-leash on the section of beach immediately north of Town Beach in Exmouth, adjacent to the golf club, plus quiet Macleod Beach, south of Exmouth Harbour.

The Cactus Garden on the Fruit Loop Drive

🍺 ENJOY A LOCAL CRAFT BEER

Exmouth is home to two craft breweries. Schnitzel and I visited Whalebone Brewing Company, in the industrial area on the southern side of town. It's very dog-friendly, with a large outdoor yard of tables, although dogs are now only permitted before 5pm and need to be kept on a leash. It's also very kid-friendly, with play equipment and a sandpit.

At the time of our visit, there were seven locally brewed beers on tap, plus three guest brews. Tasting paddles come in three different sizes, ranging from five to nine generously sized tasting glasses. If you're feeling peckish, choose from the fantastic range of pizzas; some are also served in kid sizes.

The other brewery in town is Froth Craft Brewery. Located next to the main shopping mall, this brewery includes a restaurant offering a more extensive menu. There's still plenty of outdoor tables, where well-behaved dogs are welcome. Both Froth and Whalebone also have live music on selected nights.

📍 WATCH THE SUNSET AT VLAMINGH HEAD LIGHTHOUSE

For excellent views along the coast, visit Vlamingh Head Lighthouse, a 15 minute drive north-west of Exmouth. This lighthouse is no longer in operation, but can still be reached by a steep sealed road. There's no restriction on dogs, although they should always be kept on a leash.

The carpark next to the lighthouse is a popular spot for watching the sunset. Just be warned that after rainy periods there can be a lot of mosquitoes that arrive before sunset – keep an eye out and retreat inside your car if they appear! The lookout is also the best on-shore location for spotting the whales that visit Ningaloo Reef each winter.

📍 STAY AT A LOCAL STATION

Despite its coastal location, the Ningaloo region is part of outback Australia, surrounded by sheep and cattle stations. Many of these stations offer the chance to stay for a night or longer, with most welcoming dogs at their campsites.

The closest option to Exmouth is Bullara Station, a working cattle station about a 1 hour drive back down the highway towards Perth, and easily accessible by 2WD. The station is open to visitors between April and October each year. Dogs are permitted on sites, but only in the campground area and on the walking tracks.

Further to the south, between Exmouth and Coral Bay, is Ningaloo Station. While to the south of Coral Bay other station stays include Warroora Station, Gnaraloo Station and Quobba Station. Double-check the details in advance, as many campsites are only accessible by 4WD, especially beachfront sites, and sometimes self-contained vehicles are required.

SEE THE QUOBBA BLOWHOLES

A few hours' drive south of Coral Bay, close to the town of Carnarvon, is the turn-off to Quobba Blowholes. The 50km road to the blowholes is a good sealed road, so it's an easy spot to visit on the coast even if you don't have a 4WD.

There are multiple blowholes situated close together along a short strip of coastline. They're best viewed on a rising tide, from the raised boardwalk above the rocky ground. The waves here can be dangerous, so keep both yourself and your dog on the boardwalk, well away from the water's edge.

After visiting the blowholes, I recommend heading just a kilometre south to the Aquarium, a popular snorkelling site with plenty of colourful fish to spot. While definitely not a dog-friendly activity itself, there's no prohibition on dogs in the area, so take turns with travelling companions to go snorkelling between the beach and the small island.

FOLLOW THE FRUIT LOOP DRIVE IN CARNARVON

The regional centre of Carnarvon on the southern edge of the Ningaloo Coast is an important produce growing region in Western Australia. Along both sides of the Gascoyne River on the eastern edge of town are a multitude of fruit and vegetable plantations, supplying much of the state's fresh produce.

But don't wait for it to arrive in supermarkets. Instead go for a drive on the Fruit Loop Drive Trail. Along the way stop at the small farm shops and roadside honesty stalls to sample and purchase fresh produce. Your dog is welcome to join you, although it's best to leave them in the car when going onto farms.

One can't-miss stop is Bumbak's, to pick up some of their irresistible mango jam – my favourite! Another interesting landmark along the Fruit Loop is the Cactus Garden, located midway along South River Road. It's a great stop for photos.

Another popular photo spot in Carnarvon is the OTC Satellite Dish, visible from the highway on the edge of town. While no longer in operation, the gigantic dish is still an icon of the town. For the best photo op, turn off towards the Space and Technology Museum and drive right under the dish.

How to get there

The Ningaloo region is about halfway along the Western Australia coastline. Exmouth is a 1250km drive north of Perth, and Coral Bay is about 150km south of Exmouth.

When to visit

Peak holiday time on the Ningaloo Coast is during winter, particularly when whale sharks visit between March and August, while the whale-watching season is from June to November. Temperatures are warm but mild; but temperatures during summer can be extreme, with a chance of cyclones.

Dog-friendly dining

Dog-friendly accommodation

The Shack,
Exmouth

Formerly at Bundegi Beach, this cafe is now located in the town centre, open for breakfast and dinner. I highly recommend the local prawns cooked in garlic – half a kilo goes a long way shared between two!

Mutts Cafe,
Exmouth

This dog-friendly cafe in Exmouth is open in the mornings, plus selected evenings. Head here for coffee, light meals and vegan ice-cream. It also has a handy listing of local dog-sitters – a necessity if you want to swim with the whale sharks or whales.

Sunsets Cafe,
Babbage Island

Located adjacent to the One Mile Jetty in Carnarvon, this cafe is open for brunch and lunch from Wednesday to Sunday, with a large outdoor dining area where dogs are welcome.

Ningaloo Caravan & Holiday Resort,
Exmouth

One of the two caravan parks in Exmouth, the park is dog-friendly year-round, but dogs are only allowed on selected sites. Advance bookings are essential for the winter school holidays.

Ningaloo Coral Bay – Bay Camp,
Coral Bay

The only dog-friendly option in Coral Bay. Dogs are allowed on selected powered and unpowered sites. Up to two dogs are permitted per site, with an additional nightly fee and bond. Note that only weekly bookings are accepted during most school holidays.

Discovery Parks,
Carnarvon

The most dog-friendly caravan park in Carnarvon, this park has an off-leash dog exercise area at the rear of the park. Dogs are allowed in selected cabins, as well as on sites.

Bill's Bay at Coral Bay

Broome/Rubibi

Despite its isolation, Broome is one of the most popular holiday destinations in Western Australia, thanks to the long white sandy stretch of Cable Beach and plenty more stunning natural scenery.

But what about if you're visiting Broome with a pet? Despite previously not being a pet-friendly destination, there's no shortage of things to do these days with your dog, whether you simply want a relaxing break or to enjoy an adventure with your pup.

Sunset at Cable Beach

Camel rides along Cable Beach

SWIM AT CABLE BEACH

While the bays closest to the centre of Broome are mangrove mudflats, across town is the delightful 22km stretch of white sand known as Cable Beach. Deservedly famous, it's a must-visit destination in Broome, whether to swim, laze on the sand or go 4WDing along it.

Luckily, dogs are allowed along most of Cable Beach, except the section between the surf club and boat ramp. If you want to let them off leash or enjoy a dip in the water with them, head south of the surf club and look out for the sign indicating the start of the dog exercise area. North of the boat ramp, where 4WDs are permitted, dogs need to be kept on-leash for 1km before they can be let off-leash. Note that there are not many rules along this stretch of Cable Beach – it's also a designated nudist beach.

It can get hot on the sand, even during the winter months, so consider setting up an umbrella to provide shade for your pup, and don't forget a water bowl. Cable Beach can also be closed if crocodiles are spotted in the vicinity.

WATCH THE SUNSET AT CABLE BEACH

Cable Beach isn't just the place to go for a swim in Broome, it's also the place to soak up tropical views, as the sun slowly sinks into the Indian Ocean stretching before you.

If you've got a 4WD, this is the most popular time to head to the sand, accessed from the northern end of the Cable Beach carpark. Once you find a spot, it's time to set up your chairs and watch the sunset with a beer in hand, your dog at your feet.

No 4WD? Perhaps set up a picnic blanket on the grassed reserve next to the carpark, or just stay on your beach towel on the sand and enjoy the spectacle on a warm, tropical night.

Sunset is also the most popular time of day for the camel rides on Cable Beach. These rides have taken place on Cable Beach for decades. Even if you don't take part, they're still a sight to behold, as the camels walk along the beach north of the rocks. Just be careful to keep your dog well away, particularly if your dog becomes alarmed by the camels.

LOOK FOR DINOSAUR FOOTPRINTS

Broome contains some of the best dinosaur footprints in Australia. One of the most popular spots to view them is Gantheaume Point, at the southern end of Cable Beach, where leashed dogs are permitted.

Gantheaume Point can be reached by road, which is surprisingly unsealed for the last 600m. Take it easy if you're in a 2WD, as it can be bumpy. Or you can park at the Turf Club instead, then follow the walking track over to the rocks.

The dinosaur footprints are only visible at low tide, or very low tide, and no directions are provided. I think I spotted some of them, but I wasn't sure. It's easier to check out the plaster cast of three prints located at the end of the walking path.

In any case, Gantheaume Point is a beautiful spot, with its red rocks starkly contrasting against the turquoise blue water below, and well worth a visit.

CHILL AT MATSO'S BREWERY

Matso's Brewery is a Broome institution, established over 20 years ago in Matso's Store. The brewery is most famous for its Mango Beer (my favourite!) and alcoholic Ginger Beer, although these aren't the only beers typically on tap.

Beer also isn't the only thing on the menu, with the on-site restaurant offering casual yet chic dining for lunch and dinner. While dogs are not allowed on the verandah immediately surrounding the restaurant, they are welcome (on-leash) in the beer garden.

The beer garden is also home to a food truck, at least during the busy dry season. If lounging in the beer garden, you can choose between ordering from the main restaurant menu or just grab simple takeaway style dishes from the food truck, accompanied by a tasting paddle.

VIEW THE STAIRCASE TO THE MOON

Another iconic Broome experience is watching the optical illusion of the Staircase to the Moon. This natural phenomenon occurs at Roebuck Bay, around each full moon period between March and October, as long as the full moon rising coincides with a low tide. Check online for the expected dates for the coming year.

One of the best dog-friendly spots from which to watch the Staircase is Town Beach. Just be prepared for crowds and keep your dog leashed!

While Town Beach doesn't have the white sand of Cable Beach, it's still a great spot to visit with your dog during the day. Leashed dogs are allowed at Town Beach Reserve, and the large mature trees provide some welcome shade during the hot days. The reserve is also

home to a huge playground and splash park for kids.

SHOP AT THE LOCAL MARKETS

It's not a true visit to Broome without visiting at least one of the markets held regularly in town. The largest markets are the Courthouse Markets. These markets are held year-round on Saturday morning, from 8am to 12pm. During the busier months from April to October they are also held on Sunday and don't end until 1pm.

The bustling markets have a huge number of art, jewellery, local products and hot-food stalls. On the morning of my visit, the drink stalls had very long queues! After trawling through the stalls, relax on the grass with a drink or lunch, while listening to live music. Well-behaved dogs on a leash are welcome at the markets.

From June to September, the Town Beach Markets are also held every Thursday evening. These smaller markets focus more on food, with a wide variety of food trucks set up, although there are some stalls with jewellery, clothing and homewares too. A special edition of these markets is also held during the Staircase to the Moon event.

WANDER THROUGH CHINATOWN

The historic heart of Broome is known as Chinatown; here you'll find many of the pearl outlets and shopping boutiques, as well as cafes, tour-booking shops and more.

Wander through the streets of Chinatown with your pup, keeping an eye out for the many signs explaining the history of Broome. Along the way glance inside at Sun Pictures, the world's oldest operating picture gardens (although sadly dogs are not allowed during screenings).

It's also worthwhile detouring to Streeter's Jetty, a jetty constructed in the late 19th century through the mangroves, to allow access for the merchants and pearl dealers. Further along the waterfront, climb up to Roebuck Bay Lookout for beautiful views over the mangroves and bay.

GO CAMPING NORTH OF BROOME

Camping in Broome itself isn't the only way to experience this region. If you want the Broome experience but without the crowds, head to one of the many camping spots located along the coast north of town.

Two of the most popular dog-friendly campgrounds are James Price

Point (Walmadan) and Quandong Point (Kardilakan). Both of these free campgrounds are only accessible by 4WD, and you need to be self-contained – no facilities are provided. There is a three-night limit enforced by the local council.

Further north again is the Dampier Peninsula, home to the Bardi, Nyunyul and Jabirr Jabirr peoples. Previously only accessible to 4WDs, the 200km road to the tip is now almost entirely sealed, although some access roads to campgrounds and communities are still only suitable for 4WD vehicles.

While some locations on the peninsula prohibit dogs, there are at least a few pet-friendly campgrounds. Banana Well Getaway permits pets, while Gambanan Wilderness Retreat allows small to medium dogs in its campground.

How to get there

Broome is in far northern Western Australia and best visited on a Big Lap. It's over a 2000km drive north of Perth, nearly 2500km if you take the scenic coastal route. And it's still nearly another 1900km from Darwin along the sealed highway.

When to visit

The best time to visit Broome is during winter, when temperatures are milder but still balmy, and rain is rare. Campgrounds are usually at capacity, so book in advance or prepare to use the overflow parks. During summer, temperatures are very high, with cyclones and floods a real possibility, and roads frequently cut off.

Right: **Schnitzel at Gantheaume Point**
Opposite: **Staircase to the Moon at Roebuck Bay**

Top: **The red rocks of Gantheaume Point** Bottom: **The white sands of Cable Beach**

Dog-friendly dining

Dog-friendly accommodation

Good Cartel,
Djugun

Reputedly serving the best coffee in Broome, this cafe near the main Chinatown strip also offers breakfast, sandwiches and burgers. Open seven days a week from early to late-ish; dogs are welcome in the outdoor area.

Cable Beach General Store & Cafe,
Cable Beach

Grab a bite at this dog-friendly cafe near Cable Beach. Open daily until early evening, there's a wide variety of food options for dine-in or takeaway.

Tarangau Caravan Park,
Cable Beach

A quieter park close to Cable Beach where pets are allowed on selected sites and there are pet wash facilities. Just be mindful that there is no swimming pool.

Broome Pistol Club Overflow Site,
Minyirr

If all the caravan parks in Broome are fully booked, like during my visit with Schnitzel, arrive first thing in the morning at this pet-friendly overflow campground to nab a site. Both powered and unpowered sites are on offer.

Broome's Gateway Pet-Friendly Caravan Park,
Broome

Originally the only caravan park that allowed pets near Broome, this park 30km out of town is still the most pet-friendly option, with a fenced off-leash exercise area. Note there are only unpowered sites.

Chill out at Lake Argyle

In northern Western Australia lies Australia's second largest freshwater man-made reservoir, the massive Lake Argyle. With a huge surface area of 703 square kilometres, it was completed in 1971 as part of the Ord River Irrigation Area.

For almost as long as the lake has existed, there has been a campground near the dam wall, high on the cliffs above the lake. When comparing notes recently with my parents, I discovered that they stayed there back in 1979! These days known as Discovery Resorts – Lake Argyle, it's still an idyllic spot to camp with your dog.

The resort is just a short 50 minute drive from the regional centre of Kununurra, with the turn-off to the lake close to the Northern Territory border. While some sites can be booked in advance, these are quickly snapped up during the peak winter season. If you don't have a booking, I recommend arriving early in the morning to queue for one of the remaining sites like I did. An overflow area exists if you miss out on a regular site.

Pets are permitted on the grassy caravan sites and campsites, but not in cabins. While I paid a deposit for my dog at the time of my stay, this is no longer required. It's just requested that you keep your dogs on a leash, in particular around the beer garden and restaurant area.

The resort is famous for its infinity pool overlooking Lake Argyle. While naturally dogs are not allowed in the pool, it's a common practice to tie dogs to the outside of the pool fence, where you can keep an eye on them while enjoying a swim in the refreshing waters.

Alternatively, follow the steep route down the hillside from the resort to the swimming pontoon below, where I spotted some dogs swimming in the lake water, perfect for water-loving pups. There's also a number of walking trails in the area, which allow dogs on-leash.

For a different vantage point, head out onto the lake for a cruise, with sunset cruises especially popular. I recommend contacting Lake Argyle Cruises. It has two pet enclosures next to the office where guests can leave their pets while on a cruise. Check to confirm one is available for your pet when making a booking.

Or you can head out onto the lake with your pup by your side. Lake Argyle Cruises offers a range of watercraft for hire, from barbebcue pontoon boats to kayaks to stand-up paddleboards. All of the equipment is pet-friendly, with advance bookings recommended during the peak season.

While in the area, I also recommend driving across the dam wall and taking in the views from Vista Lookout. Just across the dam wall next to the Ord River outlet is the Lake Argyle Picnic Area, with a grassy lawn for you and your pup to picnic upon.

Come sunset hour, there's often live music on the lawns or at the beer garden at the Lake Argyle Resort, with dogs permitted at selected tables along the edge of the beer garden. Sit back and relax with your dog at your side.

The shore of massive Lake Argyle

05

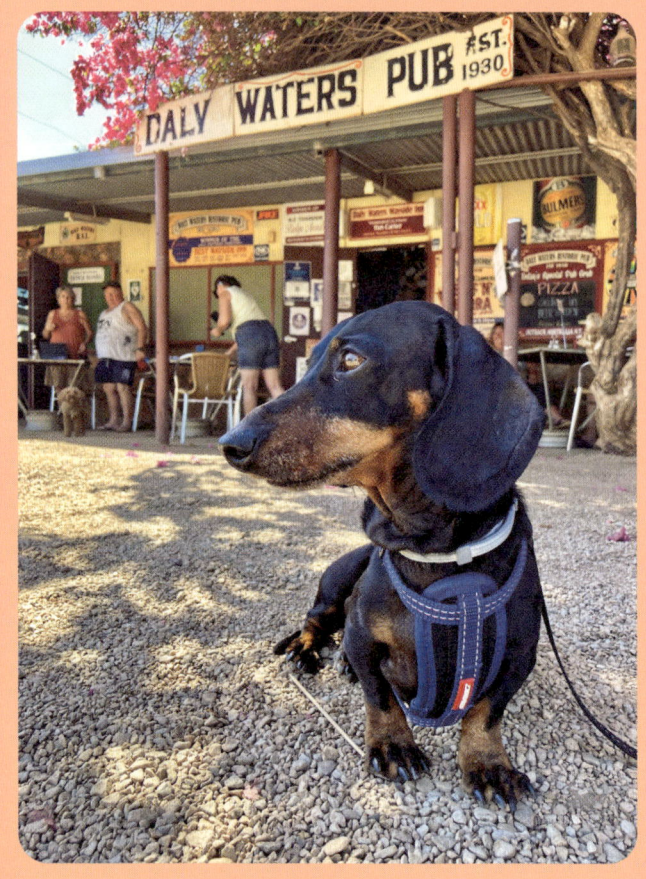

Northern Territory

Darwin/Garramilla	208
Stop off at Daly Waters	214
Central Australia	216

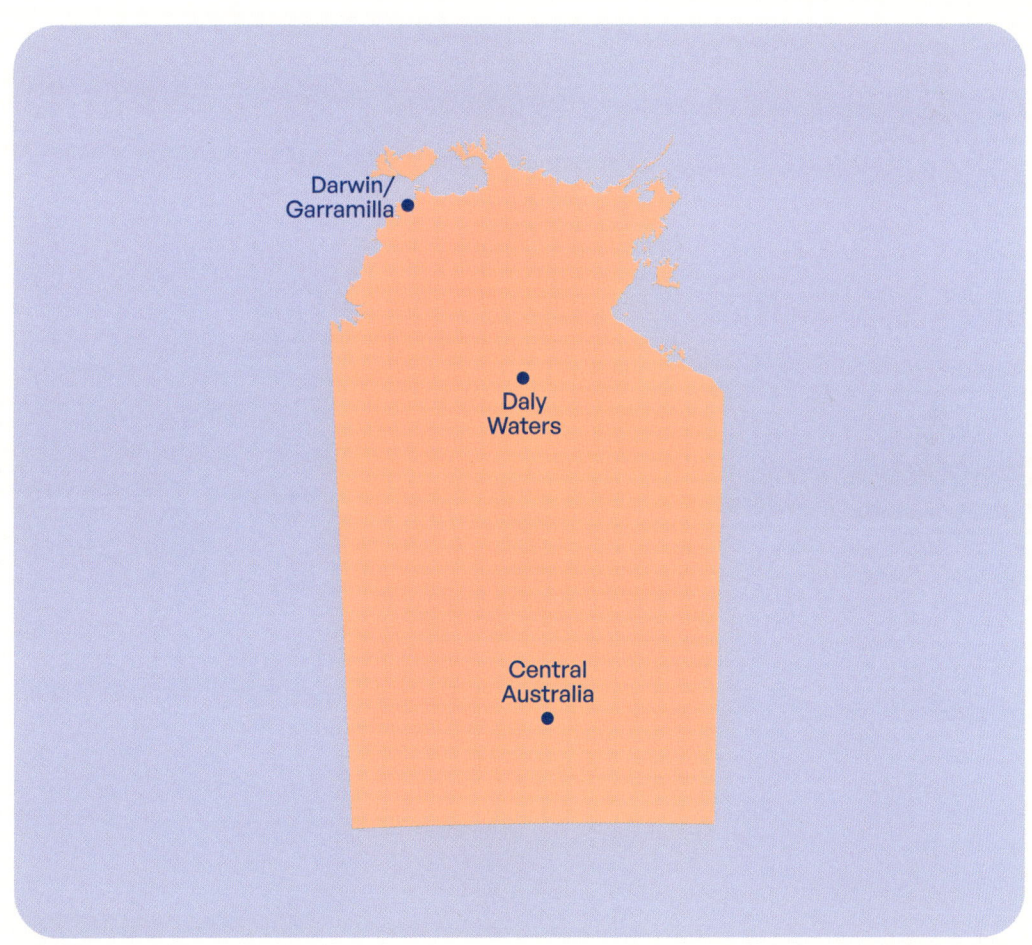

Darwin/ Garramilla

Located in Australia's Top End, the tropical city of Darwin is most often used as a jumping off point to the nearby national parks of Kakadu and Litchfield. However, with these national parks off limits to dogs, when visiting Darwin with your dog, it's best to stay within the city and nearby Palmerston. Take a stroll through the botanic gardens, find out more about the city's role in World War II, visit an impressive dog park and explore dog-friendly natural reserves.

Schnitzel on Mindil Beach

The George Brown Darwin Botanic Gardens

👣 STROLL THROUGH THE GEORGE BROWN DARWIN BOTANIC GARDENS

Darwin is home to many lush green gardens and parks, perfect for escaping the Top End heat. One of my favourite spots to visit in Darwin is the George Brown Darwin Botanic Gardens.

Located not far from the city centre and Mindil Beach, dogs are allowed off leash in the gardens (the default rule for most parks throughout Darwin). Just note that your dog still needs to be under your control – as emphasised by a sign I saw during my visit noting a recent dog-bite incident.

One of the most cooling sections of the garden to stroll through is the Rainforest Loop and adjacent Shade Forest. Or head to the Cycad Garden and Dinosaur Trail. It's worthwhile stopping off afterwards at the dog-friendly Eva's Cafe (*see* p. 212) also in the gardens.

📍 HEAD TO MARLOW LAGOON DOG PARK

One of the best dog parks Schnitzel and I have visited anywhere in Australia is in Darwin: the Marlow Lagoon Dog Park. Located in the city of Palmerston, to the south of Darwin proper, this dog park should not be missed when visiting the Top End with your pup.

As well as a huge, fully fenced area along one side of the lagoon, there are also three smaller fenced areas for smaller and quiet dogs, with double-gated entrances. There's a selection of agility equipment scattered throughout all areas, plenty of shade and water, and even a barbecue and picnic table in the main area.

To visit the dog park, part of the larger Marlow Lagoon Recreation Area, skip parking in the main carpark and instead head towards the BMX track. The entrance to the dog park and plenty of car parking is next to the BMX track.

Just be aware that this is the Top End, so there is the possibility of a crocodile in the lagoon. Check the latest signs or ask other dog owners at the park, or just keep your dog away from the water's edge.

VISIT CASUARINA COASTAL RESERVE

Another great spot to enjoy some off-leash time with your dog in Darwin is Casuarina Coastal Reserve. This large coastal reserve stretches for over 5km between Nightcliff and Lee Point. As well as a long sandy beach, it also features a grassy reserve, multiple picnic areas and a variety of walking tracks.

Restrictions on dogs vary throughout the reserve, from areas where dogs are allowed off-leash to areas where dogs are prohibited. The easiest way to find out the relevant restrictions is by checking the signs at the park.

If you'd like to play on the beach with your dog, dogs are allowed off-leash between Rapid Creek and Lee Point Rocks, except between the Cliffs and Dripstone Point and around Sandy Creek where they need to be leashed. It's best to keep your dog away from the creeks and the water, where crocodiles are sometimes sighted.

Dogs are also allowed off-leash in the Rapid Creek Open Space, but must be leashed on walking trails. Some of the picnic areas allow dogs, or consider dropping by the dog-friendly De La Plage Cafe at the Surf Club.

Walking in the Botanic Gardens

EXPLORE DARWIN'S WORLD WAR II HISTORY

Darwin is a city with a tumultuous recent history, particularly during World War II when the city was bombed multiple times. While the main museums (and the entire East Point Reserve) are off limits for dogs, there are still multiple dog-friendly places where you can explore Darwin's World War II history.

Near the war memorial in Bicentennial Park, adjacent to the city centre, there are multiple information panels explaining the city's World War II history, including extensive photographs from the era. I found them worthwhile to check out and reflect on how the city has changed.

Many of the World War II remnants around the city and to its south are also dog-friendly. For instance, you can visit the Quarantine Anti-Aircraft Battery at East Arm. The Strauss Airstrip near Berry Springs is also a popular spot to stop at, with informative panels along the former World War II airstrip.

CHECK OUT THE LANEWAY STREET ART

One of the biggest surprises when I last visited Darwin were the many large murals painted on the sides of the city's buildings. Not particularly known as a street-art destination, the murals are the result of the Darwin Street Art Festival, which has run every year since 2017.

Each year new murals are added, with a map on the festival's website showing the locations of each of the murals. You can also download an app that will take you on a self-guided tour. Many of the artworks are painted by local artists, including Larrakia artists, with wildlife a prominent theme.

Most of the murals are located around Austin Lane, as well as West Lane and Shadforth Lane. As they are relatively quiet and shady, it was fun to walk along the laneways with Schnitzel, discovering the street art. Just note that dogs are not permitted along The Mall (which doesn't actually contain any street art).

WATCH THE SUNSET ON MINDIL BEACH

One of the best beaches closest to the Darwin city centre is the wide expanse of Mindil Beach. Dogs are allowed off-leash along the beach, although look for signs about recent crocodile sightings. It's also best to avoid swimming during stinger season which is between October and May.

Mindil Beach is, however, a great spot to watch a tropical sunset in Darwin with your dog by your side. Although perhaps skip visiting the beach on Thursday and Sunday evenings during the dry season, when it becomes crowded with visitors to the popular Mindil Beach Sunset Markets. The markets take place in the adjacent reserve, with dogs not permitted to join you, although they continue to be allowed on the beach.

When to visit

Darwin has a distinct wet and dry season. It's best to visit during the dry season, between May and August, when temperatures are slightly cooler, but still hot. The wet season sees tropical downpours, high humidity and a chance of cyclones.

Dog-friendly parks

Dog-friendly dining

Muirhead Dog Park,
Muirhead

Located along Mahoney Street, on the north-eastern edge of Darwin, this park has two separately fenced areas, both double-gated. There's plenty of seating, a water fountain for dogs and agility equipment in the smaller area.

Lakeside Drive Park,
Alawa

This fully fenced dog park next to the Lakeside Drive Community Garden has two separate areas, along with water troughs and poo-bag dispensers.

Eva's Cafe,
The Gardens

Dogs are welcome to join you on the large front and back verandahs of this cafe in the George Brown Darwin Botanic Gardens, open daily until mid-afternoon. Order from the breakfast and lunch menus, with water bowls provided for dogs. The mango smoothies are delicious!

Frying Nemo Fish and Chips,
Stuart Park

Find a seat for you and your dog at the waterfront tables of this casual seafood cafe – one of my favourite dining spots in Darwin. The focus is on locally wild-caught fish, plus there's a great range of burgers, including crocodile burgers. Beer and wine are also available.

Darwin Ski Club,
Fannie Bay

Dogs are allowed in the beer garden of the water ski club, another popular spot to watch the sunset.

Dog-friendly accommodation

Mercure Darwin Airport Resort,
Darwin City

This resort-style hotel offers a Bow Wow Package, with no size restrictions. It includes accommodation in a pet-friendly bungalow, buffet breakfast for two, and a free dog toy.

Quest Palmerston,
Palmerston City

Pets are permitted to stay in the self-contained apartments on the first and second floors. Only small and medium dogs are permitted, for an extra fee per night.

Coolalinga Tourist Park,
Coolalinga

Although it's a 25 minute drive south of Darwin, this pet-friendly park has a fenced dog run and an all-important swimming pool. With the affordable rates, it is a convenient option for extended stays.

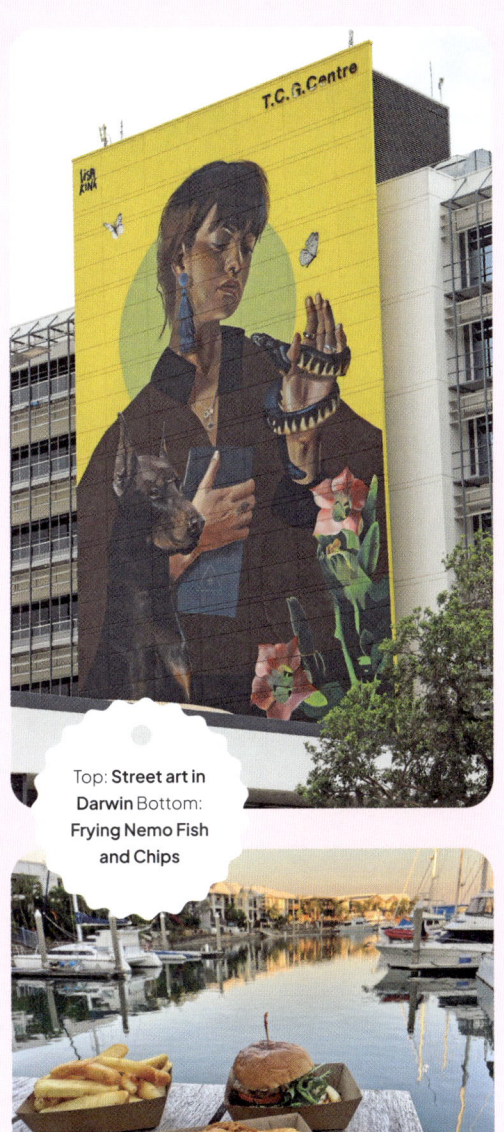

Top: **Street art in Darwin** Bottom: **Frying Nemo Fish and Chips**

Stop off at Daly Waters

The Australian outback is home to some very quirky and unforgettable pubs – a welcome spot to break up the long drives. One of the most iconic and colourful outback pubs in Australia is the Daly Waters Pub. Located about 600km south of Darwin, you can't miss stopping off at Daly Waters when travelling with your dog in the Northern Territory.

While the pub is housed in a rather unassuming building, except for the oddly placed traffic lights outside (as the sign declares, they're Australia's most remote traffic lights!), it's a different story inside. The pub's bar is decked out with copious bras and other assorted memorabilia left behind by patrons over the years – no-one is quite sure when the tradition started!

Dogs are not permitted in the bar (or the main beer garden outside), but they are welcome at the tables along the front verandah. Pull up a seat at a table and put in an order for lunch or dinner. I was impressed by the quality and prices of the pub's burgers and beers. They even had their own house brew on tap, the Outback Brew, during my visit! In the evenings, the most popular options are the plates of beef or barramundi (or both), together with a buffet salad bar.

The quirky memorabilia continues outside the pub. There's even a junkyard across the street with an old helicopter on its rooftop. Head further afield to the edge of the 'town' and its historic aviation complex. The complex is home to the oldest airport hangar in the Northern Territory and was also used as a base during World War II. Schnitzel and I wandered around and through its open doors.

Also on the edge of town is the even older Stuart Tree. This historic tree is where the European explorer John McDouall Stuart carved an 'S' while exploring a route north from Adelaide to the northern coastline of Australia. These days the long highway from Port Augusta to Darwin is named after him.

The pub is also a popular spot to spend the night, with not one but two refreshing swimming pools to cool down in. If you're planning to camp in the adjacent caravan park during the peak season, it's advisable to arrive by lunchtime to have a chance of grabbing a site, especially for powered sites. Dogs are also welcome in three of the pub's motel rooms and one of the cabins on-site, for a small additional fee.

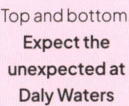

Top and bottom: Expect the unexpected at Daly Waters

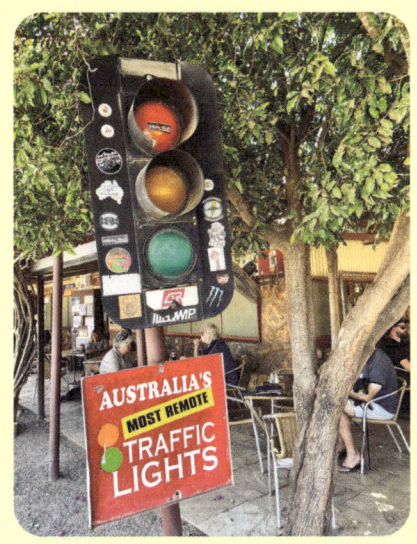

STOP OFF AT DALY WATERS

Central Australia

Central Australia is a vast desert landscape, dubbed the Red Centre after its red desert sands. However, from the vast sands and endless plains of scrub rise some wondrous sights, like Uluru, the largest monolith in Australia; the MacDonnell Ranges either side of Alice Springs; and the smaller Karlu Karlu/Devils Marbles.

While many of these attractions are off limits to dogs, it's still possible to visit the region with your dog and be impressed by its sights, including some that you can enjoy with your dog from a distance.

Boulders at Karlu Karlu/Devils Marbles

View of Uluru from a distance

📍 GAZE UPON ULURU

One of the highlights of Central Australia is visiting Uluru – the monolith often considered the spiritual heart of Australia – and the nearby Kata Tjuta rock formations. Not surprisingly, both sit within a national park where dogs are prohibited, but it's still possible to get a good view of Uluru with your dog.

Pets are permitted in the nearby resort township of Yulara, including on sites in the Ayers Rock Campground, where you can stay in a caravan or tent with your pup. Inquire with the campground staff about dog-sitting, or swap dog-sitting shifts with other campers, so that you can visit Uluru up close, but also make time to enjoy a sunset with your dog at your side.

There are a couple of lookouts around Yulara outside the national park that you can visit with your dog. On the hill at the centre of Yulara is Imalung Lookout, or alternatively head slightly further out to Ewing Lookout. While the views aren't as spectacular as from inside the national park, they're still magnificent spots to enjoy the special treat of watching the sun rise or set over Uluru, its colour changing minute by minute, with your dog by your side.

📍 SEE KARLU KARLU/DEVILS MARBLES

Uluru isn't the only impressive rock formation to check out in the Northern Territory. About 400km north of Alice Springs, in the centre of the Territory, is Karlu Karlu/Devils Marbles. Located just off the Stuart Highway, which runs the length of the Territory, it's a must-stop destination on a roadtrip through Central Australia.

The distinctive granitic boulders are located in Karlu Karlu/Devils Marbles Conservation Reserve (a Park Pass is required), which has limited access for dogs. Dogs are permitted within the carpark and

CENTRAL AUSTRALIA 217

the day-use areas, but not on the walking trails or at the campsite. Luckily, some boulders are located right next to the carpark and day-use area – I could see more than I expected, plus take some great photos with Schnitzel.

Ideally, if you're travelling with someone else, take turns to follow one or two of the short walks – both are only about 10 to 20 minutes long. There's a handy sheltered picnic table and an information shelter (with limited wifi) for the person staying behind in the carpark with your dog.

As the adjacent campsite doesn't permit dogs, if you want to stay the night nearby, head 10km south to the Devils Marbles Hotel in Wauchope. Dogs are allowed in the caravan park and the beer garden, although not in motel rooms.

CLIMB UP ANZAC HILL IN ALICE SPRINGS

The largest town in Central Australia is Alice Springs, and you'll likely pass through the hub at least once on your visit to Central Australia. While the majority of attractions around Alice Springs aren't dog-friendly – including the Telegraph Station Historical Reserve and the Desert Park on the edge of town, as well as the many sights within Tjoritja / West MacDonnell National Park to the west – you and your pup can take in the view of Alice Springs from ANZAC Hill.

This hill is located at the northern edge of the town and is home to a 1934 Anzac Day Memorial, plus a lookout. Drive or walk up the hill to Trevor Reid Park, which has excellent views looking south over the town, towards The Gap in between the MacDonnell Ranges. It's also a great spot to watch the sunset. Dogs are allowed on a leash.

VISIT THE NATIONAL ROAD TRANSPORT MUSEUM

Another dog-friendly spot around Alice Springs is the National Road Transport Museum, located just south of the town. The massive trucks on display at the museum are particularly impressive, which is also home to the Old Ghan Train Museum.

Allow plenty of time to visit the museum, with last entry at 1.30pm, and closing time at 3pm daily. Pets are also welcome to join you in camping for the night next to the museum in the paid campground.

CAMP AT GLEN HELEN

While dogs are not permitted to visit Tjoritja/West MacDonnell National Park, it's fine for them to be in your vehicle while you drive through the park to the dog-friendly caravan park and lodge at Glen Helen. Discovery Parks – Glen Helen is surrounded by the national park but pet dogs are allowed on camping sites in the caravan park. Note that dogs aren't allowed to accompany you on the walk to the nearby Glen Helen Gorge, which is located just inside the national park.

Glen Helen is about a 90 minute drive west of Alice Springs, along the fully sealed Larapinta and Namatjira drives. It's a beautiful scenic drive, and if you're in a 4WD, you can continue along the Mereenie Loop to Watarrka National Park and Kings Canyon – just buy a permit in advance. At Watarrka National Park, dogs are allowed in the campground at Kings Canyon Resort, plus on a leash at the Kings Canyon and Kathleen Springs carparks.

📍 GO 4WDING AT OWEN SPRINGS RESERVE

A former cattle station, Owen Springs Reserve is located south-west of Alice Springs. With its stretches of red sand and rocky gorges, it's popular for 4WDing and bush camping. Pets are prohibited in the northern part of the reserve, but they are allowed south of Waterhouse Range, as long as they remain on a leash.

To access this part of the reserve, enter the reserve from its southern entrance, located 66km south of Alice Springs on the Stuart Highway. A Park Pass is required. This section of the reserve includes the bush campground at Redbank Waterhole, which fills with water after rain, plus 22km of 4WD track north to the Range, as far as you can drive with a dog. A high-clearance 4WD is essential.

Sunset at Anzac Hill, Alice Springs

How to get there

Alice Springs, the largest town in Central Australia, is located roughly halfway between Darwin and Adelaide. It's about a 1500km drive south of Darwin or 1530km north of Adelaide. And Uluṟu is a further 5 hours drive south-west of Alice Springs.

When to visit

Head to Central Australia during winter. Daytime temperatures are generally warm but mild, although it can drop to freezing overnight. But you'll avoid the summers that are scorching hot.

 ## Dog-friendly parks

 ## Dog-friendly dining

Rotaract Park,
Braitling

This fenced dog park next to Angguna Avenue in Alice Springs has separate areas for small and large dogs, as well as a water fountain and shady seating.

Mary Anne Dam,
Warumungu

Just north of Tennant Creek, I recommend detouring to this great reserve and picnic area next to the man-made dam. Make sure you keep your dog on a leash and well away from the resident peacocks.

Page 27 Cafe,
Alice Springs

Located just off Todd Mall, many visitors comment on the cafe's similarity to Melbourne-style cafes. Open daily for breakfast and lunch, dogs are welcome in the outdoor seating area.

Watertank Cafe,
Ciccone

This cafe on the outskirts of Alice Springs has a great atmosphere. It is open for breakfast and lunch from Thursday to Monday. Dogs are welcome at the outdoor tables on the terrace.

Schnitzel at Karlu Karlu/Devils Marbles

Dog-friendly accommodation

Alice on Todd Apartments,
The Gap

Selected studio and one-bedroom apartments are pet-friendly. Each pet-friendly apartment is located downstairs with a fully fenced private backyard. Bowls and a welcome pack are provided.

Heritage Caravan Park,
Ross

This caravan park on the southern side of Alice Springs is popular with dog owners thanks to its fenced off-leash dog exercise area and K9000 dog wash. All sites and cabins allow pets.

Ayers Rock Campground,
Yulara

The only campground close to Uluṟu. Dogs are permitted on powered and unpowered sites. Ask the staff whether dog-sitting is currently available.

A stroll through Discovery Parks – Glen Helen caravan park

06

Queensland

Brisbane/Meanjin	224	Capricorn Coast	258
Gold Coast	232	Take a daytrip to Great Keppel Island/Wop-pa	264
Granite Belt	238	Whitsundays	266
Toowoomba	244	Townsville	272
Sunshine Coast	250	Cairns/Gimuy	278
Hit the waves at Agnes Water	256	Drive to Cape York	286

Brisbane/ Meanjin

Brisbane is often overshadowed as a tourist destination by the Gold Coast to the south and the Sunshine Coast to the north. However, there's still plenty to enjoy in this sunny, modern city, especially with your dog.

Make a beeline for the city centre and the Brisbane River, with plenty of fun dog-friendly activities on offer. Or head offshore to one of the surrounding dog-friendly islands, each offering a different experience.

Schnitzel on the Riverwalk

FOLLOW THE RIVERWALK

One of the best ways to experience the city of Brisbane with your dog is to follow the Riverwalk, the suspended walkway above the Brisbane River. The walkway offers excellent views of the Story Bridge, the city skyline and Brisbane's inner city suburbs.

Also known as the New Farm Riverwalk, the walkway starts at Riverview Circuit in New Farm, where I had no trouble finding a parking space. It then follows the eastern bank of the river until the Howard Smith Wharves. From there it's possible to continue along the edge of the river on the riverside boardwalk, as far as the City Botanic Gardens.

Leashed dogs are welcome on the Riverwalk. Just make sure you don't block the popular path, which is also shared with cyclists and joggers. Consider stopping at Howard Smith Wharves for a drink or a snack, with dogs welcome at Felons Brewing and on the comfy beanbags scattered across the lawn.

VISIT THE CITY BOTANIC GARDENS

The City Botanic Gardens are a green oasis next to the skyscrapers of the Brisbane city centre, with the historic gardens taking up the southern end of the city peninsula. Dogs are welcome inside the gates of the gardens.

Some highlights of the gardens include the palm-surrounded lagoon, the towering bamboo stand and the rainforest section. Schnitzel was most intrigued by the water dragons around the lagoon.

I also found it worthwhile to wander along the western edge of the gardens, where the colonial Parliament House and Old Government House buildings stand. While pets aren't allowed to join you in visiting their interiors, the exterior facades are still impressive to ponder.

 STROLL ALONG SOUTHBANK

Another popular pocket of parkland in inner city Brisbane is the Southbank precinct, located on the south-western side of the city, across the river from the city centre. Southbank is home to a huge swimming lagoon, plus multiple museums and galleries – although naturally those are off limits to dogs.

Instead, when visiting with your dog, don't miss the Rainforest Walk or the adjacent stunning Nepalese Peace Pagoda. Plus of course stroll along the length of the riverfront. At the northern edge of Southbank, don't miss taking a selfie with your dog at the popular Brisbane sign.

RIDE ON THE BRISBANE RIVER FERRIES

The most scenic form of public transport in Brisbane is the Brisbane River ferries and CityCats, offering various views of the city skyline and landmarks. And dogs are welcome to join you onboard, as long as they follow some rules.

Firstly, dogs are only permitted onboard outside peak hours, so between 8.30am and 3.30pm on Monday to Friday or any time Saturday to Sunday. Your dog will also need to be both leashed and muzzled, or alternatively ride in an enclosed carrier, and you'll both need to sit on the outside deck.

Best of all, this extends to the CityHopper service, a free ferry that runs roughly every half hour between North Quay and Sydney Street. It's a convenient option for hopping between the sights of the inner city for tourists, including those of us with dogs.

Top: **A stroll along the North Gorge sea cliffs** Opposite: **A ferry on the Brisbane River**

I made use of the ferry to have a fun day exploring the dog-friendly sights of inner city Brisbane with Schnitzel. After parking in New Farm, close to the start of the Riverwalk, we then strolled along the Riverwalk, through the botanic gardens and to Southbank. We then returned for free via ferry to the Sydney Street ferry stop, resting our tired feet (and paws).

🔺 HEAD UP MT COOT-THA

Just 15 minutes west of the centre of Brisbane is the beautiful Mt Coot-tha Forest, the largest conservation reserve in Brisbane. Home to more than 1600 hectares of open eucalypt forest, it's a terrific destination for an easy day out amongst nature.

Unlike the adjacent Mt Coot-tha Botanic Gardens, leashed dogs are welcome in Mt Coot-tha Forest. This includes the popular Summit Lookout, with its panoramic views across Brisbane, as well as the many hiking trails throughout the forest.

One of the most popular hiking trails is the 1.9km Summit Track. Starting at JC Slaughter Falls Picnic Area, the moderately rated paved track ascends through majestic trees and rocky outcrops to just below the Summit Lookout. Or consider following the shorter Simpson Falls Track.

🐾 DRIVE TO BRIBIE ISLAND

For another fantastic day out with your pup, head north of Brisbane to Bribie Island. A sand island sheltering the northern end of Moreton Bay, this island is easily reached by crossing a bridge – there's no need to fuss around with ferries.

The highlight of Bribie Island for four-legged visitors is its excellent off-leash dog beach. Located between Woorim Beach and

Red Beach, the off-leash dog exercise section stretches for over 4km, perfect for long beach walks. In my opinion, it's the best dog beach in the entire Brisbane area, thanks to its beautiful golden sand and extensive size.

It's easiest to access the off-leash area from the end of Lowry Street in Woorim, where there's also a handy dog-washing station with a hose. Woorim Beach is known as a surf beach, although the waves were minuscule on the day I visited, making it great for dogs of all swimming abilities.

Alternatively, head to the access point at calm Red Beach. From the carpark, you'll need to walk across a few hundred metres of on-leash beach until you reach the start of the off-leash section. After a visit to the beach, consider stopping off at the nearby Bribie Island RSL Club, one of the few RSL clubs I've encountered with a dog-friendly outdoor-dining area.

CATCH THE FERRY TO COOCHIEMUDLO ISLAND

Bribie Island isn't the only dog-friendly island close to Brisbane. There are multiple other dog-friendly islands that you and your dog can reach by ferry, including the small Coochiemudlo Island, a relatively hidden gem.

Coochiemudlo can be reached on a quick 10 minute passenger ferry from Victoria Point. On my ferry trip there were multiple dogs onboard, with dogs travelling for free and no requirement to wear a muzzle. A vehicular barge also crosses to the island but less frequently.

Once on Coochiemudlo Island, the seasonal off-leash dog beach on the island is just a 5 minute walk from the ferry jetty. Follow the footpath behind the beach (where dogs are not permitted) next to the ferry jetty,

with the dog beach starting 100m after the boat ramp and continuing for about 200m. Depending on the month and potential presence of migratory birds, dogs are either allowed off-leash or on-leash on this pretty sand beach; check the signs.

CAMP ON NORTH STRADBROKE ISLAND

Another larger dog-friendly island, also accessible by ferry, is North Stradbroke Island. Rather than a daytrip, this island is better suited for a longer visit, ideally by camping at one of the dog-friendly foreshore camping areas.

Dogs are allowed in the camping areas at Main Beach and Flinders Beach, with up to two dogs permitted per site. Note that these areas are only accessible by 4WD, with a 4WD permit also required. If you don't have a 4WD, there are some other dog-friendly accommodation options, including some of the cabins at Sea Shanties in Amity Point.

During your days on North Straddie, enjoy the beaches, walks and fishing with your pup by your side. Dogs are allowed off-leash on a section of Home Beach at Point Lookout, between Rocky Point and Rocky Headland. Dogs are allowed on-leash on a number of other beaches, including Main Beach, Flinders Beach and Deadmans Beach.

Don't miss walking along the Gorge Walk with your dog. Starting almost at the end of Mooloomba Road in Point Lookout, the 1.2km boardwalk follows the headland of Point Lookout. While just a short walk, the views are spectacular, with a chance of spotting whales between June and November.

Popular dog-friendly dining options on the island include the wide grassy lawn at the Little Ship Club in Dunwich and the pet-friendly area at the Straddie Brewing Co near the ferry terminal. The Stradbroke Island Hotel also has a dog-friendly dining area.

To get to North Stradbroke Island with your dog, it's best to take your car across on the car ferry operated by Sealink, regularly departing from Toondah Harbour in Cleveland. Dogs are also allowed onboard the quicker passenger ferries. However, while dogs are allowed onboard the buses on Stradbroke Island, it's up to the discretion of the driver. The limited services are often full on busy days, so are likely to turn away dogs.

WATCH A MOVIE BY MOONLIGHT

Every summer, the Moonlight Cinema sets up at the Roma Street Parklands in Brisbane, with different movies screening outdoors nightly.

Best of all, the Moonlight Cinema in Brisbane is dog-friendly (as is also the case in Adelaide, Melbourne and Sydney). Quiet, friendly dogs on a leash are welcome to join you, including in premium areas.

When to visit

Any time of the year is a great time to visit Brisbane, with the temperatures not too hot in summer (although rain is more common) and mild temperatures in winter.

Top: **Schnitzel on Bribie Island** Bottom: **Walking in the City Botanic Gardens**

 ## Dog-friendly parks

 ## Dog-friendly dining

Victoria Park Off-Leash Dog Park, Spring Hill

One of the closest off-leash dog parks to the centre of Brisbane, this park features two fenced off-leash areas, including one for small dogs, plus agility equipment.

Kroll Gardens Dog Park, Clontarf

This huge dog park is completely fenced, perfect for longer off-leash walks but without the danger of your dog dashing onto a road. There's also agility equipment and a smaller section for small dogs.

Rainbow Forest Park, Indooroopilly

This popular park south-west of the city allows dogs off-leash. There are bush tracks and a creek, great for cooling down on warm days.

Cafe Diversity, Redcliffe

Dogs are welcome in the large outdoor dining area at this beachfront cafe, open daily for breakfast and lunch. Your pup can choose from their own dog menu – Schnitzel loved his doggy ice-cream and licked his bowl clean!

Little Black Pug, Mount Gravatt

I loved the flavoursome fusion-cuisine options at this brunch cafe, named for the owner's two pugs. The menu changes each season, plus there's a dog-treats menu for your own pup.

Eat Street Northshore, Hamilton

Open every Friday, Saturday and Sunday from 4pm, these street food markets charge a small entry fee, but pets are welcome for free. Pets should be people-friendly, kept on a short leash and ideally carried in congested areas.

Dog-friendly accommodation

W Brisbane, Brisbane City

For a luxe stay in the centre of Brisbane, look no further than the glamorous W. Smaller dogs up to 18kg are welcome in their pet-friendly rooms, for an additional nightly fee plus a one-off cleaning fee.

Spicers Balfour Hotel, New Farm

Two of the suites at this small boutique hotel near the Riverwalk are pet-friendly, with small and medium dogs up to 25kg permitted to join you, for a one-off cleaning fee.

Alcyone Hotel Residences, Hamilton

These luxury one- and two-bedroom apartments are located in the Portside Precinct. Book a Pamper Your Pooch package directly. It includes a plush dog bed, blanket, bowls and a doggy goodie bag.

Pine Rivers Showgrounds, Lawnton

There are limited pet-friendly options around Brisbane if you're travelling with a campervan or caravan. I stayed 30 minutes north of the city at Pine Rivers Showgrounds, which has good facilities and reasonable prices.

Dogs are welcome at Redcliffe Markets

Gold Coast

As the Gold Coast is one of the most popular holiday destinations in Australia, thanks to its beaches, theme parks and nightlife, you could be forgiven for expecting that it would be a no-go zone for holidays with your dog. But you can head to one of the wonderful dog-friendly beaches on the Gold Coast for some off-leash fun on the sand, or journey inland to Tamborine Mountain for a day of quality time with your pup.

Plenty of fun at The Spit Dog Beach

🐾 HAVE FUN ON THE SAND AT THE SPIT

When heading to the Gold Coast for a beach holiday, your dog shouldn't miss out on some fun on the sand and in the water! By default, dogs are allowed on-leash on most Gold Coast beaches outside patrolled areas, but there are also some off-leash dog beaches along the coast you can visit with your pup.

One of the most popular off-leash dog beaches is The Spit Dog Beach. Located on the ocean-facing side of The Spit in Southport, just north of Seaworld, dogs are allowed off-leash from the entrance opposite Muriel Henchman Park, north to the breakwall. It was very popular on the sunny Saturday morning I visited!

It's easiest to park in the large carpark near the Seaway Kiosk, which offers doggy ice-cream – the perfect post-beach treat. Next to the walkway from the kiosk to the beach is also a convenient wash-down area for sandy dogs.

If the waves are too much for your pup, head to the opposite side of The Spit. Dogs are allowed off-leash on the eastern side of Marine Stadium with its calm, enclosed waters, between Doug Jennings Park and Muriel Henchman Park.

🐾 ... OR VISIT PALM BEACH DOG BEACH

On the southern end of the Gold Coast, another very popular off-leash dog beach is Palm Beach Dog Beach, thanks to its extensive size and its calm lagoon.

Dogs are permitted off-leash around much of the Palm Beach Parklands, including the lagoon beach on the northern side of the Currumbin Creek entrance, the ocean-facing beach as far north as lifeguard tower 13 and Rockview Public Park between the two beaches, but not on the breakwall.

Dogs can choose between paddling in the gentle and shallow waters of the creek, frolicking in the surf at South Palm Beach or walking along the sandy tracks through the park. Or they can do all three!

Just stay clear of the southern side of Currumbin Creek, where dogs are not permitted. At the carpark, there's a convenient map showing where dogs are and aren't allowed, plus I noticed some handy arrows you can follow from the carpark.

There's also another off-leash dog beach at the other end of the suburb of Palm Beach. Dogs are permitted off-leash at Tallebudgera Beach, between Tallebudgera Creek entrance and lifeguard tower 16 at Ronnie Long Park, although time restrictions sometimes apply.

📍 HEAD INLAND TO TAMBORINE MOUNTAIN

While visiting the Gold Coast, don't miss heading inland to the beautiful Gold Coast hinterland, with its rugged mountains, lush forests and cute villages. While pups will unfortunately miss out on the national parks and their walking trails, one of the best dog-friendly spots to visit is the town of Tamborine Mountain.

At Tamborine Mountain make your way to The Gallery Walk, a strip of cafes and boutiques, most specialising in locally made products. I found the shop owners quite friendly, even permitting Schnitzel inside some of the shops – although you should wait for your pup to be invited.

Just south of The Gallery Walk is Fortitude Brewing, where dogs are allowed in part of the outdoor area while you enjoy a beer or pizza. The brewery is generally open daily for lunch. Alternatively, for dog-friendly wine tasting, head to Witches Fall

Winery – don't forget to make an advance booking for a tasting.

For a non-alcoholic beverage tasting, instead head to the Tamborine Mountain Coffee Plantation. There you can order a coffee-tasting board, with Australian-grown coffee served four ways. I enjoyed a delicious lunch with Schnitzel by my side at the cafe, which has a huge outdoor area with a variety of tables where well-behaved dogs are welcome. The cafe is open from Thursday to Monday for breakfast and lunch, and also serves local beers and wines.

While at Tamborine Mountain, don't miss stopping at Rotary Lookout along Main Western Road, which offers stunning views over the mountains of the Scenic Rim. As it's situated outside national parks, dogs are allowed to join you.

RUN FREE AT THE BOTANIC GARDENS

The Gold Coast Regional Botanic Gardens in Benowa are a relatively new botanic gardens (only established in 2000) but home to a range of attractions, from a Sensory Garden to a feature lake. Dogs are welcome to join you throughout most of the gardens.

The gardens are a particularly popular destination for dog owners thanks to the large off-leash area on the western side, adjacent to a lake. If visiting this area, it's easiest to park at the western carpark. Just keep your dog on a leash while walking to the off-leash area, particularly as the gardens are a popular spot for picnics.

Dogs are not permitted in the section of gardens around the feature lake on the eastern half of the site, although there is a designated dog-walking route to bypass the lake shown on maps. Instead, I recommend visiting the pretty Butterfly Food Plants Garden or walking part of the Mangroves to Mountains Walk.

 ### TASTE LOCAL CRAFT BEER

There's a number of craft breweries dotted around the Gold Coast, from the seaside to the hinterland, with many of the breweries welcoming four-legged friends to join you for a tasting session or a meal.

I visited the award-winning Burleigh Brewing, whose taphouse is located in an industrial estate inland from Burleigh Heads. Open Friday, Saturday and Sunday afternoons, there's plenty of outdoor tables to relax at, with multiple dogs joining their owners on the sunny afternoon I visited with Schnitzel.

The beers on tap change regularly, so perhaps order a tasting paddle to sample a few. I found their Wild Flower beer, made with Wildflower Gin's signature botanical spice mix, an unusual highlight. The on-site Burleigh Eats stand offers snacks ranging from burgers to tacos to fries.

How to get there

The Gold Coast extends for about 30km along the coastline south of Brisbane towards the New South Wales border. Surfers Paradise, the heart of the Gold Coast, is an hour's drive south of Brisbane.

When to visit

The Gold Coast is a popular destination year-round – even in winter it's still warm enough to hit the beaches. However, it's best to avoid the school holiday periods if you don't love the crowds.

Dog-friendly boutiques at Tamborine Mountain

A tasting paddle at Burleigh Brewing

GOLD COAST 235

Dog-friendly parks

Saltwater Fenced Dog Park, Hope Island

This excellent large, fully fenced off-leash dog park has its own swimming lagoon, as well as agility equipment, picnic tables and water fountains. Dogs can also be walked on-leash on the path around the adjacent lake.

Tallebudgera Off Leash Agility Dog Island, Elanora

Located at the Eddie Kornhauser Recreational Reserve, there are two walkways connecting to the island, where dogs are allowed off-leash. There's also dog agility equipment on the island.

Dog-friendly dining

Le Cafe Gourmand, Mermaid Beach

This casual French cafe is open for breakfast and lunch from Tuesday to Sunday, plus for dinner on Friday. Treat your dog to some doggy ice-cream, with a range of flavours to select from.

Miss Moneypenny's, Broadbeach

This upmarket restaurant is open daily for lunch and dinner, serving modern Mediterranean cuisine and an extensive list of cocktails. Dogs are welcome on their outdoor deck – just note it's only child-friendly during the day.

Surf's up at Tallebudgera Beach

Dog-friendly accommodation

Goldie relaxing at the beach

QT Gold Coast,
Surfers Paradise

For a touch of luxury, stay at the QT Gold Coast, just metres from the beach. Book a Pup Yeah! package, available for dogs up to 20kg. As well as a bed, dogs have their own minibar and in-room dining menu.

Quest Robina Apartment Hotel,
Robina

There are six pet-friendly ground-floor terrace apartments available for up to two vaccinated dogs under 20kg. An additional charge per pet per night applies, with a bed, toys and treats provided.

BIG4 Gold Coast Holiday Park,
Helensvale

There are no size restrictions or extra charges for dogs at this pet-friendly park that welcomes dogs on sites and in cabins. There's also a fenced off-leash dog park with agility equipment, a DIY dog wash and even kennels, all on-site.

Kirra Beach Tourist Park,
Coolangatta

Just a short walk from the beach, dogs are welcome year-round on selected powered sites and in two dog-friendly cabins, both with enclosed balconies. Generally, only one small dog is allowed per booking.

GOLD COAST

Granite Belt

The Granite Belt region, in inland south-eastern Queensland, is one of the only wine-growing regions in the state. Centred around the town of Stanthorpe (also the coldest town in all of Queensland), it's a delightfully dog-friendly destination to visit, and a unique spot for a weekend away with your dog.

Left: The dog-friendly Summit Estate Opposite: At Donnelly's Castle

VISIT DOG-FRIENDLY WINERIES

The Granite Belt wine region is home to over 40 wineries, located both north and south of Stanthorpe. Many of the wineries are dog-friendly; some even allow dogs inside the cellar door. Check with the local visitor centre for their latest list of dog-friendly wineries.

One of my favourite wineries that I visited with Schnitzel was Summit Estate, about a 10 minute drive north of Stanthorpe. I was warmly greeted with a sign at the door letting me know that they're fur-baby friendly.

Once inside, a staff member will take you through a tasting of their range, including sparkling, white, rosé and red wines, with the small tasting fee waived if you purchase a bottle or more. In addition to opening during the day from Friday to Monday, they also often stay open late on Friday and Saturday evenings, when you can enjoy a sunset session next to the vines.

Other dog-friendly cellar doors in the region include Hidden Creek Winery (where we enjoyed a delightful tasting on the lawn overlooking the dam), Ridgemill Winery, Robert Channon Wines and Balancing Heart Vineyard (*see* p. 242). Note that the latter two have resident dogs, so it's best if your dog is relaxed around other dogs.

... OR A DOG-FRIENDLY BREWERY

If you'd prefer to try some beer instead, head to the Granite Belt Brewery. Located just outside Stanthorpe, the brewery is in a beautiful setting, surrounded by bushland – although be wary of the local magpies during spring!

Dogs are allowed at the tables on the lawn, plus quiet dogs are allowed at the tables up on the back verandah. Order a tasting paddle, with two sizes of glasses on offer, or just one of their many beers and ciders. If you don't want to leave, some of their on-site cabins are pet-friendly.

FEAST ON LOCAL APPLES

The region surrounding Stanthorpe is home to more than just vineyards. One of the other major crops in the region is apples, thanks to the cold climate.

You can't skip stopping at Sutton's Juice Factory, in the village of Thulimbah, to the north of Stanthorpe. Their famous apple pie, served as a big wedge with spiced apple cider ice-cream, cream and apple syrup, is unmissable in my opinion.

While dogs aren't allowed inside or in the main outdoor area, there's a 'dog parking' area just before the main door, with multiple tables for dogs and their owners. You can also buy juices and other products inside.

EXPLORE DONNELLY'S CASTLE

The Granite Belt region is named for the distinctive granite boulders that pepper the landscape. Many of the most famous outcrops are found in Girraween National Park, to the south of Stanthorpe. However, the park is of course off-limits to dogs.

One of the best outcrops around Stanthorpe that can be explored with a dog is Donnelly's Castle – not really a castle, but an impressive cluster of granite boulders. The reserve is about 20 minutes drive north of town. Note that the final few kilometres of the road is unsealed, whether approaching from the south or north, although the gravel road was in good condition when I visited.

At Donnelly's Castle you and your pup can choose between two short walks: the 50m walk to the caves area or the 100m walk to the lookout, located at the top of a huge boulder. It doesn't take long to walk both! There are also picnic facilities on-site. While there are no signs about dogs, it's advisable to keep your dog on a leash, given the steep drop-offs.

If your time is limited, there's also plenty of beautiful granite boulders to check out around town. For example, head to Jardine Street on the southern edge of Stanthorpe. About halfway along the road on the left-hand side is a short 200m walk, starting at the Land for Wildlife sign. It winds through a cluster of boulders known as Sentimental Rocks.

Enjoy a tour at Hidden Creek Winery

👣 STROLL ALONGSIDE QUART POT CREEK

Another beautiful dog-friendly walk in Stanthorpe is along the paved path next to Quart Pot Creek. This lush creek meanders through the centre of town, dotted with wetland areas and edged by parks.

A good option is to walk along the section adjacent to the fenced dog park, located next to Connor Street, just north of the town centre. Or else head further south to Heritage Park and follow the path to Red Bridge – a historic railway bridge on the edge of town. Dogs need to be kept on a leash along the path and in the adjacent parks, except the fenced dog park.

How to get there

The Granite Belt region is under a 3 hour drive south-west of Brisbane, close enough for a long weekend away.

When to visit

Head to the Granite Belt during winter for a rare experience in Queensland – the chance of snow flurries. It's an ideal place for sipping wine next to an open fire. Alternatively, both spring and autumn offer mild and pleasant temperatures.

Left: **A scenic walk in nature** Bottom: **Apple pie at Sutton's Juice Factory**

 ## Dog-friendly parks

 ## Dog-friendly dining

Stanthorpe Dog Park, Stanthorpe

Stanthorpe is home to one off-leash dog park, on the southern side of Connor Street, near the Talc Street intersection. It's fully fenced with picnic benches, chairs and a water fountain; just be wary of burrs underpaw. Until the nearby trees mature and provide shade, it's best to visit early or late in the day if the weather is warm.

Balancing Heart Cellar Door, Wyberba

This cellar door is well-known for its wood-fired pizzas, available daily at lunch and during the sunset dinners from Friday to Sunday. Dogs are welcome both on the verandah and at the tables next to the lake.

Stanthorpe Cheese and Jersey Girls Cafe, Thulimbah

I recommend paying the small fee to taste the complete cheese range, then order a ploughman's platter with your favourite. Cheese toasties are also available. Dogs are welcome at the outside tables.

Zest Pastries, Stanthorpe

Choose from the wide range of gourmet pies, either for dine-in (there are tables and a water bowl out the front to accommodate four-legged friends) or takeaway to a local park. I loved the cider pulled pork pie, but the sandwiches also looked delicious.

Dog-friendly accommodation

Alure,
Stanthorpe

Treat yourself and your pup to a stay in one of these luxury villas in the countryside south of Stanthorpe. Dogs are welcome with prior approval and an additional fee per stay. They'll be treated to their own bathrobe, plush dog bed, toiletries and treats.

Straw House B&B,
Dalveen

A farmstay just outside Stanthorpe. Stay in one of the luxurious cottages constructed from straw, with well-behaved dogs welcome for an additional fee. Don't miss out on the famous breakfast.

Top of the Town Tourist Park,
Stanthorpe

A popular caravan park on the edge of town. Pets are welcome at the powered and unpowered campsites, plus in selected pet-friendly standard and family cabins, surrounded by bush.

Foxbar Falls,
Amiens

About 15 minutes out of Stanthorpe, enjoy a stay in the bush, with dogs permitted on the walks and in the dam. Up to two dogs are permitted at most campsites, plus there's free use of kayaks and a fire-pit on each site.

Left: **A pie from Zest Pastries** Opposite: **Alure in Stanthorpe offers a luxury experience for dog and owner**

Toowoomba

The second largest inland city in all of Australia, Toowoomba is a relatively undiscovered tourism gem, especially for those travelling with dogs.

Aside from its many dog-friendly attractions – from gardens to walks and street art – its close proximity to Brisbane makes it perfect for a quick weekend away or even just a daytrip.

The Japanese garden, Ju Raku En

EXPLORE THE QUEENS PARK AND BOTANIC GARDENS

Toowoomba is known as the 'Garden City' because it is home to over 250 gardens and parks. Luckily, dogs are welcome to visit many of the gardens.

The best-known gardens in Toowoomba are the Botanic Gardens, part of the centrally located Queens Park. The heritage-listed botanic gardens were established in the 1870s and are still a highlight of the city. Wander around the gardens and view the formal garden beds, stately trees and memorials.

Dogs are welcome to join you on-leash in the gardens, plus in the adjacent Queens Park with its expanses of lawn and large shady trees. Best of all, there's also an off-leash area in Queens Park, not far from the edge of the Botanic Gardens. Your pup can have a run around off-leash after walking through the Botanic Gardens with you.

CELEBRATE THE ANNUAL CARNIVAL OF FLOWERS

Each year during September the city of Toowoomba celebrates the spring season and its gardens with the Carnival of Flowers. There are mass plantings of flowers in many of its gardens, plus other events, including a Floral Parade through the streets and a Festival of Food and Wine.

Dogs are warmly welcome at many of the festival events. In recent years the organisers have put together a Petals and Pups program, with suggested itineraries for four-legged attendees and information on dog-friendly accommodation and cafes.

If you're attending the Toowoomba Carnival of Flowers with your dog, make sure you visit some of the beautiful dog-friendly gardens around the city. You'll also find some perfect spots to take selfies with your pup.

While the Queens Park and Botanic Gardens are the focal point of the carnival, another beautiful garden (on the western side of Toowoomba's town centre) where leashed dogs are also allowed is Laurel Bank Park. Less formal than the Botanic Gardens, this park contains many interesting features, including beds of bulbs in spring, a wisteria arbour, a scented garden and a topiary *Thomas the Tank Engine* train – a favourite with children.

Note that dogs are not permitted in some of the featured gardens, including Spring

The Botanic Gardens in Toowoomba

Statue of Puppy, the first canine ambassador of Toowoomba

Bluff Park and Boyce Gardens, plus likely the private exhibition gardens (although you can always ask). Dogs are also not permitted inside the Festival of Food and Wine when it takes over part of Queens Park for a weekend.

STROLL THROUGH A JAPANESE GARDEN

For a different type of garden, head to the southern part of Toowoomba and the campus of the University of Southern Queensland where you'll discover Toowoomba's Japanese garden, Ju Raku En.

Entry to this delightful garden is also free, with dogs on a leash permitted. Schnitzel and I enjoyed strolling over the many red bridges that cross the garden's water features. This garden is particularly wonderful to visit during autumn, when the leaves change colour.

HEAD UP TO PICNIC POINT

While visiting Toowoomba, make sure you head up to the Picnic Point Parklands. As well as being great for picnics, it's a wonderful spot to enjoy views of the Lockyer Valley and Main Ridge, plus enjoy a dog-friendly walk or two.

There are multiple bushwalks on offer, from short strolls to a 6km complete circuit. The 1.85km Pardalote Walk is a lovely option that connects the main lookout point and the lookout at the end of Tobruk Memorial Drive.

While at Picnic Point, don't miss getting a selfie with the bronze statue of Puppy, the first canine ambassador of Toowoomba. The parklands are also home to a pretty waterfall, situated on the opposite side of the main lookout from the cafe.

ADMIRE THE LOCAL STREET ART

Many of the building walls in inner city Toowoomba are covered in beautiful street art murals. Some of them date from the street art festivals held between 2014 and 2017, but there are also more recent additions that regularly pop up. And since they're located outside, this is one type of art that's perfect to view with your dog at your side.

One of my favourite artworks is the stunning mural of an Indigenous child by Adnate on the edge of the Neil Street carpark, near the Empire Theatre. I also recommend heading around the corner to Union Street, just off Ruthven Street, to check out the charming elephant mural by Fintan Magee.

Other highlights include the colourful First Nations mural on the wall of the Toowoomba Regional Art Gallery highlighting the diverse local First Nations communities (also check out the sculptures in the park), and the many works along Domestic Lane. There's a map available on the local tourism website or pick up a brochure from the local visitor centre. Or just head out for a wander and see what you discover!

How to get there

It's just over a 90 minute drive west from Brisbane to Toowoomba.

When to visit

Visit Toowoomba in September, during the annual Carnival of Flowers. Alternatively, follow the Autumn Leaf Trail during the autumn months for an equally colourful display.

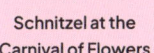

Schnitzel at the Carnival of Flowers

Dog-friendly parks

Dog-friendly dining

North Ruthven Reserve, Harlaxton

One of the recently constructed fenced dog parks in the region, this park on the northern edge of Toowoomba has big, separately fenced areas for small and large dogs, plus plenty of shady trees.

Garnet Lehmann Park, Rangeville

Dogs are allowed off-leash in nearly all of this park that surrounds a lush creek. Schnitzel and I enjoyed the popular walk looping around the park, following both a paved walking path plus a section of dirt path.

Park House Cafe, Toowoomba City

This popular dog-friendly cafe is located opposite Queens Park (*see* p. 245) on Margaret Street. Open daily until late afternoon, there are plenty of outdoor tables with large umbrellas for dining (or just enjoying a coffee) with your pup.

Ground Up Espresso Bar, Toowoomba City

This highly rated cafe is located down a narrow alleyway full of street art murals, perfect for a coffee break or lunch stop while exploring the city's street art. It's open daily for breakfast and lunch.

Street art by Adnate

Dog-friendly accommodation

The off-leash area in Queens Park

Quest Toowoomba,
Toowoomba City

Choose from a range of self-contained rooms varying in size from studios to three-bedroom apartments. Selected rooms are pet-friendly for a small additional fee – call reception to make a booking.

Toowoomba Showgrounds Caravan Park,
Glenvale

Stay with your caravan or motorhome at the showgrounds, except during the annual show. While facilities are basic, I found the prices reasonable, plus no pre-bookings are required.

Banksia Cottage,
Toowoomba City

Enjoy a stay in this beautiful old cottage built in 1898. Up to two quiet, well-behaved dogs over 12 months old are allowed with prior approval. There's a fully fenced backyard, plus a kennel and dog bowls.

Sunshine Coast

Stretching north of Brisbane, between Caloundra and Noosa, the Sunshine Coast is more than just a fabulous beach destination, thanks to the equally beautiful hinterlands in the hills behind.

You'll be spoiled for choice when visiting the region with your dog. Along with plenty of dog-friendly beaches, don't miss climbing a mountain or two – taking in the views from the hinterland – or shopping at cute markets, all with your furry friend.

The Caloundra Foreshore

🌊 HEAD TO THE BEACH

The Sunshine Coast is home to many beautiful beaches, and fortunately there are plenty of dog-friendly options to enjoy with your pup. It wouldn't be a visit to the Sunshine Coast without visiting at least one of these beaches for a play on the sand and a paddle in the water!

These are some of my favourite dog-friendly beaches along the Sunshine Coast.

Noosa Spit,
Noosa Heads

Just behind Noosa Main Beach, dogs are allowed off-leash on a whole section of the spit extending into the Noosa River and the beaches on either side. While the northern side is most popular for paddles with your pup, I found the southern side to have a wider stretch of sand, perfect for a good run or slow trot.

Sunshine Beach North,
Sunshine Beach

Dogs are allowed off-leash at the northern end of Sunshine Beach, between the small carpark on Seaview Terrace North and the Noosa National Park boundary. It's a particularly good beach when the wind is from the west thanks to it being sheltered on that side, although the water is too rough for most dogs to swim.

Castaways Beach & Marcus Beach

This huge stretch of off-leash beach extends for nearly 4km, between beach access 38 (near Orient Park South) and beach access 47 (at Tasman Trespasser Park). It's a great spot for off-leash walks, although small dogs should be wary of the often rough surf.

Stumers Creek,
Coolum Beach

Dogs are allowed off-leash at this beach on the northern end of Coolum Beach between beach access 67 and 72. A highlight of this dog beach is the calm water of the lagoon, perfect for doggy paddling. There's also a handy dog-washing station next to the carpark.

North Shore Beach,
Twin Waters

Access this dog beach from the carpark at the end of North Shore Road. Dogs are allowed off-leash from 140m north of beach access 132 down to beach access 136, including the calm waters at the entrance of the Maroochy River.

FLOAT ALONG THE NOOSA RIVER

One of the prettiest spots on the Sunshine Coast is the Noosa River, along which the towns of Noosa Heads, Noosaville and Tewantin are located. I highly recommend getting out onto the river with your pup!

The easiest way to head out on the Noosa River, if you have a smaller dog, is by taking the Noosa Ferry. Dogs are allowed on the Noosa Ferry, except on the sunset cruises, as long as they can sit on your lap. There's no extra charge for pups and no muzzles are required. I enjoyed a beautiful trip sitting with Schnitzel in the sunshine on the open-air top deck watching the scenery go by, from the wooded north shore to waterfront mansions.

The ferry runs approximately every half hour between Tewantin and Noosa Heads. I recommend getting off the ferry at Noosa Heads and going for a walk, before returning.

If you walk to your left along the boardwalk and don't turn towards Noosa Main Beach, you'll soon reach the Noosa Spit and the sign for the off-leash exercise area, including the popular dog beach.

If you have a larger dog or are feeling more energetic, hire a boat or kayak for an hour or the day. One dog-friendly boat hire company along the Noosa River is O Boat Hire. It offers a range of boats, including barbecue pontoons, kayaks and stand-up paddleboard hire.

 CLIMB A MOUNTAIN

The Sunshine Coast is dotted with mountains, including the famous Glass House Mountains. It's worth climbing one or two, partially to enjoy the beautiful views from the top, but also for a great walk with your pup.

Although some of the mountains are located within pockets of national parks, you and your dog can climb Mt Ninderry, located in a dog-friendly bushland reserve. Not far from Yandina and the freeway, the start of the Mt Ninderry Walking Track can be found on Eucalyptus Crescent in Ninderry. It's a 2.8km return track to the summit. The sign at the entrance recommends to allow 3 hours, but you'll likely finish it in under 90 minutes, even less if you and your dog are enthusiastic walkers. It took Schnitzel and I about 30 minutes to climb to the junction at the top, where the trail splits into two, heading to the east and west lookouts.

Dogs are required to be on-leash on the trail, but this wasn't strictly followed by many of the locals and their dogs on the track on the morning I hiked it. Note that there's a lot of rocky stairs during the ascent, so make sure you wear proper walking shoes.

... OR JUST DRIVE TO A LOOKOUT

Of course, climbing a mountain isn't the only way to enjoy spectacular views on the Sunshine Coast, with many lookouts also accessible by road and a few short steps.

The most famous lookout in the region is the Glass House Mountains Lookout, located just off the Glass House Woodford Road. Dogs are allowed at the lookout, although not on the adjacent walking trail. This lookout is most impressive for the number of mountains you can see, with signs naming each of the surrounding peaks.

Another lookout I enjoyed was Dulong Lookout, located just behind Nambour on

Schnitzel on the Noosa Ferry

the way to the villages of Mapleton and Montville. In fact, drive along the Blackall Range Tourist Drive and you'll be spoiled with endless vistas off towards the coast.

Make sure you stop off at the picturesque village of Montville. Go for a wander with your pup along the main street, browsing the many interesting galleries and boutiques. Plenty of the shops have water bowls for pets outside; some even have 'pet parking' areas.

SHOP AT THE EUMUNDI MARKETS

There are many markets that take place all over the Sunshine Coast, and most are dog-friendly. However, the most renowned is the Eumundi Markets, which take place in the town of the same name every Wednesday and Saturday, between 7am (8am on Wednesday) and 2pm.

Pets on a leash are welcome at the markets, with plenty of water bowls to keep your dog cool. During my visit, Schnitzel of course sniffed out the two pet stalls offering up samples! There's also plenty of pet-related things to buy at the homeware stores, such as the colourful prints and cushions at Tracey Keller Gallery.

Two-hour parking spots are available on nearby streets for free, or else head to the paid parking lot. If you're feeling hungry, there's plenty of food stalls located just off Memorial Drive, plus a few more options dotted around the rest of the market.

EXPLORE MALENY BOTANIC GARDENS

One of the jewels of the Sunshine Coast hinterland is the stunning Maleny Botanic Gardens and Bird World. When stepping out of the reception centre, I was amazed by the beautiful view of the gardens, with the spectacular Glass House Mountains in the distance. The gardens are dotted with countless waterfalls and ponds, taking advantage of the steep slope.

Leashed dogs are welcome to join you on a stroll around the gardens for no additional charge, although they are not allowed to join the guided tours to the walk-through aviaries in Bird World. It's possible to rent a golf cart for an hour to explore the gardens, with dogs likely to be allowed to join you.

RIDE THE MARY VALLEY RATTLER

For a different type of daytrip when visiting the Sunshine Coast, particularly if you're staying around Noosa, take a pet-friendly steam train ride on the lovingly restored *Mary Valley Rattler*. The *Mary Valley Rattler* departs from Gympie and traverses the scenic Mary Valley.

Pets are allowed to join you on the weekly Wednesday, Saturday and Sunday excursions (just not the Rattler Tasting Train on Thursday), for an additional charge. There are two specific booths available for families with pets, each accommodating up to two dogs and six people. Make sure you book well in advance!

How to get there

It's about a 90 minute trip north from Brisbane to Caloundra at the southern end of the Sunshine Coast. Noosa is a 2 hour drive north of Brisbane.

When to visit

The Sunshine Coast is ideal to visit year-round. Even during the middle of winter it's still usually warm enough to enjoy a swim, although the mornings in the hinterland can be chilly.

Dog-friendly parks

Weyba Creek Park, Noosaville

This long stretch of park lies on the banks of Weyba Creek, a tempting spot for a dog paddle, with plenty of shady trees to walk under and handy picnic benches.

Brightwater Dog Park, Mountain Creek

One of the few fenced dog parks on the Sunshine Coast, this secure park has double gates, plenty of shade and dog agility equipment.

Top: **Eumundi Markets** Bottom: **The Glass House Mountains Lookout**

 # Dog-friendly dining

 # Dog-friendly accommodation

Land & Sea Brewery,
Noosaville

Open daily for lunch and dinner, except on Monday. Combine one of the beer or gin tasting paddles with a meal from the wide-ranging menu – my Roast Field Mushroom Burger was amazing. There's plenty of dog-friendly outdoor seating, and even a gas fireplace for cool evenings.

The Velo Project,
Mooloolaba

Allow your dog to order from their own menu at this highly rated cafe that is open daily for breakfast and brunch. They can feast on a donut treat, while you take your pick from the breakfast options, crepes and long list of drinks.

Lane 32 Woodfired Pizza,
Maleny

As well as allowing dogs at outdoor tables (and spoiling them with dog biscuits), this restaurant has its own enclosed dog pen – perfect for when puppy dog eyes become too much at the dinner table! Open selected evenings – check in advance for their latest hours.

Saltwater Villas,
Mooloolaba

Enjoy a waterfront stay on the Sunshine Coast with your dog. All villas are pet-friendly, including the waterfront villas with fully-fenced private courtyards. Dog-sitting and walking can also be arranged.

Sunshine Valley Cottages,
Woombye

These three cottages set in a beautiful tropical garden are truly pet-friendly, with no size limit and multiple pets allowed per cottage, with prior approval. There are multiple off-leash areas, and pet-sitting is available on request.

Spicers Clovelly Estate,
Montville

For a taste of luxury, enjoy a stay at this sprawling French-style estate. Book the Pooch Package, which includes accommodation in the French cottage, plenty of dog supplies, including a bed and bowls, plus a long-lasting bone. Note that a 25kg limit applies.

Coolum Beach Holiday Park,
Coolum Beach

This beachfront caravan park is adjacent to the popular off-leash area at Stumers Creek. Dogs are permitted on application, at the discretion of the manager.

Hit the waves at Agnes Water

Just under 500km north of Brisbane, the laidback tourist town of Agnes Water is best known for having the northernmost surf break on the Queensland coast. Along with the neighbouring town of Seventeen Seventy, both towns are popular destinations with dog owners thanks to their abundance of pet-friendly accommodation.

Naturally, the top attraction of Agnes Water is its wonderfully long surf beach. The long sandy stretch of Agnes Water Beach and its surf break is largely dog-friendly. While dogs aren't allowed in the bathing area at the southern end of the beach, dogs are allowed along the rest of the beach.

In between the bathing area and the Surf Club Avenue access point, about 2km north, dogs need to stay on-leash; dogs are allowed off-leash along the northern section of the beach, which stretches for several kilometres. I recommend parking at the end of Surf Club Avenue.

The rules are a little more restrictive at Seventeen Seventy, with dogs required to stay on a leash on the protected beach inside the peninsula – the default rule in the local area. Note also that dogs are not allowed on Chinamans Beach and Spring Beach, to the south of Agnes Water, during the turtle nesting season between November and April.

A popular pastime at Agnes Water is learning to surf, though it's probably beyond most dogs! However, there are other watersports options you can enjoy with your pup. You can hire a kayak from 1770 Liquid Adventures. Dogs are welcome on hired kayaks, although skip the guided tours that visit the nearby national park. Alternatively, hire a paddleboard from 1770 SUP.

There are a number of national parks around Agnes Water where dogs are not allowed, so instead head out for a short dog-friendly bushwalk on the Discovery Trail. This 800m trail starts next to the Agnes Water Museum and meanders to a lookout overlooking Workmans Beach, with dogs on a leash welcome to join you.

Alternatively, walk along the paved path that connects Agnes Water and Seventeen

Seventy. I found the section that runs along the foreshore of Seventeen Seventy, passing through the Air Sea Rescue Park and Endeavour Park, the most scenic section thanks to its waterfront views. Turn around once you reach the Joseph Banks Conservation Park, where dogs are not permitted.

One of the best spots to stay the night with your pup is at The Summit 1770. In addition to three gorgeous dog-friendly one-bedroom cottages, there are also powered and unpowered campsites on the rural property. Some sites have private dog pens behind them, plus there are two fenced dog runs for all holidaying dogs, and regular dog-training sessions.

Closer to the beach, another dog-friendly caravan park is the Captain Cook Holiday Village. Pets are permitted on sites, but not in cabins, and the park has its own walking trail to the off-leash section of Agnes Water Beach which Schnitzel and I used often.

As the afternoon light fades, make a beeline for Seventeen Seventy, one of the few places in Queensland where it's possible to watch the sun both rise and set over the ocean. Find a seat at the marina or a local park, and enjoy a wonderful sunset with your pup by your side.

Sunset at Seventeen Seventy

Capricorn Coast

The Capricorn Coast lies in central Queensland, just inside the Tropic of Capricorn. At the centre of the region lies the sprawling country city of Rockhampton. Located on the banks of the Fitzroy River, this historic city is also the gateway to the string of beach towns along its nearby coast, while offshore lies the tropical delights of Great Keppel Island. Far enough south to be relatively free of the threat of crocodiles, the Capricorn Coast is a great destination to visit for a relaxing beach getaway with your dog.

The dog-friendly Lammermoor Beach

Heritage-listed building, Rockhampton

🐾 VISIT THE BEACHES ALONG THE COAST

One of the top attractions of the Capricorn Coast is its many beautiful beaches, spread out between Yeppoon to the north and Emu Park to the south. Luckily, by default dogs are allowed on-leash at all beaches, plus off-leash before 8am and after 4pm, unless otherwise signposted. So nearly all beaches in the area are dog-friendly!

The main exceptions are the beaches in national parks, such as Byfield National Park to the north of Yeppoon.

There are also some beaches where dogs are allowed off-leash all day long on weekdays – both Fishermans Beach at Emu Park, starting 150m north of the boat ramp; and Farnborough Beach at Bangalee.

One of my favourite beaches in the region is Lammermoor Beach, with its long stretch of golden sand, great for on-leash dog walks.

Schnitzel and I also enjoyed Cooee Bay Beach for off-leash fun in the evening – it was close to our accommodation in Yeppoon.

While crocodiles are rarely an issue this far south, marine stingers may be a risk during summer. Also be alert during turtle nesting season from October to March. If turtles are around, keep your distance and keep your dogs on a leash or completely off the beach.

📍 EXPLORE ROCKHAMPTON'S HISTORIC SIDE

Rockhampton is home to a charming city centre along the southern banks of the Fitzroy River. I was impressed by the collection of historic buildings still standing. Some of the key buildings you should check out include Customs House, The Criterion Hotel, the Rockhampton Post Office and the multiple court buildings.

Exploring the beach in Yeppoon

Most of these heritage-listed buildings are located along the riverfront Quay Street, although the Post Office and court buildings are a block back on East Street.

The Riverbank Precinct alongside Quay Street has recently been revitalised and is a lovely spot for a riverside stroll with your dog, with plenty of shady trees to keep you cool. Just keep your dog on a leash.

STROLL THROUGH KERSHAW GARDENS

A highlight from my visit to Rockhampton with Schnitzel was visiting the Kershaw Gardens in North Rockhampton. While dogs are not permitted in the main botanic gardens in Rockhampton, including the adjacent zoo, dogs are welcome at Kershaw Gardens.

Don't miss the waterfall area in the gardens. It features multiple man-made waterfalls beautifully cascading into a pool below, surrounded by lush palms and many fast moving water dragons – Schnitzel was intrigued! The waterfall area is closest to the High Street carpark.

In most of Kershaw Gardens dogs need to stay on a leash. However, there's an off-leash area close to the Dowling Street carpark, plus a small fenced off-leash park with agility equipment at the Charles Street carpark.

LISTEN TO THE *SINGING SHIP* AT EMU PARK

Emu Park, a 15 minute drive south of Yeppoon, is home to an unusual landmark – the *Singing Ship*. Up on the hill above the jetty this sculpture and memorial to Captain Cook was erected in 1970. Wait for the wind to blow, then listen for the sound of it singing.

Adjacent to the *Singing Ship* is the more recent Anzac Memorial Walk. This memorial and short section of boardwalk was erected to coincide with the centenary of World War I and is a poignant spot to visit. Underneath a large shelter are information panels about key battles, highlighting the involvement of local Queenslanders.

Dogs on a leash are welcome along the boardwalk and in the park surrounding the *Singing Ship*, although treat both sites with the respect that they deserve.

WALK ALONG THE YEPPOON FORESHORE

If you want to enjoy the beautiful coastline without getting your feet sandy, a popular walk for both humans and dogs is the Yeppoon Foreshore. Take your time, with plenty of picnic benches and sun lounges along the way, not to mention the many cafes opposite the beach that are mostly dog-friendly.

Dogs are required to stay on-leash, plus I noticed multiple reminders to pick up after your dog – luckily there are plenty of bins and poo bags available. Note that dogs are not allowed at Yeppoon Lagoon (but are fine to walk behind it) or in the Keppel Kraken water play area.

How to get there

Rockhampton is about a 650km drive north of Brisbane. While Rockhampton lies well inland, Yeppoon is a 40km drive north-east of Rockhampton on the coast.

When to visit

Located on the edge of the tropics, head to the Capricorn Coast during winter to take advantage of the warm weather that is great for visiting the many beaches and dining outside.

The waterfall in Kershaw Gardens

Dog-friendly parks

Olive Dorey Park,
Lammermoor

This excellent fenced dog park is the only one close to Yeppoon. There are three separately fenced areas. One contains agility equipment, while the other two have plenty of shade and seating.

Customs House in Rockhampton

Dog-friendly dining

Lure Living,
Yeppoon

Located opposite the waterfront in Yeppoon, this cafe is open daily for coffee and brunch. Pets are welcome outside, although keep them off the lounges; instead ask the pet-loving staff for a pet bed.

The Waterline Restaurant,
Rosslyn

This award-winning restaurant is open all day long at the Keppel Bay Marina. One section of the outdoor tables is reserved for owners dining with their pets.

Riverston Tea Rooms,
Rockhampton

This charming cafe is in one of Quay Street's historic buildings, with dogs allowed at the verandah tables. Open from Tuesday to Sunday for breakfast and lunch. The pancakes are highly praised.

Dog-friendly accommodation

Island View Caravan Park, Kinka Beach

This popular pet-friendly caravan park is located just metres from the long expanse of Kinka Beach. Dogs are welcome on sites, just check with management before booking.

Poinciana Tourist Park, Yeppoon

I stayed at this great small park, on the southern side of Yeppoon and close to Cooee Bay Beach (*see* p. 259). Pets are allowed on caravan and camping sites only, not in the new glamping tents.

Archer Park Motel, Rockhampton

Located in the centre of Rockhampton, this motel has selected ground-floor queen rooms that are pet-friendly. The motel has a swimming pool and is just a short walk from the riverfront.

A good sitting spot along Fitzroy River, Rockhampton

Take a daytrip to Great Keppel Island/Wop-pa

Queensland is home to countless lush tropical islands surrounded by reefs; many are home to luxury resorts. While most such islands and resorts are off limits to pets, Great Keppel Island is a dog-friendly tropical island paradise.

Located just off the coast of Yeppoon, it's a short 30 minute ferry trip out to Great Keppel Island. Two ferry companies operate the route, both permitting dogs onboard. I travelled with Keppel Konnections, which transports dogs for free. There's also the larger Freedom Fast Cats, which charges a small fee per dog.

The main attraction of Great Keppel is its beautiful beaches. Just like on the mainland, dogs are allowed on-leash on the beaches all day long, plus off-leash before 8am and after 4pm.

Your boat will drop you on Fishermans Beach, the hub of the island. Stroll along the beach to its southern end for the start of the walking track to other beaches nearby. The next easiest beach to visit is Shelving Beach, a 10 minute walk from the end of Fishermans Beach, although the track is quite rough. It's a great spot to swim or snorkel above the coral reef.

Further along the coast is Monkey Beach, which is regarded as having the best snorkelling on the island. I ran out of time to visit this beach, partially because I added a lunch at Great Keppel Island Hideaway to my ferry booking. The lunch and drink deal was great value and tasty, with plenty of outdoor tables and water bowls for Schnitzel.

Other dining options include the Tropical Vibes Cafe at the main island store and Great Keppel Island Pizza. The outdoor tables at both are likely to be dog-friendly, or order takeaway and head to the beach. But consider packing a picnic lunch instead if you want to maximise your time exploring the island.

After lunch, Schnitzel and I hiked to Long Beach, a gorgeous long stretch of white sand on the southern side of the island. Great for doggy paddling and swimming – Schnitzel and I had nearly the whole beach to ourselves. Just be warned: the hiking trails to the beach are not well maintained. And keep your dog on a leash while on the trails – I spotted a goanna, an echidna and plenty of birdlife.

For now, there are limited accommodation options on the island, with just a single beach house listed as pet-friendly last time I searched. It's best to visit the island with your dog on a daytrip, staying back on the mainland.

There are plans every year or two for a resort to be rebuilt on the island. (You can still see the ruins of the previous resort.) Redevelopment may also mean that it's no longer dog-friendly. So visit this dog-friendly paradise before you miss out!

Sandy beaches on Great Keppel Island

Whitsundays

The Whitsundays are a delightful stretch of tropical coastline and adjacent islands in central Queensland. Since the region's star attractions lie offshore and are largely off limits to dogs, when visiting the Whitsundays with your dog you'll need to stick to the mainland part of the region, stretching between the tourist gateway of Airlie Beach and the often overlooked town of Bowen. However, you'll be rewarded with some stunning beaches, scenic dog-friendly walks and relaxed holiday parks by the water.

Horseshoe Bay in Bowen

WANDER ALONG THE BICENTENNIAL WAY

Explore the coastline around Airlie Beach with your dog by following the Airlie Beach boardwalk and walkway, also known as the Bicentennial Way. This easy yet scenic walk starts at the Port of Airlie Marina and extends 3.5km north to Cannonvale Beach.

My favourite section of the walkway is the raised boardwalk between Whisper Bay Boat Ramp and Shingley Drive, dubbed 'Turtle Boardwalk'. Keep an eye out for the local turtles while walking along it, although ideally stick to the early morning or evening, as the dark wooden boards may be too hot for doggy paws during the middle of the day.

A section of the walk passes by Airlie Beach Lagoon, where dogs are not allowed. Instead follow the alternative 'dog track' thoughtfully marked with paw prints, plus follow the other rules signposted. Along the rest of the walk, dogs need to stay on-leash.

Once you reach Cannonvale, the eastern end of Cannonvale Beach allows off-leash dogs for most of the day – check the local signs for the current times. Also keep an eye out for signs about recent crocodile sightings – a sign was displayed during my visit, although crocodiles aren't that common this far south. For another option, head instead to the nearby Fat Frog Beach Cafe (*see* p. 270).

On the way you'll also pass by Shingley Beach, adjacent to the Coral Sea Marina. Dogs are allowed off-leash on the eastern end of the beach all day, although it's just a small area and the water didn't look clean to me. Dogs are also permitted on-leash at other beaches in the area, unless otherwise signposted.

HIKE THE CAPE EDGECUMBE WALKING TRACK

For a more adventurous walk, a wonderful dog-friendly hike in the Bowen area is the Cape Edgecumbe Walking Track. This bush track winds up to the rocky outcrops and lookouts between the stunning Horseshoe Bay and Rose Bay, with dogs allowed along the entire length.

There are multiple places you can access the walk: at Horseshoe Bay Beach, at the end of Banyan Drive in Rose Bay and at the end of Murray Bay Road. A full circuit is about 5km long, but it's also possible to just walk part of the track.

I recommend at least walking up to Rotary Lookout at Horseshoe Bay. It's only a few hundred metres, although the final mesh ramp up to the lookout might be tricky for dogs that can't be carried – I carried Schnitzel. In return you'll be rewarded with a vista across beautiful Horseshoe Bay Beach, one of the most beautiful beaches I've visited in Queensland, although sadly off limits to dogs.

RELAX ON THE BEACHES OF BOWEN

While dogs aren't allowed on the sand at the popular swimming and snorkelling spots of Horseshoe Bay Beach and Rose Bay Beach, or the nearby Grays Bay, dogs are welcome on many of the other beaches around Bowen.

The most beautiful off-leash dog beach in Bowen is Kings Beach, located between Rose Bay and the town centre of Bowen. It's a long sandy beach that is great for dogs large and small. On the day I visited the water was shallow and calm – perfect for little Schnitzel! It's easiest to access Kings Beach by following the signs to Flagstaff Hill and parking in the carpark just past the hill, at the southern end of the beach.

Another popular dog-friendly beach is Queens Beach, a golden stretch of sand on the northern side of town. The off-leash section starts at Mount Nutt Road and continues to the western end. On-leash dogs are also permitted along the rest of the beach. It's a convenient option if you are staying at one of the nearby caravan parks.

HEAD TO HIDEAWAY BAY

My top pick amongst the off-leash dog beaches in the Whitsundays area is the gorgeous Hideaway Bay. This bay is a stunning yet quiet stretch of coastline located between Airlie Beach and Bowen. You likely won't share the beach with more than a handful of people.

It's about a 45 minute drive north of Airlie Beach to Hideaway Bay, or allow an hour for the drive from Bowen. It's hidden away well off the highway! There's a single caravan park close to the beach, where dogs are allowed, or visit the spot on a relaxing daytrip.

The off-leash section of the beach officially starts after the rocks at the eastern end of the beach and extends around to the 'island'.

ENJOY A DIP AT CEDAR CREEK FALLS

Away from the beaches, one of the prettiest spots in the Whitsundays is Cedar Creek Falls. While the waterfall usually dries up during winter, the driest time of the year, this scenic spot is still home to a swimming hole year-round. And thanks to being located outside national parks, dogs on a leash are permitted to join you at the falls.

Cedar Creek Falls is about a 25 minute drive south of Airlie Beach, accessed by a winding road starting close to the Bruce Highway turn-off. It's just a short walk from the carpark to the waterhole. You can also explore the area on the other tracks winding through the forest.

VISIT THE BIG MANGO

Just south of Bowen, stop off at the Big Mango – next door to the Bowen Visitor Information Centre – for a classic tropical selfie with your pup!

Don't also miss ducking inside to pick up a tub of delicious mango sorbet to enjoy outside with your pup. There's also a fenced dog park behind the building.

How to get there

Airlie Beach is about a 1100km or 12 hour drive north of Brisbane, with Bowen an hour's drive further north.

When to visit

The Whitsundays are a popular winter escape from the cold weather in southern Australia. Skip visiting during summer, when the weather is hot and rainy, with cyclones a risk and marine stingers a danger at the beaches.

Top: **Coastal view of Hideaway Bay, Whitsundays** Bottom: **Aerial view of Cedar Creek Falls**

 # Dog-friendly parks

 # Dog-friendly dining

Wildlife Estate Park,
Jubilee Pocket

This park near Airlie Beach is home to the only fenced dog park in the region. Just be warned it's quite small, although at least there's a water tap and bowl. Dogs are also allowed on-leash in most of the surrounding park.

Bicentennial Park,
Cannonvale

Dogs are allowed off-leash in the flat grassy area along the centre of this park, with plenty of room for running around.

Fat Frog Beach Cafe,
Cannonvale

Open daily for breakfast, and for lunch on weekends, four-legged guests are treated to their own section of the menu, plus there's plenty of water bowls on hand.

Horseshoe Bay Cafe,
Bowen

While dogs are not allowed on the sand at Horseshoe Bay Beach, you can visit the cafe opposite. With a focus on the plentiful local produce, this cafe is open daily for breakfast and lunch, plus dinner on Tuesday, Friday and Saturday.

Whitsunday Gold Coffee,
Hamilton Plains

Located adjacent to the Whitsundays Visitor Information Centre, dogs are allowed in two designated areas; one is under shelter. Don't miss tasting their own coffee (grown on-site), including frappes for hot days.

Dog-friendly accommodation

BIG4 Whitsundays Tropical Eco Resort, Flametree

Pets are welcome on designated sites at this park. A lush resort surrounded by trees, halfway between Airlie Beach and Shute Harbour, it has a beautiful swimming pool and plenty of activities for kids.

Queens Beach Tourist Village, Bowen

Just a short stroll from the off-leash Queens Beach, this caravan park is highly praised for its big sites and immaculate amenities. Dogs are welcome on sites, plus there's a washing machine for dog blankets.

Coastal Cottage, Cannonvale

This three-bedroom holiday rental allows pets inside and has a fully fenced yard. It's only a short walk from the off-leash beach and dog park in Cannonvale.

Relaxing at BIG4 Whitsundays Tropical Eco Resort

Townsville

Townsville is the largest city in northern Queensland and an important regional hub. While it may not have the big tourist attractions of Cairns to the north, it still has plenty of fun things to do with your dog. Take a walk along the waterfront, hike up the imposing Castle Hill or visit one of the botanic gardens scattered around the city. For a change of pace, take a daytrip with your pup to Magnetic Island, just off the coast, or head inland to former gold-rush towns.

Walking along The Strand

WALK ALONG THE STRAND

The Strand is a beautiful stretch of sand close to the Townsville city centre, running alongside the suburb of North Ward. It's the only patrolled beach in the area, and is home to a rockpool at the northern end.

Not surprisingly, dogs aren't allowed onto the actual beach. However, as long as they stay leashed, they're welcome to stroll with you on the waterfront path through the park behind the beach. When I visited with Schnitzel, there were plenty of trees that provided shade, as well as convenient picnic tables and outdoor cafes scattered along its length.

I recommend detouring onto the short jetty about halfway up The Strand. Just off the jetty is the *Siren* sculpture, part of the Museum of Underwater Art. It's best viewed at sunset when you can view its colour changing to show the current water temperature of a nearby reef, highlighting the effects of climate change on the Great Barrier Reef.

While dogs are not allowed on the beach at The Strand, there are two off-leash beaches nearby. You can head north to Pallarenda Beach where dogs are allowed off-leash between access points 8 and 9. Alternatively, head to the sand adjacent to Benwell Park Road in South Townsville, between Archer and Boundary streets.

 DRIVE OR HIKE UP CASTLE HILL

Townsville is dominated by Castle Hill, the 286m high outcrop that looms above the city centre and The Strand. Don't visit Townsville without heading to the top and taking in the views from its multiple lookouts.

There are two options for getting to the top of Castle Hill: driving up the steep windy road, which isn't suitable for caravans; or hiking up, with a variety of trails to choose from. The most popular hiking trail is the Goat Track, which starts at Hillside Crescent. Allow about an hour for the 1.3km return walk – it includes an astounding 1300 steps! Some walkers make use of the road, but I don't recommend this option if you're walking with a dog.

If you would prefer to drive up, there are still three short walking trails you can follow on the summit: the Summit, Radar Hill and Pill Box walks. Use them to access the different vantage points overlooking different parts of the city below.

Dogs should be on a leash while in Castle Hill Reserve, both at the lookouts and on the walking trails. At the time of my visit, I noticed a sign about rangers carrying out checks for unleashed and unregistered dogs.

 VISIT THE BOTANIC GARDENS

Townsville is home to three botanic gardens scattered around the city, each with its own personality. The largest botanic garden is Anderson Gardens. The smallest is the historic Queens Gardens, which sits close to the road going up Castle Hill and provides beautiful vistas of the peak above.

However, my pick of the gardens is The Palmetum, on the southern side of the city. It's home to a huge collection of palm trees – one of the largest and most diverse in the world. The Palmetum also features a beautiful rainforest section, plus a lagoon surrounded by a savannah zone.

Dogs are allowed in all three botanic gardens, but need to be kept on-leash. Schnitzel particularly loved his walk through the rainforest area of The Palmetum, stopping and sniffing constantly!

Queens Gardens with its view of Castle Hill

EXPLORE THE JEZZINE BARRACKS PRECINCT

On the outcrop at the northern end of The Strand is Kissing Point Fort, built during the early colonial days of Townsville. For many years afterward the surrounding area, known as the Jezzine Barracks, was defence force land. However, since 2009 the precinct has been repurposed for public use, except for the Army Museum in the centre.

While dogs are not allowed inside the museum, they're welcome, on-leash, in the rest of the precinct. Head up to the former Kissing Point Fort, which still features two cannons, plus an interesting map depicting the Battle of the Coral Sea.

Then walk along the Coastal Boardwalk to the start of the Ethno-Botanical Trail, with signs detailing the local bushfoods used by the Wulgurukaba and Bindal peoples of the area, who still call the area Garabarra. There are also some beautiful sculptures to see along the way.

TAKE THE FERRY TO MAGNETIC ISLAND

One of the most popular tourist spots to visit in Townsville lies just off the coastline: Magnetic Island. Reached by a 20 minute ferry crossing, your dog is welcome to join you in visiting the island, whether on a daytrip or overnight – although they are not allowed inside the national park that covers large parts of the island.

There are two options for making the crossing. The Sealink ferry only accepts passengers on foot, while the slower Magnetic Island Ferry also has a car barge. Dogs are permitted on both ferries for free, either on the outside decks or in your car. Make sure you keep your dog leashed while outside your car. On the Sealink ferry dogs need to be either muzzled or in a pet carrier.

On Magnetic Island, dogs are allowed on most beaches outside the national park, as long as they are on a leash. Dog-friendly beaches include Geoffrey Bay and Nelly Bay, both close to the ferry terminal; the popular Horseshoe Bay; Picnic Bay with its jetty; and the remote West Point.

I recommend taking your car so that you can tour all around the island – it's larger than you expect. I skipped taking a car, so only made it as far as Geoffrey Bay and Nelly Bay beaches with Schnitzel. If on foot, the Gabul Way boardwalk to Geoffrey Bay is a beautiful easy walk.

HEAD INLAND TO CHARTERS TOWERS AND RAVENSWOOD

From Townsville, it's less than a 2 hour drive south-west to Charters Towers, one of the most charming cities in all of inland Queensland. Once a gold-rush town, during the late 19th century it was the second largest town in Queensland. These days it's still home to a magnificent collection of well-preserved buildings and remains.

A stroll through the city's streets, known as One Square Mile, is a great opportunity to appreciate how grand this city once was. Don't miss the Stock Exchange Arcade – one of the few arcades in Queensland – plus the historic Post Office, the World Theatre (originally the Australian Bank of Commerce) and the mural on the wall of the Arthur Titley Centre.

For a sensational view looking out over the city, plus plenty of information about its early goldmining days, I recommend heading up Towers Hill. Drive to the top or follow the walking trail from the centre of town or from the carpark at its base. Make sure you stop to visit the World War II bunkers situated about half-way up the hill. Two of them are open to the public. They contain audio and visual presentations that brings the period to life. Leashed dogs are okay to join you.

About an hour's drive from Charters Towers is Ravenswood, where gold was first discovered in the region. While Charters Tower is still thriving, Ravenswood is almost a ghost town, although two pubs remain open. Follow the self-guided trail around town, with plenty of signs about its dusty historic sites, from old goldmining workings to original miners' cottages.

How to get there

Townsville is a long 1350km drive north-west from Brisbane. Alternatively, it's a 350km drive south from Cairns.

When to visit

Head to Townsville during winter, when the weather is mild and sunny, although it can get chilly when you go inland. The city is surprisingly dry for northern Queensland, with rain unlikely, except during summer.

Dog-friendly parks

Murray Paw Park, Annandale

This excellent 'paw park' is fully fenced with double-gated entrances, agility equipment, seats and water, plus convenient parking. There's also a second smaller area recommended for dogs under 8kg, which Schnitzel appreciated.

Rossiter Park Off-Leash Dog Park, Aitkenvale

Another excellent fenced dog park in Townsville, this dog park is located in Rossiter Park along the banks of the Ross River. There are also agility equipment and handy benches under the shady trees.

Schnitzel on Castle Hill

Dog-friendly dining

Dog-friendly accommodation

Juliette's Gelateria,
North Ward

This popular cafe is located next to the beach along The Strand. It's the perfect spot to enjoy an ice-cream or hot drink while walking with your pup. The main Juliette's Cafe nearby, with some more substantial food options, is also dog-friendly.

Tobruk Kiosk,
North Ward

Another delightful spot to stop for a coffee or light meal while walking along The Strand with your pup, this kiosk also offers drinks and treats for four-legged guests.

Absolute Cravings,
Annandale

This cafe at The Palmetum (*see* p. 273) was being renovated during my visit, but it has since re-opened to excellent reviews. Dogs are welcome at the outdoor tables and water bowls are provided.

Shoredrive Motel,
North Ward

This motel is conveniently located right on The Strand, close to Jezzine Barracks. Pet-friendly rooms are offered for a reasonable price.

City Oasis Inn,
Townsville

While this four-star hotel is close to the city centre, it's a lovely oasis thanks to its beautiful grounds and gardens. Select Standard Double Rooms have been designated as pet-friendly and are all on the ground floor.

Saunders Beach Park Rest Area,
Saunders Beach

Townsville has a great system of free camping at selected reserves that can be booked online. Dogs are welcome at most locations, including Saunders Beach, where Schnitzel and I spent two nights. Just beware of the sand flies on still nights, as I discovered from my bites!

Cairns/ Gimuy

The northernmost city in Queensland and the gateway to the Tropical North, Cairns has long been a popular tourist destination thanks to its star attractions of the Great Barrier Reef and the Daintree Rainforest. While your dog will need to stay behind if you take a daytrip to the Reef, there's plenty of other dog-friendly attractions to tick off your bucket list.

Take a stroll along the Cairns waterfront with your pup, or visit the beaches of Palm Cove and Port Douglas further north. Head inland to the markets of Kuranda, and allow plenty of time to visit the Atherton Tablelands. You can even take a Daintree River cruise with your pup!

Walking along the Cairns Esplanade

Schnitzel at Flagstaff Hill in Port Douglas

 WANDER ALONG THE CAIRNS ESPLANADE

A stroll along the Esplanade that runs beside the Cairns waterfront and through tropical parklands is popular with both local and visiting dog-owners. There's a combination of boardwalks and cycle paths along the waterfront, with on-leash dogs permitted, and plenty of cafes and bars nearby.

Just note that the popular lagoon swimming area is off-limits to dogs, as well as the central blocks in the Cairns city centre, bordered by the Esplanade, Aplin Street, McLeod Street and Wharf Street.

 HIT THE BEACHES OF CAIRNS

While the city centre of Cairns is located next to mudflats and mangroves, if you head to the northern suburbs you'll encounter a string of beautiful sandy beaches.

One of the most popular spots with tourists is the resort enclave of Palm Cove. Across the road from its 1km stretch of beach are many high-end hotels and restaurants. I enjoyed walking with Schnitzel along its golden sand. We then returned along the path behind the beach, shaded by palm trees. Just keep your dog leashed, both on the beach and along the path, and avoid the sand near the surf club.

CAIRNS/GIMUY

Left: **The Original Rainforest Markets**
Opposite: **Historic Village Herberton**

Another beautiful beach near Cairns is Trinity Beach, an area quite popular with locals. At Trinity Beach there are off-leash sections at both the northern and southern ends of the beach. I headed to the northern end, which starts just after the playground. The only downside is that this beach is usually quite narrow at high tide.

 DRIVE NORTH TO FOUR MILE BEACH

If it's fun on the beach that you're after, you can't miss visiting the resort town of Port Douglas, a scenic hour-long drive north of Cairns and only 40 minutes from Palm Cove.

Port Douglas is home to the beautiful long expanse of Four Mile Beach, running along the southern side of the town. While dogs are not allowed on the easternmost end of the beach, close to the surf club, dogs are allowed off-leash on its western end, starting at the Four Mile Beach Park.

There's a handy hose for washing down your dog at the Cowie Street access point. Just be aware, sometimes crocodiles are spotted in the area, in which case you should be wary of visiting the beach with your dog.

HEAD UP FLAGSTAFF HILL

While in Port Douglas, an excellent on-leash walk that you can do with your dog is the Flagstaff Hill Walking Trail. This 1.1km path loops around the imposing headland at the northern end of Four Mile Beach, with gorgeous views of the Coral Sea and Low Isles from a number of viewing platforms along the way.

There are steps up to the track from the end of Four Mile Beach, but the easiest starting point is at Rex Smeal Park, where there's plenty of parking. Along the way, don't miss the steep 175m detour up to the lookout at the top of the hill, for more beautiful views looking back along Four Mile Beach.

If you just want to appreciate the views without climbing up the hill, you can also drive up Flagstaff Hill, although the initial incline might be too steep for some caravans.

BROWSE THE MARKETS IN KURANDA

Up in the mountains immediately behind Cairns is the rainforest village of Kuranda. While you won't be able to visit it using the Skyrail or Scenic Railway – which don't allow dogs – it's just a 20 minute scenic drive along the highway from the suburb of Smithfield.

The main street of Kuranda is lined with an eclectic array of shops and cafes, plus there's not one but two markets! Well-behaved, leashed dogs are allowed at both the Original Rainforest Markets and the Heritage Markets.

Note though that dogs aren't allowed on the rainforest walk behind the Original Rainforest Markets, nor in the wildlife attractions. Both markets operate from Wednesday to Sunday, although some extra shops may be open on public holidays.

My pick of the two was the Original Rainforest Markets. It has a strong hippie vibe, lots of clothing and jewellery stores and even a minigolf in the forest. The Petite Cafe Creperie was very busy at the time of my visit and allows dogs at its outdoor tables.

EXPLORE THE ATHERTON TABLELANDS

There's more to the highlands behind Cairns than just Kuranda, with the entire Atherton Tablelands region to explore. The area is particularly dog-friendly, so it's worthwhile staying a few days just on the Tablelands with your dog.

About 30 minutes inland from Kuranda is the agricultural town of Mareeba, home to the majority of coffee plantations in Australia and the nearby dog-friendly Emerald Creek Falls. There are two walking tracks you can follow to the falls: one to the bottom of the falls, while the other ascends to a lookout. Or you can just paddle in the creek near the carpark.

The Atherton Tablelands is home to many museums, some that allow dogs to join you both inside and out. A must-visit destination is the fabulous Historic Village Herberton, a 90 minute drive from Cairns. This museum complex is the largest privately owned historic village in Australia. Home to a collection of over 60 buildings, each one is bursting with memorabilia, from classic cars and carriages to sewing machines and bottles. You'll need a full day to explore everything. Best of all, dogs on a leash are welcome to join you, including inside the buildings and on the weekly steam-train rides!

For a great chance of spotting platypuses, head to the village of Yungaburra. The creek that runs past the town is home to multiple platypuses and there's a good chance of spotting one if you visit early or late in the day. One popular location to spot them is from the Peterson's Creek Walking Track, but I spotted some from the Platypus Viewing Platform on the western edge of town.

Sit or stand behind the wooden fencing at the viewing platform, peering through the gap, while keeping your dog on a leash, and try to spot a platypus down below. I was surprised and delighted to almost immediately spot a platypus at the Viewing Platform, despite not arriving until 9am on a winter's morning.

SPOT CROCS ON THE DAINTREE RIVER

For a different kind of wildlife experience, take your dog onboard a crocodile-spotting cruise on the Daintree River. I was surprised to discover that it's traditional for many of the local boat owners to bring along their dogs, and at least one company, the Daintree River Cruise Centre, offers dog-friendly cruises.

The cruises depart in small boats from the southern bank of the Daintree River – a 90 minute drive north of Cairns, with no need to board the Daintree Ferry across to Cape Tribulation. The cruises operated by the Daintree River Cruise Centre last about 60 to 90 minutes, depending on the weather conditions, with the chance to spot a variety of local birdlife and even snakes, as well as saltwater crocodiles lounging on the banks.

If you're interested in bringing your dog along, it's important that you call the cruise centre and advise them in advance, so that your dog can be accommodated.

GO KAYAKING AT BABINDA

The small town of Babinda to the south of Cairns is best known for the Babinda Boulders, a series of huge granite outcrops along Babinda Creek. Unfortunately pet dogs aren't allowed to visit the boulders or the adjacent swimming hole.

However, just downstream from the Boulders and their rapids, you can join a kayaking adventure with Babinda Kayaking. Refreshingly, adventurous four-legged guests are welcomed to join you, with no size restrictions. There are only a few 'mini' rapids along this stretch!

Kayaking on Babinda Creek

Half- and full-day self-guided kayaking and stand-up paddleboarding trips heading downstream are available. A pick-up service to return to your starting point is included, but if you have a dog, someone will need to remain behind at the finishing point with them, as they don't have the facilities to transport dogs.

How to get there

The main tourist hub of Far North Queensland, Cairns is a 1700km drive north of Brisbane and 350km north of Townsville. Allow at least 3 days or longer if driving along the Bruce Highway from Brisbane, ideally with plenty of stops along the way.

When to visit

It's best to head to Cairns and Far North Queensland during winter, when the weather is milder. During summer the weather is hot and muggy, with a chance of cyclones, and the local beaches are off limits due to marine stingers.

Dog-friendly parks

Dog-friendly dining

Goomboora Park,
Brinsmead

This is one of the most popular dog parks in Cairns; about half of the park allows off-leash dogs. There's also a safe swimming creek underneath the dense trees, with its own dog beach.

Barron Waters/Burrawungal Park,
Caravonica

Head to this fenced dog park on the western edge of Cairns, which has a large off-leash area with a man-made lagoon for safe swimming (although check the signs), plus a separate section for small dogs.

Atherton Dog Park,
Atherton

This fenced dog park near the Chinese Temple is fully fenced, with plenty of shade, water bowls and seats. There was even a collection of tennis racquets and a tennis ball dispenser at the time of my visit with Schnitzel!

Hemingway's Brewery,
Cairns City

Dogs are permitted at the tables out the front, or ask the staff to let you through to the harbourside courtyard. I recommend ordering a tasting paddle, plus there's an extensive food menu.

St Crispin's Cafe,
Port Douglas

Open for breakfast and dinner from Tuesday to Saturday, this picturesque spot overlooks a dam and the greenery of the Mirage Country Club golf course. Dogs are welcome on the verandah, with water and dog treats available.

Palm Cove Tavern,
Palm Cove

Just a few blocks back from the waterfront, this tavern is home to a huge dog-friendly beer garden and relatively cheap drinks. There's even a 'Doggy Dine-In' menu with pet-friendly pub-food options.

Mungalli Creek Dairy,
Manunda

A biodynamic dairy on the Atherton Tablelands that is famous for its cheesecakes. Dogs are welcome to join you at the tables in the garden – I particularly recommend the cheese platters!

Dog-friendly accommodation

Crystalbrook Bailey Residences,
Cairns City

Dogs are welcome in the first-floor rooms of these luxury holiday apartments, each with its own courtyard or balcony. Contact the hotel directly to book a Residential Paws package including food, a water bowl and a special treat for your dog.

Tasman Holiday Parks – Cairns Cool Waters,
Brinsmead

Pets are welcome to stay in selected pet-friendly Daintree and Reef cabins, as well as on pet-friendly sites. There's a Rainforest Creek Walk on-site, plus it's close to Goomboora Park (*see* p. 284).

NRMA Palm Cove Holiday Park,
Palm Cove

Camp opposite the beach, with up to two pets permitted on selected powered and unpowered sites. Make sure you book directly and request permission for your pets.

Top: **Four Mile Beach at Port Douglas**
Bottom: **Mungalli Creek Dairy**

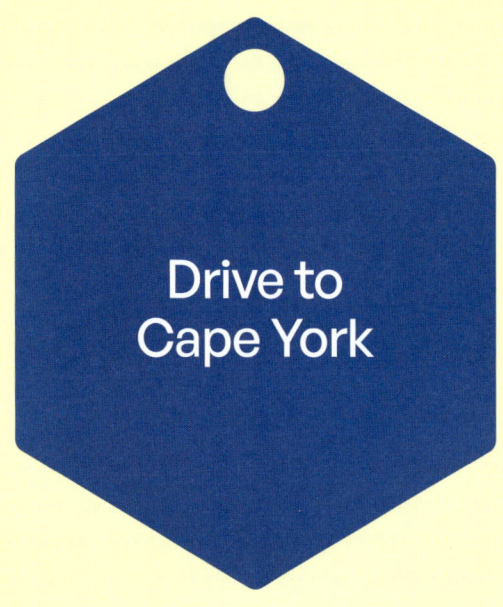

Drive to Cape York

Driving to the tip of Cape York is a bucket-list item for many Australians visiting Queensland. Luckily, there's no need to leave your pup behind because they can join you on the journey and for the final photo stop at the tip of Cape York – the most northerly point on mainland Australia.

Naturally there are some restrictions around where dogs can and can't go on Cape York, so plan your journey in advance and check the rules. In particular, you'll need to skip visiting the national parks in the area, plus make arrangements for dog-sitting if you want to take a boat across to Thursday Island. However, many of the other campgrounds allow dogs.

The tip of the Cape is just over 1000km north of Cairns. However, most of the road is unsealed and can be in a terrible condition, so allow plenty of time for your journey. The return trip generally takes one to two weeks, and shouldn't be attempted before late April, due to roads being uncrossable during the wet season. Make sure you're prepared for the remote areas you'll be travelling through; this includes packing first-aid supplies for your dog.

A 4WD vehicle with low range and high clearance is essential for the trek to Cape York. If you've only got a 2WD vehicle or even an AWD, you can travel only as far north as Cooktown, along the recently sealed highway.

The tropical outpost of Cooktown is a charming spot to spend a few days with your dog, and is surprisingly dog-friendly – I didn't spot a single sign prohibiting dogs when I visited with Schnitzel. Named after Captain James Cook (although he was only Lieutenant when he was there), who spent seven weeks in the area after running his ship aground on the Great Barrier, there are many impressive spots along the riverfront area. Don't miss the Reconciliation Rocks Precinct and Milbi Wall, both exploring the Guugu Yimithirr People's heritage.

My favourite spot around Cooktown was the Cooktown Botanic Gardens – one of the oldest in Queensland and a gorgeous spot to visit. Leashed dogs are welcome, including at the on-site cafe. Nearby you can visit the beautiful beach of Finch Bay, although stay well away from the water's edge due to the risk of crocodiles.

Another popular spot is Grassy Hill and the historic lighthouse on top, offering great views of the surrounding hills and sea. Or go for a drive along the sealed road to Isabella Falls – 30 minutes drive north and one of the safest swimming spots around, for both humans and dogs.

Instead of driving along the highway to Cooktown, which detours a long way inland, it's possible to drive up along the coast and the Bloomfield Track, if you have a 4WD. The 30km long 4WD track starts on the northern edge of the popular Daintree region. Despite being largely national park, it's still possible to visit the Daintree with a dog.

The Daintree is home to some pockets of private and council-owned land, including the beautiful off-leash Cow Bay Beach and Thornton Beach. Take your time driving through the region; there's plenty of speed bumps to protect the local cassowaries – keep your eyes open! At the southern end, there's a paid ferry crossing over the Daintree River – just stay in your vehicle with your dog.

The waterfront in Cooktown

07

Tasmania/
Lutruwita

Hobart/Nipaluna	290
Launceston	296
Relax at the larapuna/Bay of Fires	302

Hobart/ Nipaluna

The second oldest city in Australia, Hobart enjoys an enviable natural location, situated on the banks of the Derwent River, at the base of the towering kunanyi/ Mt Wellington. There's plenty to explore in Hobart with your dog, from the historic precinct of Battery Point to the city's many dog-friendly beaches and walks.

Hobart is also an ideal base for daytrips across southern Tasmania, with a surprising number of attractions in the region allowing dogs to join you.

Walking along Hobart's waterfront

📍 EXPLORE BATTERY POINT

One of the areas of Hobart that you can't miss visiting is the suburb of Battery Point. This precinct home to many colonial buildings and cottages. It's a delightful area to stroll through with your pup.

Battery Point is located immediately south of the city's centre. Head up the hill to Arthurs Circus, one of the most picturesque spots in Battery Point. Many beautiful old homes line the outside of this unusual circular street.

While exploring the area, I recommend dropping in to Jackman & McRoss Bakery. Renowned for its scallop pies, it also offers a range of delectable baked goods in the display case. Grab one of the tables out the front, where dogs are welcome to join you, or order takeaway and enjoy your food in a nearby park.

At the northern edge of Battery Point is Salamanca Place, home to the long-running Salamanca Market. One of the most popular attractions in Tasmania, the market takes place every Saturday, from 8.30am to 3pm, with a wide variety of locally made products and produce for sale.

While dogs are usually permitted along Salamanca Place and at Salamanca Square, where the market takes place, they are prohibited from the area when the market is open. Instead, when visiting the market head to the RSPCA Tasmania tent to book your dog into the 'puppy parking' in return for a donation.

📍 VENTURE UP KUNANYI/ MT WELLINGTON

Rising high behind Hobart is kunanyi/ Mt Wellington. It's a great spot to visit for stunning views over Hobart and the Derwent Estuary – although double-check to make sure the summit isn't shrouded in fog before driving up if you want to enjoy the vista!

It's about a 30 minute drive from the centre of Hobart up to the Pinnacle, the summit area on kunanyi/Mt Wellington. Dogs are technically allowed to visit the Pinnacle, but only if they are confined to a vehicle.

kunanyi/Mt Wellington is also a popular spot for hiking. Dogs on a leash are allowed on selected tracks in the Recreation Zone of Wellington Park, plus on the Radfords Track and the Pipeline Track between Fern Tree and Neika. Maps and brochures clearly indicate where dogs are and aren't allowed.

A popular dog-friendly walk just outside Wellington Park is the section of the Pipeline Track that continues to Waterworks Reserve. Starting at Fern Tree, hike with your dog to the turn-around point at the dry Gentle Annie Falls. It's a 3.1km return walk, with interpretive panels along the route highlighting historical features.

If visiting Hobart during the cooler months, snowfalls on top of the 1200m high mountain are not uncommon (and can in fact occur any time of year!). It's one of the easiest places to see snow with your dog in Tasmania.

🐾 HEAD TO KINGSTON DOG BEACH

Hobart is home to multiple dog-friendly beaches. One of the most popular options is Kingston Dog Beach, about a 15 minute drive south of the city centre. Dogs are allowed off-leash on the sand at the northern end of Kingston Beach, north of the river entrance.

The northern end of Kingston Beach is also the start of the dog-friendly Alum Cliffs Track. This coastal walk follows the cliff-tops to the

The historic Richmond Bridge

Shot Tower, an impressive 60m tall tower previously used to create shot for muskets. Dogs on a leash are allowed along the entire length of the walk. Return along the same path, which is 4km long one-way.

Another off-leash dog beach around Hobart is Short Beach at Sandy Bay, where dogs are allowed off-leash on the beach and in the adjacent Errol Flynn Reserve all day long.

Alternatively, head further south to Nutgrove Beach. Note however that dogs are only allowed off-leash before 10am and after 6pm during daylight savings time (October to March), or after 3pm the rest of the year. During the rest of the day they need to stay on-leash.

TAKE A DAYTRIP TO PORT ARTHUR

One of the most popular attractions in Tasmania is Port Arthur, a former convict settlement on the Tasman Peninsula that has been World Heritage listed. While it's ideal to stay overnight in the area to fully explore the site, it's also possible to visit Port Arthur on a daytrip from Hobart.

It's about an 80 minute drive from the centre of Hobart to Port Arthur, less if you are staying on the eastern side of Hobart near the airport. Make sure you depart early in the morning to allow plenty of time to explore the extensive site.

I was quite surprised to learn that dogs are allowed at Port Arthur, as many similar attractions of this importance in Australia don't permit dogs. Inside the visitor centre – where dogs are not allowed – ask a staff member to direct you to the special entrance to use with your dog. Note that dogs are not permitted on the harbour cruise (also best skipped if you are short on time) or in the house museums.

The majority of the buildings at the site are atmospheric open-air ruins, including the barracks and church, and you can explore them with your dog. Naturally, keep your dog on a leash and always pick up after them.

On your way to Port Arthur, a popular spot to stop is the Cubed Espresso Bar, located on Eaglehawk Neck, about 20 minutes before you arrive at Port Arthur. The coffee from this van is highly rated, and with only outdoor seating it's definitely dog-friendly.

I also recommend stopping at the Tessellated Pavement, near Eaglehawk Neck. Just a few hundred metres off the highway, this platform of fragmented rocks is an interesting sight to see, both from up above at the lookout and down upon the platform; dogs are allowed on-leash at both.

VISIT HISTORIC RICHMOND

Another spot to visit close to Hobart is the charming town of Richmond. Just a 30 minute drive north of Hobart in the Coal River region, many of the buildings in this town were established in the 1820s and '30s.

A highlight of a visit to Richmond is viewing the sandstone Richmond Bridge, the oldest stone span bridge in Australia. Also take a walk through the streets of the town where many Georgian-era buildings that were built by convicts still stand, including the Richmond Gaol and the Richmond Court House.

About a 15 minute drive further north of Richmond is one of the most dog-friendly cellar doors in Tasmania. At Wobbly Boot Winery dogs are allowed inside, plus there are three off-leash areas and complimentary treats provided. Double-check the latest opening hours before visiting – at times it's only open by appointment.

STEP OUT ONTO THE TAHUNE AIRWALK

To get a sense of Tasmania's beautiful untouched wilderness, head to Tahune Adventures, about a 90 minute drive south of Hobart and ideal for a daytrip.

The highlight of a visit to Tahune Adventures is venturing out on the Tahune Airwalk. You walk out on an elevated walkway about 30m above the forest floor, before stepping onto the cantilevered section, about 50m high. Surrounded by forest, slowly regenerating after bushfires in 2019, you'll be able to glimpse the peaks in the nearby World Heritage area.

Best of all, leashed dogs can join you on the Tahune Airwalk. They are also welcome to join you on the two other walks included in your ticket: the short Huon Pine Walk and the longer Swinging Bridges Walk. Just keep your dog on a leash. At the on-site cafe, dogs can also join you at the outdoor seats, with water bowls provided.

On your return trip to Hobart, stop off at Willie Smith's Apple Shed, just north of Huonville. Open daily, order from the menu that focuses on local produce, or just sample the award-winning Tasmanian cider. Dogs are welcome at the outdoor tables.

When to visit

Hobart is at its best during summer, when the days are long and the temperatures mild. During winter, snow is possible on kunanyi/ Mt Wellington.

HOBART/NIPALUNA   293

 ## Dog-friendly parks

 ## Dog-friendly dining

John Turnball Oval,
Lenah Valley

One of the best dog parks in Hobart, this fully fenced dog park has a separate area for small dogs, as well as agility equipment, a water fountain, lighting and bins.

Knocklofty Reserve,
West Hobart

Not your typical dog park, this bushland reserve permits off-leash dogs on many of its tracks and trails, between 6am and 8pm during daylight savings time (October to March), between 7am and 5pm the rest of the year. Check the signs on-site for more details.

Room for a Pony,
North Hobart

This cafe is open daily for breakfast, lunch and dinner. There's a large dog-friendly outdoor area with gas heaters – essential for chilly days and evenings in Tasmania.

Preachers,
Hobart

Just up the hill from Salamanca Place, this trendy bar is open until late seven days a week. The beer garden out the back is popular with dog owners, offering a rotating range of craft beers on tap and meal specials on selected days.

The Salty Dog Hotel,
Kingston Beach

Not far from the popular Kingston Dog Beach (*see* p. 291), this classic family-friendly pub is open daily for lunch and dinner. Dogs are welcome in the outdoor area.

Jackman & McRoss Bakery in Battery Point

Dog-friendly accommodation

Discovery Parks – Hobart,
Risdon Vale

The closest caravan park to the centre of Hobart. Pets are allowed on powered sites, plus in selected budget cabins that are ideal for families and include a bathroom and full kitchen.

Hobart Showground Motorhome Park,
Glenorchy

At Tasmania's largest campground, there's a range of sites available, with all types of pets welcome, as long as they stay on a leash.

Cedar Cottages,
Blackmans Bay

Choose from five pet-friendly cottages of varying size, some with their own yard. The cottages are a 15 minute drive south of Hobart, near Kingston Dog Beach (*see* p. 291).

Top: **Revamped bus turned into indoor bar seating** Bottom: **Port Arthur**

Launceston

Just like Hobart, Launceston is also situated on the banks of one of Tasmania's major rivers, this time the Tamar River in the state's north. But it's just a short drive out of the city to the surrounding countryside, home to vineyards, fruit orchards and fields of lavender, with many attractions welcoming dogs to join you on a visit.

Murals in Sheffield

TOUR LAUNCESTON'S HISTORICAL BUILDINGS

As the third oldest European settlement in Australia, Launceston is home to many significant buildings. In particular, the prosperity of the late 19th century resulted in the construction of many fine Victorian-era buildings.

Some of the finest historic buildings in Launceston can be found along Cameron Street, including the Crown Mill and the Launceston Post Office and its clock tower. One of the best ways to appreciate the architecture is by taking a self-guided walk with your dog.

The Launceston Historical Society has developed multiple audio-guided walks that you can follow. 'A Walk along Historic Cameron Street' is a 2km long walk, while the shorter 1km long 'Launceston City Walk' focuses on the city blocks to the south. Both can be followed by downloading the Cya On the Road app on your phone.

CRUISE THROUGH CATARACT GORGE

One of the top tourist attractions in Launceston is Cataract Gorge, thanks to its natural beauty, walking tracks and picturesque riverside swimming pool. However, the reserve is strictly off limits to dogs.

There is one workaround though – you can take a cruise through the gorge with your dog! Dogs of all sizes are permitted on the Cataract Gorge Adventure Cruise, operated by Tamar River Cruises. Departing multiple times per day, year-round, the cruise operates on the *Lady Launceston*, a replica steamboat.

A short cruise lasting just 50 minutes, it's the perfect amount of time to appreciate the natural wonders of the lower reaches of the gorge and the history of Launceston's Seaport, with your leashed pup at your side.

TASTE TASMANIAN SPARKLING WINE

Launceston is the gateway to the Tamar Valley, one of the main wine-growing regions of Tasmania. In particular, the region is well known for producing fine Tasmanian sparkling wines, and you should not pass up the chance to enjoy a tasting at one of the local cellar doors open to the public.

One of my favourite cellar doors in the region is Jansz, located in Pipers Brook, about a 45 minute drive from the centre of Launceston. This winery pioneered the use of the traditional Methode Champenoise in the region and is renowned for its sparkling wines.

Dogs are permitted outside at the cellar door. Make an advance booking for a curated tasting of the wines, perhaps accompanied by a Tasmanian cheese plate, and inquire about options for visiting with your pup.

PICK YOUR OWN BERRIES

Sparkling wine isn't the only fine treat to enjoy while visiting the Tamar Valley region around Launceston. The area is also dotted with a variety of farm-door outlets, from cheese factories to nut orchards. One of my favourites is the Hillwood Berries Farmgate, just over a 20 minute drive from the centre of Launceston.

While dogs are not permitted to join you in the rows of berries while you pick your own, they are allowed on the rest of the property, including the outdoor tables at the adjoining cafe.

If there are two of you, take turns filling up a punnet with luscious strawberries, blueberries, raspberries or blackberries.

Generally, pick-your-own operates from November to April. Or perhaps just enjoy the farm produce and delicious desserts on offer at the cafe. Fresh berries taste so much better!

SNIFF FIELDS OF LAVENDER

Just as summer is the best time of year to visit Launceston and pick your own berries, the height of summer is also the best time of year to visit Bridestowe Lavender Estate. This famous lavender farm is about a 45 minute drive north-east of Launceston, with peak flowering season between December and January.

If visiting during the flowering period when the fields are bursting with purple lavender, there is an admission charge to enter, although kids and dogs enter for free. Make sure you keep your dog on a leash and pick up after them, so they continue to be allowed in the fields.

During the rest of the year, you can still visit the shop and cafe, which specialises in lavender-infused products. My pick is the vividly coloured lavender ice-cream!

RIDE ON THE DON RIVER RAILWAY

To enjoy a ride on a historic train with your dog in Tasmania, visit the Don River Railway. Located in Don on the western side of Devonport, it's a 75 minute drive from Launceston and an easy daytrip with your dog.

Multiple train rides operate on Thursday to Sunday each week, starting from the museum which is open daily. A variety of trains is used, including heritage carriages hauled by a steam locomotive or a vintage diesel locomotive.

The train ride along the Melrose line between Don Village and Cole Beach lasts about 30 minutes. Entry to the museum and site is included with train ride tickets, or it's possible to just buy a ticket to explore the museum and site. Best of all, dogs ride for free, plus they are allowed in the museum. Just keep them leashed and clean up after them.

VIEW THE SHEFFIELD MURALS

Another great daytrip from Launceston is to the country town of Sheffield, about an hour's drive west. This town is famous for the many murals painted on its buildings, although it's also home to some great country-style cafes.

The first mural in Sheffield was painted in 1986. These days there are over 200 murals on walls around the town and the surrounding area. To locate them all, check out the map put together by the local visitor centre or hire a 45 minute audio tour from the centre.

Naturally, it's fine to wander around the streets admiring the murals with your pup by your side. Don't miss spotting the cute dogs in some of the murals!

How to get there

Launceston is a 200km drive north of Hobart. Allow up to 3 hours for the drive.

When to visit

Launceston and northern Tasmania are most popular with visitors during summer, when the temperatures are warm.

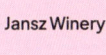
Jansz Winery

Cataract Gorge

 **Dog-friendly parks**

 **Dog-friendly dining**

Hardwicke Street Reserve,
Summerhill

This off-leash dog park is popular with locals because it is large, yet fully enclosed. Choose between the fenced open field or the bushland area with walking tracks.

Waverley Lake Park,
Waverley

Dogs are allowed off-leash in the southern area of this park. It's also a great spot for pups to enjoy a leashed walk around the lake on the walking path, followed by a paddle in the lake.

Cafe Mondello,
Launceston

Dogs are warmly welcome at this cafe in the centre of Launceston. Open daily for breakfast and lunch, with a focus on fresh, local ingredients. And there are warm blankets and heaters on offer in the cooler months.

Maple Cafe,
East Launceston

Open daily for breakfast and lunch, this family-friendly cafe has an outdoor area where dogs are welcome, plus a playground that's popular with two-legged kids.

Dog-friendly accommodation

Stillwater Seven,
Launceston

Enjoy a luxury stay at the private suites of Stillwater Seven, adjacent to the hatted Stillwater Restaurant. Make a booking for Suite 7 – with its private courtyard, pets are welcome to stay with you.

Discovery Parks,
Hadspen

One of the most pet-friendly caravan parks around Launceston. Dogs are welcome on sites as well as in selected budget cabins that can accommodate up to four people. Each cabin has its own kitchenette and ensuite.

Old Mac's Farm Stay,
Norwood

A great option for self-contained caravans and motorhomes, this farmstay just outside Launceston is open seasonally during the warmer months.

Top and opposite:
Bridestowe Lavender Estate and lavender ice-cream

Relax at larapuna/ Bay of Fires

Tasmania is renowned for its rugged landscapes and stunning natural beauty, much of it World Heritage listed. While many natural highlights such as Cradle Mountain and Wineglass Bay are located inside national parks and are off limits to dogs, a beautiful spot you can visit with your dog is the Bay of Fires, often named one of the top beach spots in the state.

More than just one bay, this area of coastline is largely contained in the Bay of Fires Conservation Area, with dogs on a leash allowed in most areas. It stretches for 50km along the north-eastern Tasmanian coastline, between Binalong Bay in the south and Ansons Bay in the north. (Skip heading further north into Mount William National Park with your dog.)

A short drive north of the town of St Helens and less than a 3 hour drive from the city of Launceston, the area is deserving of a longer stay. There are multiple free campgrounds within the conservation area, mainly in the southern end. Dogs are allowed in nearly all of them, except the Jeanneret Beach Campground. Given the campgrounds are free, facilities are basic, although most have either hybrid or pit toilets.

The bay was named for the fires of First Nations People that were spotted on the shore by early explorers. These days it's renowned for its beautiful beaches, crystal-clear blue water and striking orange lichen–covered boulders that glow like fire. Spending some time paddling at the beaches and walking along them is a must. Fishing, kayaking and snorkelling are also popular, or just lazing and taking in the scenery with your dog at your side.

Dogs are allowed on-leash at many of the beaches in the southern half of the conservation area. The main exception is the small beach next to the Jeanneret Beach Campground, where dogs are prohibited. Additionally, dogs are prohibited from Binalong Bay Beach and Taylors Beach between October and March, although they are allowed on-leash on these beaches during winter. North of The Gardens, dogs are prohibited from the beaches. Always double-check the signs.

If camping with a dog during summer, try to stay at one of the campgrounds adjacent to a beach where dogs are allowed on the sand. The top picks are Cosy Corner South, Cosy Corner North and Swimcart Beach campgrounds. Alternatively, if you camp at Policemans Point, dogs are allowed on the southern shore of the Ansons Bay river mouth.

Sparkling clear water at Bay of Fires

Index

90 Mile Beach Vic. 91, 95
90 Mile Straight WA 161

Abrahams Bosom Reserve, Currarong NSW 20
Adelaide/Tarndanya SA 130–5
Adelaide beaches SA 131
Adelaide Hills hiking SA 133
Adelaide Hills wine region SA 131
Agnes Falls Scenic Reserve Vic. 92
Agnes Waters Qld 256–7
Airlie Beach Qld 266, 267, 268
Aitkenvale Qld 276
Alawa NT 212
Albany/Kinjarling WA 178–83
Albany Heritage Park WA 179, 180
Albany historic precinct WA 179
Alexandria NSW 8
Alfred Nicholas Gardens, Sherbrooke Vic. 106–7
Alice Springs NT 218–19, 220
Alpine National Park Vic. 88
Altona Dog Beach Vic. 72
Alum Cliffs Track, Kingston Beach Tas. 292
Amiens Qld 243
Anderson Gardens, Townsville Qld 273
Annandale Qld 276, 277
Anniebrook WA 189
Ansons Bay Tas. 302, 303
ANZAC Hill, Alice Springs NT 218
Apollo Bay Vic. 123, 127
Arakwal National Park NSW 51
Arkaba Lookout, Flinders Ranges SA 155
Arno Bay Estuary Boardwalk SA 151
Ashfield Flats, Bassendean WA 167

Aslings Beach, Eden NSW 24, 26
Atherton Qld 284
Atherton Tablelands Qld 281–2
Augusta WA 186, 187
Austinmer NSW 14, 16
Autumn Festival, Macedon Vic. 111, 113
Avoca Beach NSW 31, 34
Ayers Rock Campground, Yulara NT 217, 219

Babbage Island WA 196
Babinda Boulders Qld 282
Babinda kayaking Qld 282–3
Badger Creek Vic. 109
Balcombe Estuary Boardwalk, Mount Martha Vic. 101
Bald Hill, Stanwell Tops NSW 13
Balhannah Dog Park SA 132–3
Balladonia Roadhouse WA 161
Ballarat Vic. 118, 119, 120, 121
Ballarat Botanic Gardens Vic. 118–19
Bambra Vic. 127
Banana Well Getaway, Dampier Peninsula WA 201
Bangalee Qld 259
Bangalow NSW 52, 54
Barangaroo Reserve NSW 3
Barossa Valley wine region SA 131, 132
Bassendean WA 167
Batemans Bay NSW 24, 27
Bathurst NSW 59
Battery Point Tas. 291
Bay of Fires Tas. 302–3
Bay of Martyrs, Great Ocean Road Vic. 125
Bayswater WA 168

Bayview Dog Beach NSW 5
Beauchamp Falls Reserve, Otway Forest Park Vic. 123–4
Beaumont NSW 17
Beechworth Vic. 82, 85, 86, 87
Beechworth Historic Park Vic. 82–3
Belair National Park SA 133
Belconnen ACT 65
Belgrave Vic. 106
Bellingen NSW 47, 48
Belongil Beach, Byron Bay NSW 51
Bendalong NSW 24
Bendigo Vic. 117, 119, 121
Bennett Springs WA 168
Benowa Qld 234
Bermagui NSW 28
Berri SA 144, 145, 146, 147, 148
Berrima NSW 5–6
Berry NSW 14–15
Berry Springs NT 211
Best Friend Holiday Retreat, Tarra Valley Vic. 91
Betts Beach, Murray River Vic. 79
Bicentennial Park, Darwin NT 211
Bicentennial Way, Airlie Beach Qld 267
Big Banana, Coffs Harbour NSW 44
Big Bend Lookout, Murray River SA 145
Bignalls Beach NSW 33
Bill's Bay, Coral Bay WA 193
Binalong Bay Tas. 302
Binalong Bay Beach Tas. 302
Birubi Beach NSW 33
Blackall Range Tourist Drive Qld 253
Blacksmiths NSW 35
Blacksmiths Beach NSW 31
Blanchetown SA 142, 145

Blinman SA 155
Bloomfield Track Qld 287
Blue Gum Hills Regional Park, Minmi NSW 32–3
Blue Haven Beach WA 171
Blue Lake, Mount Gambier SA 137
Blue Mountains NSW 10–11
Blue Mountains National Park NSW 10
Boambee Beach, Coffs Harbour NSW 46
Bombo Beach, Kiama NSW 14, 16
Bondi to Coogee Coastal Walk NSW 3–4
Boranup Forest WA 187
Bowen Qld 266, 267–8, 270, 271
Bowen beaches Qld 267–8
Braddon ACT 67
Braitling NT 220
Breakaways, the, Coober Pedy SA 157
Briars Community Forest, Mount Martha Vic. 100
Bribie Island Qld 226–7
Bridestowe Lavender Farm Tas. 298
Bridge to Bridge Walk, Lake Burley Griffin, Canberra ACT 64
Bright Vic. 83, 84, 85, 86, 87, 88
Bright Brewery Vic. 84–5
Brighton Beach bathing boxes Vic. 71–2
Brighton Dog Beach Vic. 72
Brinsmead Qld 284, 285
Brisbane/Meanjin Qld 224–31
Brisbane River ferries Qld 225–6
Broadbeach Qld 236
Bronte Beach NSW 4
Broome WA 197–203
Brownhill Creek Recreation Park SA 133
Brunswick Heads NSW 55
Bullara Station WA 194
Bunda Cliffs SA 161
Bundegi Beach WA 193
Bundy Creek Beach WA 171
Burleigh Heads Qld 234
Burra SA 156, 158
Burrows Park, Clovelly NSW 4

Byfield National Park Qld 259
Byron Bay NSW 50–5
Byron Bay Hinterland NSW 52

Cable Beach WA 198–9, 203
Cactus Country, Strathmerton Vic. 79
Caiguna Blowhole WA 161
Caiguna Roadhouse WA 161
Cairns Qld 278–85
Cairns beaches 279–80
Cairns Esplanade Qld 279
Callala Beach NSW 19
Callan Point Beach, Rozelle NSW 4–5
Caloundra Qld 250, 253
Camden NSW 9
Canberra/Ngambri/Ngunnawal ACT 63–7
Cannonvale Qld 267, 270, 271
Cannonvale Beach Qld 267
Canyon Walk, Bright Vic. 83
Cape Edgecumbe Walking Track Qld 267
Cape Le Grand National Park WA 170
Cape Range National Park WA 193
Cape York Qld 286–7
Capertree NSW 61
Capricorn Coast Qld 258–63
Capricorn Coast beaches 259
Caravonica Qld 284
Cardigan Vic. 121
Carnarvon WA 195, 196
Carnival of Flowers, Toowoomba Qld 245–6
Carrington NSW 34
Castaways Beach Qld 252
Castle Hill, Townsville Qld 273
Castlemaine Vic. 118
Castletown WA 173, 174, 175
Casuarina Coastal Reserve, Darwin NT 210
Cataract Gorge, Launceston Tas. 297
Cedar Creek Falls Qld 268
Ceduna SA 152, 153, 160
Central Australia NT 216–21

Central Coast NSW 30–5
Central Deborah Goldmine, Bendigo Vic. 117
Central Springs Reserve, Daylesford Vic. 110
Central Tilba NSW 26–7
Central West NSW 56–61
Charters Towers Qld 275
Cherry Walk, Bright Vic. 83
Chinamans Beach, Agnes Water Qld 256
Chinatown, Broome WA 200
Christies Beach, Murray River Vic. 79
Ciccone NT 220
City Botanic Gardens, Brisbane Qld 225
Cleveland Qld 228
Clog Barn, Coffs Harbour NSW 46
Clontarf Qld 230
Coal River wine region Tas. 293–4
Coastal Boardwalk, Townsville Qld 274
Cockle Train, Goolwa SA 133
Coffin Bay SA 150, 151, 153
Coffin Bay National Park SA 150
Coffs Harbour NSW 43–9
Colbinabbin Vic. 78
Coldstream Vic. 108
Comaum SA 141
Coniston Beach, Wollongong NSW 14
Coober Pedy SA 156–7, 158
Coochiemudlo Island Qld 227–8
Cooee Bay Beach Qld 259
Cooktown Qld 286
Cooktown Botanic Gardens Qld 286–7
Coolalinga NT 213
Coolangatta Qld 237
Coolum Beach Qld 251, 255
Coonawarra wine region SA 137–8
Copacabana Beach NSW 31
Coral Bay WA 193, 195, 196
Corin Forest snow play area ACT 65
Corindi/Pipeclay Beach, Coffs Harbour NSW 46

Cosy Corner North campground, Bay of Fires Tas. 303
Cosy Corner South campground, Bay of Fires Tas. 303
Courthouse Markets, Broome WA 200
Cow Bay Beach Qld 287
Cowaramup WA 186–7, 188
Cowell SA 152
Cowes Vic. 95
Cowra Japanese Garden NSW 58
Crib Point Vic. 103
Croudace Bay Dog Park, Lake Macquarie NSW 31
Culburra NSW 19, 22
Cupitt's Estate, Ulladulla NSW 25
Currarong NSW 19, 20

Daintree region Qld 282, 287
Daintree River crocodiles Qld 282
Dalveen Qld 243
Daly Waters NT 214–15
Daly Waters Pub NT 214, 215
Dampier Peninsula WA 201
Dandenong Ranges Vic. 104–9
Darkum Beach, Coffs Harbour NSW 46
Darwin/Garramilla NT 208–13
Darwin's World War II history NT 211
Dawes Point NSW 9
Daylesford Vic. 110–15
Daylesford mineral springs Vic. 110
Daylesford Sunday Market Vic. 113
Deadmans Beach, North Stradbroke Island Qld 228
Delicate Campground, Goolawah Regional Park NSW 41
Denham WA 191
Denmark WA 180–1
Devonport Tas. 298
Diddams Close, Belconnen ACT 65
Dinner Plain alpine resort Vic. 88–9
dinosaur footprints, Gantheaume Point WA 199
Djugun WA 203
dolphin-watching cruise, Jervis Bay NSW 19

Don River Railway, Devonport Tas. 298
Donvale Vic. 74
Dubbo NSW 58–9, 61
Dulong Lookout, Burnside Qld 252–3
Dunsborough WA 186, 187
Dunwich Qld 228
Durras Main Beach, Batemans Bay NSW 24
Dwellingup WA 167

Eagle Bay WA 186
Eaglehawk Neck Tas. 293
East Corrimal Beach NSW 14
East Launceston Tas. 300
East Perth WA 168
Echo Point Lookout, Blue Mountains NSW 10
Echuca Vic. 76–80
Echuca paddlesteamer cruise Vic. 77
Echuca wine region Vic. 77–8
Eden NSW 24, 26, 27
Elanora Qld 236
Elder Range Lookout, Flinders Ranges SA 155
Eleven Mile Beach WA 171
Elliston SA 150, 151
Emerald Vic. 106, 108
Emerald Beach NSW 49
Emerald Creek Falls, Mareeba Qld 282
Emu Park Qld 259, 260–1
Emu Point WA 180, 182, 183
Esperance WA 170–5
Esperance beaches WA 171
Esperance Foreshore WA 173
Etmilyn WA 167
Eucla WA 161
Eumundi Markets Qld 253
Eveleigh NSW 8
Ewing Lookout, Yulara NT 217
Exmouth WA 193, 194, 195, 196
Exmouth breweries WA 194
Eyre Peninsula SA 149–53
Eyre Peninsula beaches SA 150–1

Fannie Bay NT 212
Farm, The, at Ewingsdale, Byron Bay NSW 51–2
Farm Beach SA 150
Farnborough Beach, Bangalee Qld 259
Finch Bay Qld 287
Fisheries Beach, Albany WA 180
Fishermans Beach, Emu Park Qld 259
Fishermans Beach, Great Keppell Island Qld 264
Fitzgerald Bay SA 151
Five Finger Reef, Coral Bay WA 193
Flagstaff Hill Walking Trail, Port Douglas 280–1
Flametree Qld 271
Flinders Beach, North Stradbroke Island Qld 228
Flinders Ranges region SA 155
Floriade Festival, Canberra ACT 65
Forest Glade Gardens, Mount Macedon Vic. 111–12
Four Mile Beach Qld 280, 281
Fourth Beach WA 171
Frankston Vic. 99
Fremantle WA 164, 165–6, 168
Frenchman Bay Beach WA 180
Frenchman Bay beaches WA 180
Fruit Loop Drive Trail, Carnarvon WA 195
Fyshwick ACT 66

Gambanan Wilderness Retreat, Dampier Peninsula WA 201
Gantheaume Point WA 199
Gap, The, Alice Springs NT 221
Gembrook Vic. 106
Geoffrey Bay Qld 275
Geographe Bay WA 186
George Bass Coastal Walk Vic. 92
George Brown Darwin Botanic Gardens, Darwin NT 209, 212
Gerringong NSW 17
Gidgegannup WA 166
Gippsland Vic. 90–5
Gippsland Lakes cruises Vic. 92–3
Girraween National Park Qld 239

Glass House Mountains Qld 252–3
Glebe Foreshore NSW 3
Glen Helen NT 218
Glenelg Beach SA 131
Glenorchy Tas. 295
Glenvale Qld 249
Gnarloo Station WA 195
Gold Coast Qld 232–7
Gold Coast craft breweries 234
Gold Coast Regional Botanic Gardens, Benowa Qld 234
Golden Beach Vic. 95
Goldfields Vic. 116–21
Goode Beach WA 180
Googong ACT 66
Goolwa SA 133
Gordon ACT 65
Gosford NSW 31–2, 33
Gracetown Dog Beach WA 186
Grand Bendigo tour Vic. 117
Granite Belt Qld 238–43
Granite Belt wine region Qld 239
Grassy Hill, Cooktown Qld 287
Grays Bay Beach, Bowen Qld 267
Great Keppel Island/Wop-pa Qld 264–5
Great Ocean Drive, Esperance WA 171, 172, 173
Great Ocean Road Vic. 122–7
Great Ocean Road beaches Vic. 123
Great Ocean Walk, Esperance WA 171
Great Otway National Park Vic. 124
Great Southern wine region WA 180–1
Great Stupa of Universal Compassion, Bendigo Vic. 119
Greenly Beach SA 150
Greenwell Point NSW 22
Guildford WA 166
Gunghalin ACT 65
Gympie Qld 253

Hadspen Tas. 301
Hahndorf SA 132
Hamilton Qld 230, 231
Hamilton Plains Qld 270
Hams Beach, Caves Beach NSW 31

Hanging Rock Vic. 113
Harewood Forest, Denmark WA 181
Harlaxton Qld 248
Hawker SA 155, 157, 158
Hawker Beach, Mount Martha Vic. 101
Hazelmere WA 169
Head of Bight Visitors Centre SA 160, 161
Heading Cliff Lookout, Renmark SA 145
Healesville Vic. 108, 109
Hearns Lake Beach, Coffs Harbour NSW 46
Helensvale Qld 237
Henley Beach SA 131, 134
Hepburn Mineral Springs Reserve Vic. 111
Hepburn Springs Vic. 111, 115
Herberton Historic Village Qld 282
Heritage Market, Kuranda Qld 281
Hideaway Bay Qld 268
High Country Vic. 81–7
High Country breweries Vic. 84–5
High Country wine region Vic. 84
Hill End NSW 57–8
Hillarys Dog Beach WA 165
Hills Beach NSW 46
Himeji Garden, Adelaide SA 131
Historic Port of Echuca Vic. 77
Hobart/nipaluna Tas. 290–7
Home Beach, Point Lookout Qld 228
Hope Island Qld 236
Horseshoe Bay, Magnetic Island Qld 275
Horseshoe Bay Beach, Bowen Qld 267
Horseshoe Beach, Newcastle NSW 31, 32
Hotham Valley Railway, Dwellingup WA 167
houseboating, Murray River SA 142–3
Hucks Hill Lookout, Flinders Ranges SA 155
Humps, The, Hyden WA 175

Hunter Valley wine region NSW 36–7
Huonville Tas. 293
Huskisson NSW 19, 20, 21, 22
Huskisson Beach NSW 19
Hyams Beach, Jervis Bay NSW 19
Hyden WA 174–5

Ikara–Flinders Ranges National Park SA 155
Imalung Lookout, Yulara NT 217
Indooroopilly Qld 230
Isabella Falls, Cooktown Qld 287

James Price Point (Walmadan) campground WA 201
Japanese Garden, Toowoomba Qld 246
Jeanneret Beach Campground, Bay of Fires Tas. 302
Jervis Bay NSW 18–22
Jervis Bay breweries NSW 19
Jezzine Barracks precinct, Townsville 274
Johanna Beach Vic. 124
Jones Beach NSW 14
Jubilee Pocket Qld 270

Kanku–Breakaways Conservation Park SA 157
Karlu Karlu/Devils Marbles NT 217–18
Karriedale WA 189
Kata Tjuṯa NT 217
Katarapko section, Murray River National Park SA 145
Katoomba NSW 10, 11
Kennett River koalas Vic. 123
Kershaw Gardens, North Rockhampton Qld 260
Kiama NSW 12–17
Kiama Blowhole NSW 13
Kiama Coast Walk NSW 13–14
Kilcunda Vic. 92
Kimba SA 152
King George Sound WA 178, 179, 180
Kings Beach, Bowen Qld 267–8

Kings Canyon NT 218
Kings Park, Perth WA 165
Kingston ACT 66
Kingston Beach Tas. 291–2, 294
Kingston Dog Beach Tas. 291
Kingston-on-Murray SA 145
Kingston Park SA 135
Kissing Point Fort, Townsville Qld 274
Knapsack Viaduct via Lapstone Zig Zag Walk, Blue Mountains NSW 11
koala sculptures, Port Macquarie NSW 41
koalas, Great Ocean Road Vic. 123
Korora Beach NSW 46
Kronkup WA 183
Kununurra WA 204
Kuranda markets Qld 281
Kurrajong Point Beach, Yarralumla ACT 65
Kyabram Vic. 78
Kyeemagh Dog Beach, Botany Bay NSW 5
Kyneton Botanic Gardens Vic. 112

La La Falls, Warburton Vic. 107
Lake Argyle WA 204–5
Lake Bunga Vic. 94
Lake Burley Griffin, Canberra ACT 63, 64
Lake Daylesford Vic. 110
Lake Ginninderra, Belconnen ACT 65
Lake Parramatta NSW 5
Lake Tuggeranong, Greenway ACT 65
Lake Wendouree, Ballarat Vic. 118–19
Lakes Entrance Vic. 91, 93, 94, 95
Lakes Entrance Walk Vic. 91
Lammermoor Qld 262
Lammermoor Beach Qld 259
Launceston Tas. 296–301
Launceston historical buildings Tas. 297
lavender farm, Bridestowe Tas. 298

Lawnton Qld 231
Lee Point NT 210
Leeuwin–Naturaliste National Park WA 187
Leighton Dog Beach WA 165
Lenah Valley Tas. 294
Lighthouse Beach, Port Macquarie NSW 39–40
Limestone Coast SA 136–41
Lincoln National Park SA 150
Lions Park Beach, Pambula Beach NSW 24
Lipson Park, Robe SA 138
Little Austinmer Beach NSW 14
Little Beach, Stockton NSW 33
Little Creatures Brewery, Fremantle WA 166
Long Beach, Coffin Bay SA 150
Long Beach, Great Keppell Island Qld 264–5
Long Beach, Robe SA 139
Long Jetty NSW 35
Long Tunnel Extended Gold Mine, Walhalla Vic. 97
Lorne Vic. 123, 126, 127
Loxton SA 146
Lucky Bay WA 171, 172
Lucky Bay Brewing WA 172
Lyrup Flats, Murray River National Park SA 145

McCauley's Beach NSW 14
McClelland Sculpture Park, Frankston Vic. 99
Macedon Vic. 111, 114
Macedon Ranges Vic. 110–15
Macedon Regional Park Vic. 112
McLaren Vale wine region SA 131, 132
MacMasters Beach NSW 31
Madura Pass Lookout WA 161
Magnetic Island Qld 274–5
Main Beach, North Stradbroke Island Qld 228
Maldon Vic. 118
Maleny Qld 255
Maleny Botanic Gardens and Bird World, Wootha Qld 253

Malmsbury Botanic Gardens Vic. 112
Malua Bay NSW 29
Mangrove Boardwalk, Huskisson NSW 20
Manly Dam NSW 5
Mannum SA 142
Manunda Qld 24
Mapleton Qld 253
Marcus Beach Qld 251
Mareeba Qld 282
Marengo Vic. 127
Margaret River WA 184–9
Margaret River breweries WA 185
Margaret River surf beaches WA 185–6
Margaret River wine region WA 185
Marks Park, Bondi NSW 4
Marlo Vic. 93
Marlow Lagoon Dog Park, Palmerston NT 209–10
Marong Vic. 121
Mary Valley Rattler (steam train), Gympie Qld 253
Matso's Brewery, Broome WA 199
Melbourne/Naarm Vic. 70–5
Melbourne street art Vic. 71
Meribee NSW 21
Merimbula NSW 25, 26, 27
Merimbula Boardwalk NSW 25
Merimbula oysters NSW 26
Mermaid Beach Qld 236
Merricks Vic. 103
Middleton Beach WA 180, 183
Millionaire's Walk, Sorrento Vic. 101
Millthorpe NSW 59
Milton NSW 28
Mindarie WA 168
Mindil Beach NT 209, 211
Mindil Beach Sunset Markets NT 211
Minnehaha Falls Track, Blue Mountains NSW 11
Minyirr WA 203
Miss Drew's Bakery and Dog Cafe, Tyabb Vic. 99
MM Beach, Port Kembla NSW 14

Moama NSW 80
Mogo NSW 28
Mollymook NSW 25, 29
Monash SA 148
Monkey Beach, Great Keppell Island Qld 264
Monkey Mia dolphins WA 190–1
Montville Qld 253, 255
Mooloolaba Qld 255
Moonee Beach NSW 46, 48, 49
Moorak SA 141
Morgan SA 142
Mornington Peninsula Vic. 98–103
Mornington Peninsula National Park Vic. 101
Mornington Peninsula wine region Vic. 99
Mornington Vic. 101, 102
Mosman Beach WA 165
Mount Ainslie ACT 63
Mount Buninyong Scenic Reserve Vic. 119
Mount Coot-tha Forest, Brisbane Qld 226
Mount Gambier SA 137, 139, 140
Mount Gravatt Qld 230
Mount Hotham Vic. 88
Mount Macedon Vic. 111–12
Mount Macedon hiking Vic. 112–13
Mount Martha Vic. 100, 101
Mount Ninderry Qld 252
Mount Panorama, Bathurst NSW 59
Mount Schank SA 137
Mount Wellington/kunanyi Tas. 291
Mount William National Park Tas. 302
Mountain Creek Qld 254
Mudgee NSW 59, 60, 61
Mudgee Region wine region NSW 57
Muirhead NT 212
Mullaquana SA 153
Murphy's Haystacks SA 151–2
Murray Bridge SA 142
Murray River houseboating SA 142–3
Murray River lookouts, Renmark SA 145

Murray River National Park SA 143, 145–6
Murray River Reserve, near Echuca Vic. 79
Murray to Mountains Rail Trail Vic. 83
Murray's Beach, Sawtell NSW 46
Musk Vic. 114
Musk Vale Vic. 115
Mystery Bay NSW 29

Nambour Qld 252
Narooma NSW 25–6, 28, 29
Narrabeen Lagoon NSW 5
National Arboretum, Canberra ACT 64–5
National Gallery of Australia, Sculpture Garden, Canberra ACT 63
National Holden Motor Museum, Echuca Vic. 77
Nelly Bay Qld 275
Nelsons Beach, Vincentia NSW 19
New Farm Qld 226, 231
Newcastle NSW 30–5
Newcastle Harbour Foreshore NSW 32
Newrybar NSW 52
Nightcap National Park NSW 52
Nightcliff NT 210
Nimbin NSW 53
Ninderry Qld 252
Nine Mile Beach, Redland NSW 31
Ningaloo Coast WA 192–6
Ningaloo Station WA 195
Nobbys Beach, Port Macquarie NSW 39
Nobbys Lighthouse, Newcastle NSW 32
Noble Falls hiking WA 166–7
Noosa Heads Qld 251
Noosa Main Beach Qld 251
Noosa National Park Qld 251
Noosa River Qld 251–2
Noosa Spit, Noosa Heads Qld 251, 252
Noosaville Qld 251, 254, 255
Norseman WA 160

North Adelaide SA 134, 135
North Avoca Beach NSW 31
North Coogee Beach WA 165, 167
North Hobart Tas. 294
North Lambton NSW 34
North Melbourne Vic. 74
North Shelly Beach, Toowoon Bay NSW 31
North Shore Beach, Twin Waters Qld 251
North Stradbroke Island camping Qld 228
North Wall Beach, Coffs Harbour NSW 45
North Ward, Townsville Qld 277
North West Cape WA 192, 196
Norwood Tas. 301
Nullarbor, the, SA/WA 160–1
Nullarbor Roadhouse SA 160
Nutgrove Beach, Sandy Bay Tas. 292

Oak Flats NSW 16
Old Bottlebutt Tree, Burrawan State Forest NSW 40–1
Old Dubbo Gaol, Dubbo NSW 58–9
Olinda Vic. 106, 109
Olinda Tea House Vic. 106
Orana Bay, Yarralumla ACT 65
Orange NSW 57, 59, 60
Orange wine region NSW 57
Original Rainforest Market, Kuranda Qld 281
Outback South Australia 154–9
outback station stays SA 155
Ovens River, Bright Vic. 83
Owen Springs Reserve NT 219
Oyster Walk, Coffin Bay SA 151

Paddington NSW 8
Pallarenda Beach, Townsville Qld 273
Palm Beach Dog Beach Qld 233
Palm Beach Parklands Qld 233
Palm Cove Qld 279, 284, 285
Palmerston NT 208, 209–10, 213
Palmetum, The, Townsville Qld 273
Pambula NSW 24–5
Pambula Beach NSW 24, 29

INDEX 309

Parachilna SA 155
Paradise Beach, Coral Bay WA 193
Paringa Paddock, Murray River National Park SA 145
Paringa SA 142, 145, 146, 147
Parliament House, Canberra ACT 63
Patonga NSW 34
Patonga Beach NSW 31
Paynesville Vic. 91
Penong SA 160
Perkins Beach NSW 14
Perlubie Beach SA 150
Perth/Boorloo WA 164–9
Perth beaches WA 165
Peterborough Vic. 125
Picnic Bay, Magnetic Island Qld 275
Picnic Point Parklands, Toowoomba Qld 246
Pink Lake WA 173, 175
Pinnacle, the, Mount Wellington Tas. 291
Pipers Brook Tas. 297
Pittwater NSW 5
Point Hut Pond, Gordon ACT 65
Point Lookout Qld 228
Policemans Point campground, Bay of Fires Tas. 303
Porepunkah Vic. 83, 84
Port Arthur/tukana Tas. 292–3
Port Augusta SA 149, 157
Port Campbell National Park Vic. 124
Port Douglas Qld 280, 284
Port Fairy Vic. 127
Port Lincoln SA 150, 152, 153
Port Lincoln Foreshore SA 150
Port Macquarie NSW 38–42
Port Macquarie Coastal Walk NSW 39
Port Stephens NSW 33
Portsea Vic. 101, 103
Prawn Rock Dog Beach, Denmark WA 181
Prevally Beach WA 185
Puckeys Estate Nature Reserve, Wollongong NSW 14

Puffing Billy Railway, Dandenong Ranges Vic. 106
Putta Bucca NSW 60

Quandong Point (Kardilakan) campground WA 201
Queens Beach, Bowen Qld 268, 271
Queens Gardens, Townsville Qld 273
Queens Park and Botanic Gardens, Toowoomba Qld 245
Quobba Blowholes WA 195
Quobba Station WA 195
Quorn silo light show SA 155–6

Rangeville Qld 248
Ravenswood Qld 275
Rawnsley Lookout, Flinders Ranges SA 155
Rawnsley Patrk Station SA 155
Raymond Island Koala Trail Vic. 91–2
Red Beach, Bribie Island Qld 227
Red Hill wine region Vic. 99
Redcliffe Qld 230
Renmark SA 142, 143, 144, 145, 146, 147, 148
Richmond Tas. 293–4
Richmond Vic. 75
Risdon Vale Tas. 295
River Torrens, Adelaide SA 131
Riverland SA 144–8
Riverland wine region SA 147
Riverwalk, Brisbane Qld 225
Robe SA 138, 139, 140, 141
Robe Coastal Walk SA 138–9
Robina Qld 237
Rochester Vic. 78
Rockhampton Qld 258, 259–60, 261, 262, 263
Rockhampton historic centre Qld 259–60
Rocky Creek Dam NSW 52
Roebuck Bay WA 199
Roebuck Bay Lookout WA 200
Rosa Glen WA 188
Rose Bay Beach Qld 267
Rose Bay Dog Beach NSW 4

Rosebud Vic. 102
Ross NT 221
Rosslyn Qld 262
Rotary Lookout, Esperance WA 173
Rotary Lookout, Tamborine Mountain Qld 234
Royal Beach, Mornington Vic. 101
Royal Botanic Gardens, Melbourne Vic. 71
Rundle Mall, Adelaide SA 131
Rutherglen Vic. 84, 87
Rye Vic. 103

Safety Beach Vic. 100
St Helens Tas. 302
St Kilda Vic. 71, 74
Salamanca Market Tas. 291
Salamanca Place Tas. 291
Salmon Beach WA 171
Salmon Beach Wind Farm, Esperance WA 173
San Remo Vic. 92, 94
Sancrox NSW 42
Sanctuary Point NSW 22
Sandy Bay, Clontarf NSW 4
Sandy Bay Tas. 292
Sapphire Beach NSW 46
Saunders Beach Qld 277
Scarborough NSW 16
Sceale Bay SA 150
Sea Acres National Park NSW 39
Sea Cliff Bridge, Wollongong NSW 13
Sealy Lookout, Orara East State Forest NSW 44–5
Semaphore Park SA 134
Seventeen Seventy Qld 256–7
Shark Bay WA 190–1
Sharkey's Beach, Coledale NSW 14
Sheffield murals Tas. 298
Shelly Beach, Port Macquarie NSW 39
Shelving Beach, Great Keppell Island Qld 264
Shingley Beach Qld 267
Shoalhaven wine region NSW 15
Short Beach, Sandy Bay Tas. 292

silo art
   Echuca Vic. 78
   Riverland SA 147
Silver Beach, Botany Bay NSW 5
Singing Ship, Emu Park Qld 260–1
Sirius Cove, Mosman NSW 4
Snowy River Estuary Walk Vic. 93
Soldiers Point NSW 34, 35
Somerville Vic. 102
Sorrento Vic. 101, 102
South Coast NSW 23–9
South Coast breweries NSW 24–5
South Cottesloe Beach WA 165
South Fremantle WA 167
South Fremantle Dog Beach WA 165
South Lawson Waterfall Circuit, Blue Mountains NSW 10–11
South Wharf Vic. 74
Southbank Vic. 74, 75
Southbank precinct, Brisbane Qld 225
Speers Point NSW 34
Spit, The, Dog Beach, Gold Coast Qld 233
Spring Beach, Agnes Water Qld 256
Spring Hill Qld 230
Staircase to the Moon, Broome WA 199–200
Stanthorpe Qld 238, 239, 240, 242, 243
Stanthorpe apples Qld 239
Stevensons Falls, Forrest Vic. 124
Stirling SA 133
Stockton NSW 33
Stokes Hill Lookout, Flinders Ranges SA 155
Strand, The, Townsville Qld 273
Strathdale Vic. 120
Strathmerton Vic. 79
Strickland State Forest NSW 31–2
Stuart Park NT 212
Sublime Point, Blue Mountains NSW 10
Suffolk Park, Byron Bay NSW 54
Summerhill Tas. 300
sunset
   at Cable Beach WA 198–9
   at Mindil Beach NT 211

Sunshine Beach North, Sunshine Beach Qld 251
Sunshine Coast Qld 250–5
Sunshine Coast beaches Qld 251
Surfers Paradise Qld 237
Surfer's Point, Prevally WA 185
Surry Hills NSW 8
Sutton ACT 65, 67
Swan Reach SA 145
Swan Valley wine region WA 166
Swimcart Beach campground, Bay of Fires Tas. 303
Sydney/Warrang NSW 2–9
Sydney Harbour NSW 5
Sydney Harbour beaches NSW 4–5
Sydney Harbour foreshore NSW 3
Sydney hotels NSW 6–7, 9

Tahune Airwalk Tas. 293
Talia Caves SA 152
Tallebudgera Beach Qld 233
Tallow Beach, Byron Bay NSW 51
Tamar Valley berries, pick your own Tas. 297–298
Tamar Valley wine region Tas. 297
Tamborine Mountain Qld 233–4
Tassells Cove, Safety Beach Vic. 100–1
Tathra NSW 27, 29
Taylors Beach Tas. 302
Ten Mile Lagoon WA 171
Tessellated Pavement, Eaglehawk Neck Tas. 293
Tewantin Qld 251
Thornton Beach Qld 287
Thulimbah Qld 242
Thursday Island Qld 286
Timboon Vic. 125
Tjoritja / West MacDonnell National Park NT 218
Toowoomba Qld 244–9
Toowoomba street art Qld 246–7
Torndirrup National Park WA 180
Torquay Vic. 122
Towers Hill, Charters Towers Qld 275
Town Beach, Broome WA 199–200

Town Beach Markets, Broome WA 200
Townsville Qld 272–7
Townsville botanic gardens Qld 273
Trentham Falls Vic. 113
Trentham Farmers' Market Vic. 113
Trinity Beach Qld 280
Tuggerah NSW 34
Tulip Top Gardens, Sutton ACT 65
Tumby Bay SA 150, 152
Tumby Bay murals SA 152
Tuross Head NSW 28
Twelve Apostles, Great Ocean Road Vic. 124
Twelve Apostles Gourmet Trail, Timboon Vic. 125
Twilight Beach WA 171
Tyabb Vic. 99

Ulladulla NSW 25, 27, 28
Uluṟu NT 217
Umina Beach NSW 31
Umpherston Sinkhole, Mount Gambier SA 137
Upper Orara NSW 49
Uredale Point Heritage Trail, Albany WA 180
Uriarra Recreation Reserve Area ACT 65
Urunga Beach NSW 46
Urunga Boardwalk NSW 45

Venus Bay SA 152
Victor Harbor SA 133
Victoria Hill Historic Mining Reserve, Bendigo Vic. 117
Victorian Goldfields Railway Vic. 118
Vincentia NSW 19, 22
Vintage Talking Tram, Bendigo Vic. 117
Vlamingh Head Lighthouse WA 194

Waikerie SA 147, 148
Walhalla Vic. 96–7
Walhalla Goldfields Railway Vic. 96
Walkers Rocks Campground SA 151
Wallaga Lake NSW 24

Wandiligong Vic. 83, 85
Wangaratta Vic. 86
Warburton Vic. 107
Warners Bay NSW 35
Warroora Station WA 195
Washerwomans Beach, Bendalong NSW 24
Watarrka National Park NT 218
Wauchope NT 218
Wave Rock, Hyden WA 174–5
Waverley Tas. 300
Wellington Park Tas. 291
Wendouree Vic. 120
Werri Beach, Kiama NSW 14
West Beach, Esperance WA 171
West Beach, Robe SA 139
West Coast beaches WA 165
West Hobart Tas. 294
West Hoxton NSW 8
West Point, Magnetic Island Qld 275
whale-watching
 Albany WA 180
 Head of Bight Visitors Centre SA 160
 Ningaloo Reef WA 194, 195
 South Coast NSW 27
whale-watching cruise, Jervis Bay NSW 19

Whalers Cove, Albany WA 180
Whitsundays Qld 266–71
Whyalla SA 151, 152, 153
Willow Springs (station) SA 155
Wills Bend, Murray River Reserve Vic. 79
Wilpena Pound SA 155
Wimbie Beach, Batemans Bay NSW 24
Witchcliffe WA 188
Wolli Creek Regional Park, Earlwood NSW 5
Wollongong NSW 12–17
Wombat Hill Botanic Gardens, Daylesford Vic. 112
Woodend Vic. 113, 114
Woodend Farmers' Market Vic. 113
Woolgoolga Back Beach, Coffs Harbour NSW 46
Woollahra NSW 9
Woollamia NSW 22
Woolshed Brewery, Renmark SA 147
Woombye Qld 255
Woorabinda Bushland Reserve SA 133
Woorim Beach Qld 226, 227
Wyberba Qld 242
Wylie Bay WA 171

Yalata Roadhouse SA 160
Yallingup WA 189
Yallingup Beach WA 186
Yandina Qld 252
Yarra Bend Park Vic. 73
Yarra River boating Vic. 73
Yarra Valley Vic. 104–9
Yarra Valley wine region Vic. 105
Yarrabi Pond, Gunghalin ACT 65
Yarralumla ACT 65, 66
Yeppoon Qld 259, 261, 262, 263
Yeppoon Foreshore Qld 261
Yeppoon Lagoon Qld 261
You Yangs Regional Park Vic. 72
Yulara NT 217, 219
Yungaburra Qld 282

PHOTO CREDITS

All images © Shandos Cleaver, except the following:

Cover: Getty images; vi, xiii (top), 14, 18, 43, 46, 47, 49 (top), 50, 54, 56, 66 Destination NSW; vii, xii (middle) Loriana Cassarino; x, 240, 241 (top), 242, 269 (bottom), 280, 283 Tourism and Events Queensland; xiii (bottom), 68, 73, 78, 84, 87, 89, 97, 98, 104, 106, 107 (top), 109, 112, 114, 119, 123, 125, 126 (bottom) Visit Victoria; xviii, 2, 9, 30, 51, 64, 72, 79, 120 (top), 133, 146 (top), 184, 213, 217, 226, 237, 269 (top), 290, 292, 297 (top) Alamy; 29 Bannisters Hotel; 138, 167, 198, 260, 263, 265, 272, 278 Shutterstock; 150, 161 Michelle Lynn; 143, 152, 159, 174, 177, 191 (bottom), 192, 196, 200, 209, 212, 219, 221, 266, 271, 288, 299 (bottom), 300 Tourism Australia.

About the author

Shandos Cleaver is the founder of Travelnuity (https://www.travelnuity.com), a top-ranking travel website focused on dog-friendly travel. Together with her Miniature Dachshund, Schnitzel, Shandos has travelled extensively throughout Australia, the United States and Europe, including six months driving around Australia in a campervan. She's passionate about providing inspiration and information to others wanting to travel with their dogs, whether close to home or internationally. When not on the road, Shandos and Schnitzel live in Sydney, Australia.

ACKNOWLEDGMENTS:

Thanks so much to my wonderful husband, Joel, for all his support and driving 99% of the time on our road trips. And of course, thanks to the one and only Schnitzel, our amazing travel companion!

Published in 2024 by Hardie Grant Explore, an imprint of Hardie Grant Publishing

Hardie Grant Explore (Melbourne)
Wurundjeri Country
Building 1, 658 Church Street
Richmond, Victoria 3121

Hardie Grant Explore (Sydney)
Gadigal Country
Level 7, 45 Jones Street
Ultimo, NSW 2007

www.hardiegrant.com/au/explore

All rights reserved. No part of this publication may be reproduced, stored in a retrieval system or transmitted in any form by any means, electronic, mechanical, photocopying, recording or otherwise, without the prior written permission of the publishers and copyright holders.

The moral rights of the author have been asserted.

Copyright text © Shandos Cleaver 2024
Copyright concept, maps and design © Hardie Grant Publishing 2024

The maps in this publication incorporate data © Commonwealth of Australia (Geoscience Australia), 2006. Geoscience Australia has not evaluated the data as altered and incorporated within this publication, and therefore gives no warranty regarding accuracy, completeness, currency or suitability for any particular purpose.

 A catalogue record for this book is available from the National Library of Australia

Hardie Grant acknowledges the Traditional Owners of the Country on which we work, the Wurundjeri People of the Kulin Nation and the Gadigal People of the Eora Nation, and recognises their continuing connection to the land, waters and culture. We pay our respects to their Elders past and present.

For all relevant publications, Hardie Grant Explore commissions a First Nations consultant to review relevant content and provide feedback to ensure suitable language and information is included in the final book. Hardie Grant Explore also includes traditional place names and acknowledges Traditional Owners, where possible, in both the text and mapping for their publications.

Traditional place names are included in *palawa kani*, the language of Tasmanian Aboriginal People, with thanks to the Tasmanian Aboriginal Centre.

Off the Leash in Australia
ISBN 9781741178999

10 9 8 7 6 5 4 3 2 1

Publisher	Design
Megan Cuthbert	Murray Batten
Editor	Typesetting
Alison Proietto	Megan Ellis
Proofreader	Index
Susan Keogh	Max McMaster
Cartographer	Production manager
Emily Maffei	Simone Wall

Colour reproduction by Megan Ellis and Splitting Image Colour Studio

Printed and bound in China by LEO Paper Products LTD.

 The paper this book is printed on is certified against the Forest Stewardship Council® Standards and other sources. FSC® promotes environmentally responsible, socially beneficial and economically viable management of the world's forests.

Disclaimer: While every care is taken to ensure the accuracy of the data within this product, the owners of the data (including the state, territory and Commonwealth governments of Australia) do not make any representations or warranties about its accuracy, reliability, completeness or suitability for any particular purpose and, to the extent permitted by law, the owners of the data disclaim all responsibility and all liability (including without limitation, liability in negligence) for all expenses, losses, damages (including indirect or consequential damages) and costs which might be incurred as a result of the data being inaccurate or incomplete in any way and for any reason.

Publisher's Disclaimers: The publisher cannot accept responsibility for any errors or omissions. The representation on the maps of any road or track is not necessarily evidence of public right of way. The publisher cannot be held responsible for any injury, loss or damage incurred during travel. It is vital to research any proposed trip thoroughly and seek the advice of relevant state and travel organisations before you leave.

Publisher's Note: Every effort has been made to ensure that the information in this book is accurate at the time of going to press. The publisher welcomes information and suggestions for correction or improvement.